THE CAREER OF
Alphonse Daudet

A CRITICAL STUDY

THE CAREER OF

Alphonse Daudet

A Critical Study

BY MURRAY SACHS

HARVARD UNIVERSITY PRESS

CAMBRIDGE, MASSACHUSETTS · 1965

TO
MY MOTHER
AND TO
THE MEMORY OF
MY FATHER

Preface

The literary work of Alphonse Daudet is just now a most unfashionable subject in academic circles. No doubt that is because Daudet has for some time been considered too simple in his techniques, and too obvious in his meanings, to challenge an age which takes particular pride in penetrating the hermetic world of the "difficult," obscure artist. A preface is of course no place to try to dispose of the broader questions about the nature of literary art which such an attitude raises. The point needs to be made, however, that this modern tendency to dismiss significant writers like Daudet merely because they seem too easily comprehensible often has the paradoxical effect of rendering such writers more difficult and obscure. For they then become the victims of neglect and of gross oversimplifications, of hand-me-down opinions and of carelessly researched facts. It does not take many decades of that kind of treatment for direct and accurate knowledge of the works of such writers to be replaced by a commonly accepted set of distortions and imprecise clichés.

Something of that sort does seem already to have happened in the case of Alphonse Daudet. This I discovered when, armed with the vague notions about his work that were common to my generation of university specialists in French literature, I had occasion to undertake a brief foray into one aspect of his career. I was completely unprepared for the mass of contradictions and controversies about the man and his work which my research began to uncover. And that is why a brief foray has turned into a major exploration of book length. This book was written in the belief that the misconceptions about Daudet that I had when I began my research are all but universal today, and that a serious effort is now needed to restore our understanding and appreciation of Daudet's literary achievements, and of the vital role he played in the literary life of his time.

Certain ground rules and assumptions which governed the way this study has been conducted should be explained at the outset. Of first importance is the fact that the main stress has been deliberately placed on the evolution of Daudet's writing career. That fact severely limits the scope of the treatment that will be found here. For example, there has been no attempt to provide a complete biography. Biographical details are introduced only where they help reveal why Daudet's career took the turns that it did. By the same token, it has not seemed necessary to provide closely detailed analyses of all Daudet's specific works. Such analyses are provided selectively, and only as they elucidate some change or development in Daudet's artistic practice. Similarly, explanations of the times in which Daudet lived, or of the work of his contemporaries, have been considered to lie outside the confines of the discussion. Indeed, it has been assumed throughout that the reader already has some familiarity with that era's events, literary movements, and principal men of letters, and probably even some general acquaintance with elements of Daudet's writing. A working knowledge of the period has been taken for granted, in other words, so that the argument might remain steadily in the foreground. Unswerving emphasis has been put upon the way Daudet's personal career evolved, and why. The central goal of this study can be stated as follows: to penetrate the workings of the creative process in the course of Daudet's career, and thereby to assess the aesthetic worth and historical importance of his total achievement.

I am only too well aware that there are urgent needs with respect to the study of Alphonse Daudet's life and works which the present book does little to satisfy. For example, a more thorough stylistic analysis which precisely identified the characteristics and techniques behind Daudet's distinctive writing manner and his charm would be most welcome. So would a study of Daudet's personal understanding of the word "realism," and of his practice in that kind of writing, showing the areas of his agreement with and of his divergence from the ideas of his contemporaries in this domain. Knowing what I have left undone here, I can only hope that this work will help clear some of the ground and encourage others to fill the gaps which remain.

A last point needs to be emphasized in these preliminary remarks. The very existence of this study makes obvious my firm belief in the positive value to be found in Alphonse Daudet and his work as a creative artist. And these pages will accordingly try to show why and to what degree Daudet merits his fame as a writer of quality. Yet one can warmly admire an artist without necessarily deceiving oneself into believing him great. It should occasion no surprise, therefore, that these pages must also address themselves to the question of why Daudet was not a better writer than he was, and why he failed to attain greatness. Indeed, it can be said of Daudet with peculiar accuracy that his greatest talents cannot be understood apart from his failings. It was precisely the interaction between the two in him that determined the course of his creative life. Daudet is not an author whose work can be truly illuminated by an attitude of worship. In the present state of Daudet's reputation, the most useful aim is for objective understanding and a just evaluation of his career. That aim requires that the man and his works be seen entire, warts and all.

ACKNOWLEDGMENTS

It is a pleasure to record here my gratitude to all those—too numerous to be named individually—who have provided information or encouragement during the years of research and writing. I am particularly happy to thank my colleague and friend, Elliott M. Grant, who willingly criticized the study in manuscript and whose many suggestions have added to its accuracy and value. All responsibility for the content of this book, of course, rests exclusively with me. All translations provided are my own and claim only to be adequate for the intended purpose.

For access to unpublished documents my thanks are due the following: to the Goncourt Academy and its Secretary, M. Gérard Bauër, for permission to examine and quote from materials in the Fonds Goncourt deposited in the French National Library in Paris; to M. Charles Daudet and Dr. François Daudet, grandsons of Alphonse Daudet, for permission to examine selected autograph materials in their possession; and to the distinguished novelist M. Roger Ferlet, who generously allowed me to examine the wealth of unpublished letters and other material which he has collected in his Daudet museum at La Vignasse.

A grant from the "Class of 1900" Fund of Williams College helped defray the costs of one summer's research in France, and another grant from Brandeis University paid in part the expenses of preparing the manuscript.

My greatest debt I have saved for last: to Miriam Blank Sachs, who contributed to this study more hard work, good will, and astute criticism than any author has the right to expect from his wife. I am profoundly grateful to her.

Waltham, Massachusetts   M.S.
March 1965

Contents

Myth and Reality

Since Alphonse Daudet's death in 1897 a public consensus has gradually been taking shape regarding his particular contribution to literature. In all the traditional sources of critical opinion the same few ideas about Daudet, often expressed in the same words, tend to recur. It is first pointed out that as a realist and Naturalist in fiction Daudet distinguished himself from the others of that school by the pity he displayed for his characters. His style and narrative manner are then characterized as possessing an indefinable charm. Finally, the most distinctive of his literary gifts, which are conceded to be fragile, is declared to be wit. In other words, what the name of Alphonse Daudet should now conjure up in the public mind, to judge by our standard reference sources, can be reduced to just three key words: pity, charm, wit.[1]

Professional scholars are, of course, by training and temperament disposed to question all such capsule judgments. But the general reader too must, on reflection, have good cause to doubt this developing consensus. In the first place, it has the ring of condescension, conveying the notion that Alphonse Daudet was an irretrievably minor figure whose writings were trivial, though pleasant. Such a notion is at the very least a distortion of historical reality, for Daudet was, in his time, one of France's leading realistic novelists, read and acclaimed throughout Europe, North America, and South America. Even today, for that matter, Daudet is an important "presence," scarcely deserving of condescension. At least a few of his works continue to reach a vast international public, spreading his fame in the form of

popular paperbacks, gift editions, school editions, stage pro-
ductions, and cinema adaptations.

The current consensus must be challenged, in the second
place, because it is so fragmentary. It appears to be based entirely on the surface characteristics of a few regularly antholo-
gized short stories, with perhaps an echo of *Le Petit Chose* and
Tartarin de Tarascon thrown in. Even so widely read a novel
of Daudet's as *Sapho* would seem to have left little residue in
this popular stereotype of him; and it contains no hint at all
that the great bulk of his work is in a vein of somber realism.
There is good reason, therefore, to ask whether the common
capsule summary of "pity, charm, and wit" is transmitting to
posterity a reality or a myth about Alphonse Daudet.

A few recent scholarly studies, responding to this challenge
of an apparently unsatisfactory popular consensus, have reached conclusions of a surprisingly negative kind. These studies,
often impressively documented and representing the work of
well-qualified and articulate though as yet isolated scholars, pro-
pose the radical theory that Daudet's reputation is indeed a
myth, fabricated by the author himself, based on clever plagiarism of others and astute public relations. "No literary fame
was more trumped up, more manufactured, more artificially
contrived and inflated than his," claimed the well-known scholarly journalist Auriant recently. Attacking with astonishing
vehemence, he went on: "He is glorified by a legend which he
created himself, and which has been carefully maintained by his
heirs who have kept jealous watch to see that it is perpetuated
intact . . . All judgments . . . need to be revised. The moment
has come for Alphonse Daudet to take leave of his legend and,
shorn of his false prestige, to enter into literary history where
his place is not among the masters, as they tried to make people
believe during his lifetime, nor even among the minor masters
of the nineteenth century, but at the tail end of the list of dis-
credited or disqualified novelists." [2] The denunciation seems

needlessly shrill and impassioned, considering that no serious claims for a place among the literary giants have lately been lodged in Daudet's behalf. However, this passionate note of condemnation is typical of the new revisionism concerning Daudet. Auriant may be suspected of journalistic sensationalism, but there are the more deliberate academic voices, like Jacques Vier and Luc Badesco, writing in responsible learned journals, who see in Daudet "one of the most ingenious parasites in French literature" [3] and a man driven by "the carefully calculated need to redesign his own development, and to find a way, at any cost, to transform his illusions retroactively into something that really existed." [4]

The revisionist attacks have been rather too strident and too absolute not to be suspect in their turn. Yet the mass of evidence they adduce must at least compel serious students of French literature to question any comfortable image of Daudet they might feel tempted to entertain. It is now necessary at least to try and account for the fact that Daudet can arouse such sharp controversy and such passionate opposition. The revisionists have also succeeded, by the sources they quote, in reminding scholars who have been willing to forget it that the controversial aspects of Daudet are no posthumous creation of literary polemics. While he lived they were a constant factor at every stage of his career. Something about Daudet's personality, and about his work, too, seemed to breed as much antagonism as admiration. For example, in the same year (1883) in which Henry James was informing the English-speaking world that "Alphonse Daudet is at the head of his profession," another novelist, Octave Mirbeau, was telling all Paris that Daudet was guilty of plagiarism, exploitation of others, sharp and dishonest literary practices, and lack of talent and imagination.[5] It may be added that Mirbeau simply collected in one scurrilous article a whole series of charges and rumors about Daudet's character and his writings which had been current in literary circles for years. Subsequently even Edmond de Goncourt, who had long been Daudet's closest literary friend and ally, was provoked to the gravest doubts about Daudet's honesty and good faith in the matter of his rumored candidacy for the French Academy.[6] Throughout Daudet's career one can cite repeated instances of controversy over the originality and worth of his writings, and over his integrity and trustworthiness in personal dealings, which are fully as persistent, and therefore presumably as significant, as the praise, admiration, and honors that were heaped on him. Yet of this controversial Daudet, who is every bit as real as the kindly Daudet of popular fame, there is usually very little account taken.

It is, of course, the very fact that this controversial side of Daudet is so rarely mentioned and so little known which the revisionists point to for proof of their theory that Daudet's respectable reputation is no more than a myth manufactured by the author himself. Their argument seems to be that Daudet and his heirs have cleverly managed to paper over the damaging facts in his career, and have successfully propagated the false notion that he was a fine dedicated artist, an independent spirit, and a generous and kindly soul. The trouble with this argument is that it explains too much. It credits Daudet with a stunning conspiracy sustained for nearly thirty years and extended beyond the grave by his family. It convicts the public of all those years of truly monumental gullibility. And it suggests that Daudet had the secret not only of concealing his faults but also of somehow persuading the public to like his spurious creations. If one accepted the revisionist view, one would be forced not to denounce Daudet but to admire him for bringing off the most successful confidence game in the annals of literature.

Nevertheless, this revisionist view cannot be totally dismissed either, for it is based on verifiable truth. Any objective inquiry into the career of Alphonse Daudet soon encounters evidence of this myth-making in the form of deliberate attempts

to falsify the record. These have been far less systematic than
the revisionists claim, but they have been quite real. Daudet
himself regularly tidied up the details of his life in his biographical writings.[7] And his heirs have since striven even more conscientiously to shape the truth to a selected pattern. The primary sources for a biography of Daudet are still, to this day, the
accounts given by Daudet himself, his brother Ernest, and his
two sons Léon and Lucien. If it has frequently been difficult to
penetrate beyond what the family has been willing to reveal,
or to correct legends which they have been eager to propagate,
it is because important primary documents have been withheld,
or published only partially, or even destroyed, as a matter of
concerted family policy.[8] A decade ago, in a typical public instance, when the diaries of the Goncourt brothers were about to
be published in unexpurgated form at last, members of the Daudet family brought a very costly lawsuit in a desperate (and
happily unsuccessful) move to block the publication. The
motive was quite simply fear of indiscreet revelations about the
private doings and sayings of Alphonse Daudet, which might
tarnish the brightly polished image of him they had always
sought to present. It is indisputable that Daudet's career has at
times been the object of some deliberate myth-making. It has
however been far less persistent, far less organized, and far less
successful than some would have us believe.

In point of fact, the family-shaped myth, the fierce revisionist hostility, and the plainly inaccurate popular consensus, are
the least, because they are merely the most recent, of the frustrations which have plagued efforts to separate reality from
myth with respect to Daudet. These recent frustrations only
make more complex and less amenable to simple solutions the
difficulties in evaluating Daudet which have in fact long existed.
The most eloquent testimony to these difficulties is to be found
in the hesitant, shifting, and even contradictory critical judgments that have been made of his work over the years, even by

ᴦthe most scrupulously neutral and objective critics. Historians of literature, for example, have always shown a skittish discomfort over the problem of "placing" Daudet. He has never fitted without elaborate qualification into any of the conventional groupings, including the Naturalists with whom he has most readily been identified. Charles Beuchat, the indulgent historian of Naturalism who was prone to embrace every writer of fiction under that rubric, hesitated to be categorical in Daudet's case: "Must Alphonse Daudet be classified among the Naturalists . . .? By his method of working, and by the content of his works as a whole, Alphonse Daudet is certainly of the family of Flaubert, the Goncourts and Zola . . . But beyond this realist in Daudet— and that is the reason for our hesitation in classifying him—one must look for the innovator who brought a vibrant sensibility to the Naturalist doctrine and who rejected the dogma of impassibility so dear to Flaubert." ⁹ Other critics too have thus remarked uneasily on Daudet's Romantic traits, his impressionism, and his emotionalism, noting that they are at the opposite pole from the Naturalist school in which he seems most at home.

The confusion about the true nature of his work takes many other forms as well. For example, there have been attempts to see him as a purely regional novelist, whose subject is Provence—and opposite attempts to maintain that he is primarily a novelist of Paris. He has been called to task both for his moralizing and for his immorality, for his optimism and for his pessimism, for his excessive pity and for his lack of pity.

Daudet's critics, both during his lifetime and since his death, have written so chaotic a record of vacillation and contradiction that no coherent picture of the reality of what he was has been able so far to emerge. Clearly there is some complex problem in Daudet which has eluded understanding—one too complex, certainly, to be explained away by manufactured myths.

Daudet himself, we know, would have been pleased to see such endless hesitation in the critical fraternity over his work.

For he cherished nothing more, in the conception of himself he hoped to perpetuate, than the notion that he was an independent spirit in the literary world, unclassifiable and giving allegiance to no recognized school.[10] He hated to be pigeonholed. Perhaps the trouble that has been experienced in seeing and fully grasping the reality of Daudet's career has been, in some small degree, a triumph of the author's own myth-making in this regard. But there is surely a much more significant operative reason for this trouble. What Daudet liked to dignify as the virtue of independence was in reality a compulsion over which he exercised little control. He was driven to be, and became in fact, a writer of unprecedented variety. He attempted so many different kinds of writing in his career that he is genuinely unclassifiable, in the sense that any single classification would necessarily be a distortion. The range of Daudet's published writing, in subject matter, in form, and in style, probably exceeds that of every other writer of any consequence in his time. There is every reason, therefore, why even contradictory opinions about him could each have some proper validity. In forty years of active and productive literary practice Alphonse Daudet created a monument which resists exact definition, and defies attempts to find therein a coherent unity. It is necessary to accept this almost incredible diversity as a fact, if one is to begin to understand the meaning of Alphonse Daudet's career.

This diversity, however, is itself but a symptom of the general problem whose dimensions this discussion has tried to make clear. Alphonse Daudet is a peculiarly elusive figure in literary history, inconsistently portrayed and inconclusively situated in the development of French literature. We are still very far from understanding him, and no fair and honest judgment of his work is possible, of course, without that understanding. The vagueness and inaccuracy which have long enveloped public knowledge of the man and his works make Daudet one of the least "known" of familiar and famous writers. The reality of what he was and what he wrote has been obscured and distorted by his own protean and enigmatic activity, and by the series of misconceptions, half-truths, and myths that have taken hold about him.

At the present time we are confronted with at least four distinct views of Daudet. There is the broad popular consensus now current which seems to reduce Daudet to the authorship of a few youthful works, robbing him thereby of his substantial achievements in the novel of realism and in the theater. There is a revisionist point of view now forming which would deny to Daudet any creative originality or any pure motive in conduct. There exists a controversial Daudet, feared and distrusted by some, admired and idolized by others. And there is the mythical Daudet, invented by the author himself and perpetuated by his heirs, who projects an image of gentle kindliness and artistic fervor. This mythical Daudet, inspired by a zeal to cloak weaknesses, has been the most pernicious distortion of all; for it ends by sacrificing the vital qualities, resulting in a Daudet so anodyne and dehumanized as to suggest little of his complex sensitivity and major artistic gifts. Undeniably, there are fragments of truth in all of these conceptions, but a whole and believable Daudet, in conformity with all the facts, is what is urgently required, if Daudet is ever to have his rightful place in the history of his time.

It is the attempt to supply that integrated and convincing conception of Daudet, and with it a truer assessment of his artistic worth, which is undertaken in this study. The method followed is that of a systematic and detailed analysis of the evolution of Daudet's career, through all its many fits and starts and changes of direction. The analysis will be probing for the inner consistency and the meaning of that career. Before one can usefully embark on such an analysis, however, one must first dissipate the fog of myth and misconception which presently surrounds Daudet's name. That in turn requires an understanding of Daudet which convincingly reconciles and accounts for the conflicting and contradictory facets of his reputation which are the inexorable reality confronting the investigator who would interpret his career.

Since Daudet's work is so varied, and opinions about it so contradictory, one must perforce seek that understanding not in the works but in the character of the man himself—or at least in those aspects of his character which directly conditioned his creative work. The key to reconciling the difficulties, if there is one, is to be found in the man. And it is the central thesis of this study that that essential key, which goes farthest toward solving the puzzle of his career, lies in the peculiar nature of his personal commitment to literature. There was never any question of the seriousness of Daudet's vocation, of course. He began to write while still a young boy, and at the age of sixteen had composed a complete novel in addition to numerous poems.[11] He gave no sign of contemplating any other vocation than that of writer during his formative years. And yet his choice of career had no consuming inevitability for him, for it seemed to answer no urgent inner need for self-expression. A literary career was an ambitious dream, and he seemed entirely prepared to do something else if necessary. Even in the midst of his successful career he felt drawn to subliterary occupations like journalism and editing, which he sometimes thought were his true calling; and at one point he was prepared to abandon even the subliterary world in favor of a secure government post.[12]

Through literature Daudet seems to have sought status in society, public acclaim, and, perhaps more than anything else, a personal identity. It was not because he felt compelled to create, even without the status or the acclaim, that he turned to writing. In this Daudet seems to have been fundamentally different from such writers as Balzac, Flaubert, or Zola with whom he is properly to be compared. Daudet was singularly unpossessed by that passionate inner conviction, which drove each of them, that he had something utterly unique to say which had to be expressed. The truth is that Daudet was never sure of what it was he had to say as a writer. He was sure only that he wanted to be a writer—and he was not exactly inflexible even on that point. The secret of the remarkable diversity of his work is simply that he tried everything in his restless desire to find his true voice, and the form and subject by which he could best get established and attract a following. So it was that in his career he essayed poems, plays, sketches and topical commentary (called *chroniques*), short stories, novels, criticism, historical vignettes, translations, and memoirs.

Daudet's was a hesitant and conditional vocation, for reasons no doubt deeply buried in his psyche. There was no trace of fanatical dedication to art in him, in the manner of Flaubert, for example. His creative urge called to him in an irresolute voice, his muse was uncertain. With such a cast of mind, self-doubt plagued him throughout his literary career and exposed him helplessly to every influence both fruitful and injurious. It is for that reason that he left a trail of bewildering inconsistencies and contradictions and shaped a literary performance marked by indecisiveness, hesitations, constant change, and a profound fear of commitment and fixed positions. To resolve the principal difficulties which have obscured the reality of what Daudet was, one must focus on this characteristic of his hesitant and uncertain muse, and its accumulated consequences.

This trait of Daudet's can be identified as the essential creative flaw in a writer of impressive range and, at his best, of compelling power. This one flaw goes far to explain the heartbreaking impression left by a reading of his complete works. For everything Daudet wrote, including the very worst, carries the imprint of truly extraordinary talent; yet no single work, including the very best, seems wholly satisfying and inevitably "right." Daudet's career is a story of flawed genius, falling repeatedly just short of fulfillment. For that reason, a study of Alphonse Daudet's literary career promises more than a needed correction of critical focus. It offers also an especially fascinating insight into the creative process. For Daudet's flaw, and its impact on what he created, provide a case history unusually rich in implications for the study of that fragile process by which art comes into being.

Origins

The bare vital statistics are unenlightening: Alphonse Daudet was born in the meridional city of Nîmes on May 13, 1840, the third son of Vincent Daudet, who was in the silk business, and his wife, the former Adeline Reynaud, whom he had married in 1829. The vital statistics begin to take on meaning only if one adds that Alphonse was the fifth child born to the couple in the eight years from 1832 to 1840, but only the third to survive.[1] Not surprisingly the child was of delicate health. Moreover, Vincent Daudet's business affairs had been suffering a disastrous decline in the years preceding the birth of Alphonse, and his violent outbursts of temper and his passionate devotion to royalist politics had long since driven the dignified and reserved Adeline into the resigned silence of a disillusioned though piously dutiful wife. It was not a happy household into which Alphonse Daudet was born, nor one in which a new and sickly child demanding care could be particularly welcome. It was, in fact, a family living in emotional disharmony and financial disarray.

Alphonse Daudet thus probably experienced from birth the classic traumas of rejection, isolation, and deprivation of love. Terrified by his father's rages, unable to penetrate his mother's withdrawn and melancholy demeanor, too young to attract the attention of Henri, the oldest son who was eight years his senior, Alphonse spent his very earliest years in a kind of emotional solitude. His closest bond with his family was his brother Ernest, just three years older than himself, and a rather tearfully sentimental child from all accounts, who was not likely to supply the secure affection Alphonse needed. It is suggestive that Alphonse became so attached to the family of the wet nurse to whom he was entrusted that till the age of about six he seems to have spent as much of his time with them, in the village of Bezouce, a short distance from Nîmes, as with his own family. The healthy country air provided the excuse, but the fact remains that Alphonse always remembered his sojourns there with unusual pleasure. Any happy memories Alphonse had of his childhood were not, it seems fair to say, associated with his own family. And if he generally spoke of his childhood as unhappy—the tone, if not the facts, of *Le Petit Chose* is a fair expression of Daudet's own view of those years—it is not because he was mistreated by his parents physically, but because he was deprived, in that unfortunate family atmosphere, of the warm affection his nature craved.

Inevitably, the consequences of the unhappy first years of his life are visible in the man and the artist he grew up to be. Because the focus of those years was emotional suffering, one can surely trace back to that time a pattern of protective behavior in the mature man, which has at least three facets, and which developed in Alphonse Daudet as a response to that childhood suffering. The first facet of the pattern, and the most immediate, was that he learned not to leave himself emotionally exposed when he could avoid it. He developed a capacity to conceal his feelings or his desires, to withdraw into himself, and to live on the resources of his own imagination rather than depend on an unreliable world around him for emotional satisfactions. This capacity he cultivated into that fierce sense of personal independence which characterized his years of maturity, and which had in it strong overtones of the fear of commitment—whether to a person or an idea. All his life, Daudet held something of himself in reserve in even the most intimate of his relationships, and a certain detachment marked his manner in all his contacts—with literary or political movements,

with places, institutions, or events. This detachment, this independence, this reserve—a protective coating learned in the pain
of early suffering—had much to do, no doubt, with that pervasive feeling among so many of his contemporaries that
Daudet was not quite trustworthy.[2]

Yet one must live in the world of men and ideas, however
detached one remains. And so, a second facet of his behavior
was the constant habit of careful, objective observation. Aided,
indeed, by this very ability to remain detached, Daudet found
it imperative to study the world around him, to see it steadily,
and be prepared for its dangers. Some have said that his myopia
was actually a spur in this direction, forcing him to greater
acuity of observation to compensate for his weak eyes. However that may be, Daudet's psychological impulse toward this
constant, curious, probing, and astonishingly comprehensive
power of observation seems to hark back to earliest infancy,
when he felt the need to take the precise measure of his environment in order to protect himself from it.

But a child of so sensitive a nature cannot simply suppress
all need for emotional satisfaction. If one allows this need no
direct expression, it finds its own, perhaps devious, ways of
attaining its goal. Yet a third facet of Daudet's behavior, therefore, dating from infancy, was an oblique bid for affection
through pleasing behavior and winning ways. The psychological impulse at work was a craving to be liked and accepted,
all the more urgent because the more directly channeled displays of emotion had been suppressed. Daudet learned early
how to charm by his manner, and entice attention for himself
from others. There can be no doubt that in this psychological
impulse lies the origin of Daudet's famous charm, both as a
public personality and as a writer. His sympathy for the under-
privileged, his generosity, his widely attested gifts as a conversationalist, even his very writing style, can be traced back to
his need to feel liked and accepted, and to the oblique means
he developed in his personality to achieve that goal. Thus

Daudet fashioned, in earliest infancy, and in response to the position in which he found himself within his family, a basic personality which equipped him for the literary career he adopted by making him emotionally introverted and detached, keenly observant, and superficially charming.

Such a cluster of character traits within one individual obviously contains the seeds of internal conflict and tension. It is not surprising, therefore, that one can discern in the mature Daudet a permanent ambivalence, and a painful inability to make clear choices and decisions. He was himself aware, at a very early moment in his literary career, of the opposing drives that constituted his personality. In one of the very first of the many reflections he consigned to his private notebooks—published after his death under the title *Notes sur la vie*—he made the following perspicacious analysis of himself:

Homo duplex, Homo duplex! la première fois que je me suis aperçu que j'étais deux, à la mort de mon frère Henri, quand papa criait si dramatiquement: "Il est mort! il est mort!" Mon premier MOI pleurait et le second pensait: "Quel cri juste! Que ce serait beau au théâtre!" J'avais quatorze ans.

Cette horrible dualité m'a souvent fait songer. Oh! ce terrible second MOI toujours assis pendant que l'autre est debout, agit, vit, souffre, se démène! Ce second MOI que je n'ai jamais pu ni griser, ni faire pleurer, ni endormir!

Et comme il y voit! et comme il est moqueur!

(*Homo duplex, Homo duplex!* the first time I perceived that I was two persons was at the death of my brother Henri, when my father cried out so dramatically: "He's dead, he's dead!" My first self wept and the second thought: "What a perfect cry! How fine it would be in the theater!" I was fourteen years old.

That horrible duality has often set me to thinking. Oh! that terrible second self always calmly seated while the other is up, acting, living, suffering, struggling! That second self which I have never been able to get drunk, or make cry, or put to sleep!

And how well he does see! and how he does mock!) [3]

One smiles at the petty inaccuracy, so characteristic of Daudet, by which he claimed he was fourteen when in fact he was sixteen at the time his oldest brother died. It was Daudet's lifelong mania to be preoccupied with his appearance and his public image, which included a rather coquettish compulsion to make himself younger than he was. It seems related to that facet of his character which sought constantly to please and charm, to make attractive and to embellish. But the essence of the analysis is quite exact. The sensitive, emotionally responsive author protected himself all his life against his vulnerability with an unceasingly alert second self, detached, sharply observant, and often extremely ironic.

This duality is visible throughout his work, but perhaps most notably—and most rewardingly blended—in the famous *Tartarin de Tarascon*. All the warm affection for the people and territory of his native Provence is expressed in this book, yet it is hemmed in at every turn by the detached ironist who seems by his manner of presentation to suggest the faint condescension of the outsider—a tone for which his fellow Meridionals never really forgave him. If the tone is pleasing (to non-Meridionals, at least) in *Tartarin*, it is nonetheless sharply ambivalent, and the emotional conflict inherent therein was to cause many unfortunate weaknesses in other works. This conflict and this ambivalence, arising out of that complex nature formed in infancy, are at the very center of Daudet's distinctive artistic personality, producing the effect of "the uncertain muse," prodding the young Alphonse to a dedicated life of self-expression in literature while, at the same time, crippling him for the achievement of complete artistic unity in his work.

The circumstances of Daudet's youth tended to confirm and consolidate the character traits formed in infancy by his own nature and that of the family into which he was born. The family remained in Nîmes almost till Alphonse's ninth birthday, moving to Lyons in the spring of 1849. During all those years, the atmosphere of financial crisis dominated the Daudet household, deepening relentlessly. Both Ernest and Alphonse were regularly left to their own devices, and grew up with an unusual amount of freedom from parental supervision. Both parents were embroiled constantly in the futile efforts to save the factory, and the irascible nature of Vincent Daudet produced many a violent scene to which the impressionable Alphonse was a terrified witness. The factory itself became involved in one of the important childhood incidents which helped to teach Daudet the dangers of emotional attachment. He had formed the habit of playing in this factory on Sundays, imagining it to be Robinson Crusoe's island and other playgrounds of youthful fancy. As business declined, Alphonse began to have more and more weekdays to add to the Sundays on which he could disport himself in these fascinating surroundings. He had become deeply attached to these games and the premises when suddenly his father broke the news that the quarters had been sold to a religious order. The heartbreak of this loss is graphically recorded in the first chapter of *Le Petit Chose*,[4] and there can be no doubt of the deep and lasting impact the event had on Daudet, making him ever wary thereafter of becoming attached to places, as he was already wary of becoming attached to people.

The years in Nîmes encouraged in the young Alphonse a certain independence and self-reliance, because he was left so often alone. But he paid the price in the absence of a supporting affection of which he had need, and for which his mother lacked both time and temperament. The family was too dominated by a sense of urgency and despair for Alphonse to find in it a secure anchor of stability and warmth. When the move to Lyons was decided on and announced, it seemed to Alphonse, as to all the family, the promise of a new day and a happier turn in the family's fortunes.

It proved instead—and for Alphonse especially—a bitter disappointment. The idea of change and the prospect of a boat trip up the Rhone engendered excitement, but spirits were soon dampened in the drab and foggy atmosphere of their new city, so different from the bright sunny atmosphere of Nîmes. And the poverty of their circumstances added to the disappointment that quickly set in once the trip itself was over. Daudet was to regard the seven years he spent with his family in Lyons as the gloomiest time of his life, and as decisive in the molding of the irreducible pessimism in his outlook. Even allowing for some exaggeration in Daudet's estimate of those years, there seems no doubt that the impact they made on him was significant, and went far to reinforce, and perhaps even to aggravate and warp, the tendencies which had begun to form in his character and attitude as a small boy in Nîmes.

Alphonse seems to have been especially vulnerable to the humiliation of poverty. One of his most searing memories of the Lyons period, which he wrote about in *Le Petit Chose*, and which he seems to have mentioned often in conversation, concerns the shame he felt at wearing a working-class blouse to school.[5] No doubt he was teased by his bourgeois schoolmates. Yet one recognizes in this episode the sensitivity and the fierce pride of the young boy, so wounded by this humiliation which many another boy would scarcely have felt, and would soon have forgotten in any case. One senses therein something of the origins of Daudet's later concern with financial security, and the pleasure he took in the ownership of property and the wearing of good clothing—matters which were virtually obsessions with him during the last two decades of his life. There is, in this incident, an early indication also of how Daudet came to have that concern to put the best possible face on things—the concern of the myth-maker, which led to his harmless fibbing about his age, and to his many devices for concealing or altering certain facts of his biography. A person so conscious of appearances, so eager to be liked, and so skilled at projecting a charming image of himself, must certainly have suffered excruciatingly and drawn lessons for the future from a situation in which he was exposed to ridicule by the poverty of his clothing.

His scholastic career in Lyons added further to the evolution of the budding artist. His pride and independence, which had begun to be formed in Nîmes, now found systematic expression in his persistent absences from school. He took to going off by himself, partly no doubt to satisfy his need to explore and observe the world around him, but partly also out of a growing sense of protective contempt for all forms of conventional authority. He was responding to a need to escape the discipline and control of the classroom. This need ultimately became translated in the mature Daudet into a distrust of and opposition to governments, political parties, law enforcement agencies, and most forms of organized activity from literary movements to august bodies like the French Academy. His truancy from school was another form of avoiding commitments and involvements, of remaining detached and preserving independence—a way of behavior that became second nature to Daudet. Vincent Daudet, his father, who was doubtless grieved that his son never shared his passionate royalist beliefs, seems to have realized that it was not conviction but some inner need to oppose authority that motivated Alphonse. Edouard Drumont, in his *"La France juive" devant l'opinion*, reports having heard the father, shortly before his death in 1875, say to his stubborn son: "You don't like magistrates, you don't like bailiffs, you don't like policemen, you don't like members of the French Academy, in fact you don't like any organized group." [6] There is no doubt that the father thus accurately summed up one of his famous son's fundamental traits, already fully developed in his youthful escapes from the Lyons classroom.

But the absences from school were more than simple assertions of independence. They were more importantly the occasions for exercising those faculties which were to make of Daudet one of the leading novelists of his generation. Daudet himself has told us, in his various reminiscences, how such days were spent roaming and exploring, exercising his imagination and observing people. He enjoyed many outings rowing a boat on the river, developing his taste for this sport, and imagining himself an explorer discovering new worlds as he pulled his boat ashore on unfamiliar islands in the river. Or he would spend his day following some passing stranger, trying to imagine the life and character of this person, perhaps constructing in his mind an entire novel based on what he observed.

On days when he did attend school, Alphonse proved himself a good student, and, as one might expect, showed particular gifts in composition and in rendering Latin texts into elegant French. Encouraged a good deal by his older brother Ernest, Alphonse also began in those years to make up poems and stories outside of school assignments. His literary bent, the written expression of his lonely imaginings and observations, began to declare itself. Ernest affirms that his brother completed his first full-length novel in those years, at the age of sixteen.[7] No trace has ever been found of the manuscript, said to have been lost by the editor of a Lyons newspaper who had promised to publish it; and nothing is now known of its contents but what Ernest recalled in print years later. But if Ernest can be believed, Alphonse showed very early a sustained capacity for imaginative writing as an activity in which he could win both inner satisfaction and the approval and interest of others. His future vocation, and the nature of its attractiveness to him, were revealed at an unusually early age.

Of this apparent vocation, however, his parents took no note and offered no encouragement. The end of the Lyons years was also the end of Daudet's formal education. Not yet seventeen, the young Alphonse was taken from school by his impoverished parents and sent to the Provençal town of Alès, where, thanks to the good offices of a relative, he was to have the post of *pion*, or study assistant and supervisor, in the local secondary school. For the family this was a windfall, solving a pressing financial problem. But for the young man himself it was an inauspicious launching into the uncertainties of life. Though there is every evidence that the lad was well treated by his superiors at the school, Daudet seems to have suffered greatly in his pride and sense of independence, feeling constantly that he was there on sufferance, out of charity. This resentment conflicted, however, with the desire he had, because of his nature, to succeed with the school's pupils, to win them over and be liked by them in the job he was doing. These contradictory feelings were doubtless more than his tender years could readily handle.

The months in Alès are shrouded in some mystery. The account given in *Le Petit Chose* suggests ill-treatment by his superiors of a kind that does not accord with verifiable facts, and M. J.-H. Bornecque is certainly right in maintaining that the novel is not to be trusted as truth on this point. The abrupt departure in the middle of a school year, in November of 1857, may very well have been precipitated by some precocious scandal in which the young *pion* had become involved, as M. Bornecque suggests.[8] At any rate, the objective truth of Daudet's experience there is surely much less grim than *Le Petit Chose* suggests. What seems significant, however, is not so much the probably objective truth of the matter, but rather that Daudet always looked back on those months as unhappy, and on his departure as a deliverance. Daudet's memory of that period must surely have been colored by his inner conflict, rendering intolerable for him a situation which would have seemed a lucky opportunity for many another boy.

His abrupt departure from Alès was not merely flight from pain, nor wholly a matter, either, of deciding to take the plunge into the literary life in Paris. It was also, and perhaps most importantly, a desperately needed return to the nearest form of family security he had: it brought him again under the protective wing of his older brother Ernest. Alphonse Daudet was particularly fortunate in having so motherly an older brother as Ernest. The account of this relationship in *Le Petit Chose* seems hardly exaggerated. Ernest had the rare quality of modesty, as well as a strong sense of family loyalty. He appreciated his brother's gifts, acknowledged them to be superior to his own, and cheerfully undertook to support his younger brother while the latter devoted his energies to writing. Ernest's temperament was ideal for his brother's needs, providing the support and affection Alphonse needed, without imposing on him any sense of obligation at which his proud and independent spirit would have balked. Under such favorable circumstances, at the tender age of seventeen, Alphonse Daudet thus began in earnest the active shaping of a literary career. Within a year he was to experience the heady triumph of becoming a published author. Yet the triumph quickly proved illusory, and more than a full decade of trial and apprenticeship was to go by before he was to have sufficient achievement, self-confidence, and recognition to feel that his career was successfully established.

The wide-eyed and hopeful young man who came to Paris on that chill November morning in 1857 possessed already the essential traits and habits which would later constitute his literary personality once the experience of apprenticeship had set the mold. The practiced and observant eye, the intense curiosity, the detached and ironic manner, the capacity to charm and beguile—all the hallmarks of his later fame were already present in embryo when Ernest greeted him at the railroad station, cold, hungry, and tired, but eager and curious about Paris. The beginnings of these traits go back to his earliest infancy, and the profound impact on him of the family into which he was born. Daudet himself may be quoted here, in summation of the lasting importance of those earliest beginnings on his entire life and career. In his notebooks he has recorded this observation: "Plus je regarde, plus je vois et compare, plus je sens combien les impressions initiales de la vie, de la toute enfance, sont à peu près les seules qui nous frappent irrévocablement. A quinze ans, vingt ans tout au plus, on est *achevé d'im-primer*. Le reste n'est que des tirages de la première impression. La lecture d'une observation de Charcot me confirme là-dessus." ("The more I observe, the more I see and compare, the more I feel how much one's initial impressions of life, those of earliest infancy, are almost the only ones which strike us irrevocably. At the age of fifteen, twenty at the latest, one is already *set in print*. After that there are only more editions of that first printing. The reading of a remark by Charcot confirms my feeling on that point.")[9]

Not only Charcot, but all of modern psychological knowledge, bears Daudet out. As the content and style of all his works, in a long and productive career, were to demonstrate, Alphonse Daudet was, at the age of seventeen and trembling hopefully on the threshold of his career, already *achevé d'im-primer*. The ingredients of his success—and of his failure—were already formed and assembled, waiting to find expression.

The Apprentice Years

1 8 5 7 – 1 8 6 8

At the beginning of his volume of reminiscences, *Trente ans de Paris*, Alphonse Daudet speaks of the "involuntary terror" he felt on arrival in Paris for the first time.[1] We may well believe him. Eager though he was to conquer the big city and win a place for himself in the literary world, he was not of a temperament to feel unshakably confident of success. Further on, *Trente ans de Paris* speaks with the distortions of hindsight about his poverty and his early struggles to get started. However, the objective truth is that the young man, not yet eighteen years old, enjoyed remarkable luck during that first winter in Paris. It is true that the two brothers had barely a subsistence from what Ernest was earning, but they did not starve. Alphonse worked away at his poetry, happily and fruitfully. They made friends rapidly among the aspiring young artists, in the bohemian circles of left bank cafés. Alphonse soon had a mistress, Marie Rieu, to whom the volume of poems which marked his debut the following summer was dedicated. He gained entree into a few literary salons, was invited to read some of his poems, and tasted the first pleasures of acclaim. And before long he had a contract with the publisher Jules Tardieu, who happened—as by some prearranged destiny—to be his neighbor, for the publication of a volume of poems. All of this took place during Daudet's first six months in Paris—hardly a tale of suffering in obscurity!

His very success, however, promptly turned to a sense of

failure. His relationship with Marie Rieu soon became stormy, painful yet somehow also inescapable. His "vogue" in the literary salons did not last beyond the one season. And his publisher had the poor judgment to bring out his slender volume of poems, *Les Amoureuses*, in July of 1858. Whether because of the vacation season, or because of the inherent slightness of the book's contents, it received virtually no notice, and sold not at all. It was mentioned twice in reviews that summer—once unfavorably—and a third time in a year-end article the following December which complimented the author on his skill but unkindly pointed out the triviality of his themes.[2] His "glorious" entry into literature had turned into a rout.

Thus, Daudet's first triumph was swiftly converted into the first wounds to his vanity. This was but the first episode in what became a pattern in his career: apparent quick successes in every genre, which nevertheless were to leave as their residue the taste of ashes. In spite of the accumulating fame and fortune of his later years, Daudet was to grow steadily more embittered and cynical about the literary life. As with *Les Amoureuses*, so with most of his other "triumphs," enduring personal satisfaction seemed destined always to elude him. The triumph, having been too easily won, was inevitably and promptly followed by disillusionment. To his credit Daudet always learned artistically from his disillusionments. At the personal level, however, the pattern which began to be established with the publication of *Les Amoureuses* had to result in the author's increasing isolation, independence, and disengagement from the mainstream of literary endeavor.

A more significant disillusionment than that caused by the indifference of the public and the reviewers to *Les Amoureuses* was that occasioned by Daudet's own gradual realization that his verses lacked quality, that he was not a poet. Perhaps it might have been better for Daudet if he had not had the encouragement of publication at so immature a stage in his development. He was before long able to face the fact that his true bent lay in prose, rather than verse. But it was characteristic of him, at that age as throughout his career, to have to flounder and grope toward his achievements, suffering the vagaries of his uncertain muse. *Les Amoureuses* was the work of a groping apprentice, seeking his way. And yet, for the attentive reader, concerned to trace and comprehend the trajectory of this career, *Les Amoureuses* can be studied with interest and profit. If *Les Amoureuses* became the symbol of Daudet's earliest disappointment in himself, it contains nevertheless the record of his artistic sensibility as it was when his public life as a writer began.

A proper perspective on the poems of *Les Amoureuses* requires that their date of composition be borne in mind. The earliest among them were composed when Daudet was a mere boy of sixteen in Lyons; and the latest of them were written during that first Paris winter of 1857–58, when he was still short of his eighteenth birthday. That the volume should be of weak quality is less surprising than that it should have any quality at all. And it does have certain unmistakable qualities: a light and delicate touch, verbal wit, an engaging manner, and a flair for technical virtuosity. The two best known poems of the collection, "Les Prunes" and "Trois jours de vendange," contain a concentrated sampling of all the good qualities scattered through this uneven volume. Both poems have a catchy sing-song rhythm and a challengingly intricate versification, the one in eight-syllable lines, the other in ten. Both achieve their effect by suggestion and evocation, rather than by direct statement. "Les Prunes" is a fine example of Daudet's delicate charm and gay wit; "Trois jours de vendange," in a more elegiac mood, handles a sentimental theme with finesse. Both exhibit a genuine tenderness of emotion which is completely winning. If neither poem is great nor yet original, each can claim at least the merit of being moving and effective within the limits of its simple theme and small scope.

The talent of the poet, and the virtues of his poetry in *Les Amoureuses*, are real and incontestable. But neither the talent nor the virtues, even at their very best, possess weight and substance enough to support any serious critical analysis. For the history of French poetry, there is nothing in *Les Amoureuses* to detain the student. For the history of Alphone Daudet as a man of letters, however, there is much in the collection which is revealing and suggestive. In particular, Daudet's manner of handling certain themes shows the directions in which the traits of his personality were beginning to find literary expression.

The poem which opens the collection, called "Aux petits enfants," is probably also the earliest in date of composition. It is a sentimental poem, reminiscent of Victor Hugo who pioneered the celebration of infants as a theme in French poetry. It was natural enough, of course, for a teenaged novice to follow the example of an admired master in his first efforts. But what will strike the reader most about this poem is its utter lack of feeling. It suggests a schoolboy's mechanical exercise on an assigned theme, and it is entirely conventional in conception except for a mildly venturesome verse pattern:

> Enfants d'un jour, ô nouveau-nés,
> Petites bouches, petits nez,
> Petites lèvres demi-closes,
>   Membres tremblants
>   Si frais, si blancs,
>   Si roses; [3]

The reason for the wooden effect is obvious: Daudet is not seeking to express a personal emotion (a boy of sixteen is not likely to know the emotions of fatherhood), but merely to produce something resembling that which he learned in school to call a poem. Hence the choice of so conventional a theme, hence the succession of banal, obvious, generalized images, and hence, too, the showy verse pattern without special appropriateness to the subject. The callow inexperience of the writer is patent. Only the unpracticed can suppose that the subject alone is enough to assure a poetic emotion: since babies are reputed to be universally irresistible, a diligent application of the rules of prosody suffices to make a poem about newborn infants. Or so the young poet appears to have reasoned. The sole aspect of the poem which relates it to the personality of Daudet is the instinctive gravitation to sentimental subject matter. In his compulsive desire to please and charm, Daudet was always to show a predilection for describing in his works those details and experiences which are by their very nature charged with sentiment. In so doing, he often fell into the dangers of facile sentimentality, of course. But with such material he nevertheless learned the art of evoking genuine emotion. Even in *Les Amoureuses* he managed to progress beyond the mechanical and emotionless composition of "Aux petits enfants," as can be seen in the very next poem, "Le Croup."

"Le Croup" also takes as its theme infancy, in this case the effects of illness on a helpless baby. But now Daudet allows the material itself to have its impact, instead of smothering it in generalized rhetoric. He evokes specific details and particularized people, so that a personal drama emerges. The reader is thus brought emotionally closer to the material, is allowed some involvement with the subject in a direct way. To increase this involvement, the poet underlines with rhetorical questions the pathos of the situation: "Qui est le bourreau qui le fait souffrir?" "Qui sait égorger un petit enfant?" ("Who is the tormentor who makes him suffer?" "Who knows how to slaughter a tiny infant?") The device, here used by Daudet for the first time, was to become almost a trademark: instead of the impersonal manner which constituted an aesthetic principle with most of his contemporaries, Daudet adopted an intimate tone produced chiefly by such intrusions on the part of the author. It is because of this mannerism that Daudet became known as a "different" naturalistic author because he showed pity. As this earliest use of the device shows, however, Daudet's goal is not

so much to show pity as to draw the reader into a more intimate
relationship with his material. In this poem we have a portrait
not only of the dying child, but also of the fearful and attentive mother, the despairing father ashamed that he cannot bear
to watch, and the senile grandfather hoarsely croaking a lullaby
in the corner. The details particularize, humanize the scene,
and give it some power to move us as it could not in a more
abstract presentation. "Le Croup" marks a step in the evolution
of Daudet who, fatally attracted to the sentimental, developed
strategies of art to render such material with effectiveness and
tact.

The principal theme of *Les Amoureuses* is, of course, love,
and it is in Daudet's manner of handling this theme that the
collection is most revealing. With astonishing consistency, the
situations involved in the love poems are variations on one basic
theme: a love-sick male who suffers at the hands of a proud or
cruel female. The very consistency of this theme compels us
to see in *Les Amoureuses* the expression of a very deep-seated
conviction in the mind of their author, a personal vision of love
as one of the inescapable sorrows of man. Every tale of love
takes shape in Daudet's imagination as the story of a tenderhearted male, victimized by the combination of his imperious
need for affection and the hardhearted nature of women. It is
too simple to explain this pattern in *Les Amoureuses* as but a
reflection of Daudet's relationship with Marie Rieu, to whom
the first edition is dedicated and with whom he had a stormy
and painful liaison that lasted nearly ten years. For the fact is
that Daudet's later relationship with his wife Julia was also
one in which her iron-willed personality dominated. And more
significant, the love situations in all Daudet's subsequent fiction
were of the same basic order. It was the very essence of his
play *L'Arlésienne*, and of his novel *Sapho*, to mention only the
two best-known examples. What we find in *Les Amoureuses*
is not the reflection of a love relationship of that moment, but

something basic to Daudet's view of the world, a view that remained consistently his until he died.

Perhaps the collection's most complete expression of this theme and outlook is to be seen in the poem "A Célimène." It is not really Molière's coquette of whom he speaks, in this mannered literary exercise. It is rather Daudet's private image of woman—and of his own masculine weakness. The personal truth in the poem fairly screams through the artifice. The final stanza is representative of the poem's quality:

> Je ne vous aime pas, c'est dit; je vous déteste.
> Je vous crains comme on craint l'enfer de peur du feu,
> Comme on craint le typhus, le choléra, la peste;
> Je vous hais à la mort, Madame; mais, mon Dieu!
> Expliquez-moi pourquoi je pleure, quand je reste
> Deux jours sans vous parler et sans vous voir un peu.[4]

Of course, accompanying the pain there is a certain amused self-mockery underlying this poem. Alceste, or the poet, is after all made to cut a comic figure here: pompous, boastful yet completely helpless in the spell of Célimène. In spite of its grim theme, the poem is designed to evoke a smile. This, too, is most characteristic of Daudet, and the same tone may be seen in many—even most—of the other poems of the collection: "La Rêveuse," "Les Prunes," "Les Cerisiers," "Les Bottines," and so forth. The picture of love is dispiritingly pessimistic, but the tone is light, amused, and ironic. It was Daudet's way of disarming for himself and for the reader the thrust of the theme. His preferred way of dealing with love was to deflect into laughter the inevitable sadness of the situation. Not that all the poems are light in this way. A few are solemn, associating love with death, as in "Trois jours de vendange," "Miserere de l'amour," "Dernière amoureuse." But most are humorous. The salient fact, however, is that all treat love as inherently painful, especially to the male. So far as this theme is concerned, the Daudet of the major works of fiction was already fully evolved in *Les Amoureuses*.

Other themes which forecast the mature artist-to-be can also be found in *Les Amoureuses*—less fully developed than the love theme, yet readily discernible. In "La Vierge à la Crèche," for example, there is already detectable the rather tender, sentimentalized notion of motherhood that Daudet would expand eventually into such a character as Rose Mamaï of the play *L'Arlésienne*. Thereafter similar types recur often enough in his works so that a publisher was eventually able to issue an anthology of extracts from Daudet's work called *Les Mères*.

The sonnet "L'Oiseau bleu" also presents the earliest version we have of a favorite Daudet theme: the self-destructive force latent in the artistic gift. The image of beauty, the bluebird, which the poet clasps to his bosom in this poem, ends by draining his blood and destroying him. One naturally thinks of Musset's pelican in "La Nuit de mai"; and it is true that other reminiscences of Musset are evident all through the collection, culminating in the poem called "Le Ier mai 1857—Mort d'Alfred de Musset." Yet "L'Oiseau bleu" seems far from a mere echo of Daudet's youthful admiration for, and imitation of, his favorite poet. Its theme was one with which Daudet was too obsessively concerned all his life: not only in the famous story from *Les Lettres de mon moulin*, "L'Homme à la cervelle d'or," but also in *Le Petit Chose*, in the stories of *Les Femmes d'artistes*, in *Jack, Sapho, L'Immortel*, and all the other works in which artists play any role. Daudet returned again and again to the idea that the artist's gift of genius is the source of suffering and disorder for himself and those around him. His ambivalent feelings about the literary life—its rewards and its high cost, its gift which is also a curse—are expressed in "L'Oiseau bleu" in their earliest form.

But perhaps the most characteristic note of all struck in the collection is that of broad diversity. In a poet so young and inexperienced the varieties of tone and mood, of versification, and of theme might have seemed puzzling to contemporaries. No sharply defined literary personality emerged from the pages of this first publication. Instead one sensed a talent capable of going in any number of directions, and groping restlessly to find the right path. But nothing about this collection, as one sees in retrospect, was a surer augury of the Daudet who was to be. Haunted by his uncertain muse, Daudet's entire career was to be marked by that same restless search for themes and forms that would express the best that was in him. *Les Amoureuses* gives us, in miniature and in an embryonic stage of development, the contours of Daudet's essential temperament as an artist, with both its strong and its weak points. And that is the only interest the collection still holds today.

In launching his career with poetry, Daudet had chosen the most traditional of all entry permits into the Paris literary world, even for writers of prose. Such diverse writers as Sainte-Beuve, Anatole France, Maupassant, and Gide all launched their careers with a volume of verse. For a young man seeking his way, and sensitively alive to the practices and standards around him, the first *recueil de poésies* seemed indispensable. But when the volume met with no success, Daudet characteristically relied on his sensitivity to the literary scene, rather than on his inner urges, in choosing a new direction. He had, however, a laudable purpose.

As early as 1859 Daudet was able to sell occasional pieces to newspapers and journals of the time. These pieces, mostly prose, were in the vein of what was then successful in Paris journals, and represented no original contribution by Daudet of style or content. They were compositions of a chatty tone on topical matters, which went by the name of *chroniques*. Some *chroniques* were in verse, though Daudet seems to have been persuaded by 1859 that poetry was not his medium. His success in writing *chroniques* is attested to by his entry into one of the most prestigious of the journals, *Le Figaro*, late in 1859.

This new departure in his career reveals more than his resilience and his versatile talent. It reveals also his self-conscious attention to his own development. For he made the writing of these *chroniques* a consciously chosen training ground for the serious business of learning to write. With remarkable lucidity for his age he treated his journalism as an apprenticeship. Daudet did not become a full-time journalist, as did so many of his contemporaries, now forgotten, who dissipated their talents in this facile way. He used the practice of journalism to teach himself to write, and as a valuable source of income, without ever losing sight of his goal, and without ever confusing what he was doing with art. He was aided, to be sure, by another stroke of luck: the windfall of a sinecure as secretary to the Duc de Morny. This post, providing regular income while demanding little in the way of time and effort, shielded Daudet from the kind of dire necessity that made full-time journalists out of others. And it is also true that Daudet filled out his apprentice years with considerable writing for the theater, some of it productive of moderate income and fame. But in the main, the decade of apprenticeship which Daudet served took the form of occasional journalism. This kind of writing was the proving ground for his métier, and the means by which he first made himself known as a practicing man of letters.

A significant bridge between the poet and the *chroniqueur* of these early years is provided by the last poem of any consequence that Daudet composed, a work of considerable length published in *Le Figaro* in 1860, with the title "La Double conversion." The story itself is little more than an anecdote, but Daudet's manner of expanding it into a long dramatic narrative is suggestive of his developing psychology and of his artistic methods. The fact that he composed the story in eight-syllable verse of indifferent quality can be regarded as nothing more than the last gasp of his initial apprentice phase. Thereafter he was to compose almost exclusively in prose.

What engages our interest in "La Double conversion" is precisely the nonpoetic talent it reveals. It is, in the first place, the longest work Daudet had published up to that moment, running to more than twenty densely packed pages, and suggesting tentative feelers on the part of the young author toward the more sustained forms of literature and away from the very brief poems and anecdotes that had occupied him exclusively till then. The beginnings of a certain self-confidence, still very hesitant but real, are visible in "La Double conversion."

Then, the very length of the work afforded the author his first published opportunity at creating characters in depth. Since the story involved the love between a young Jewess, Sarah, and a young Catholic, André, each of whom offers spontaneously to convert to the other's religion, there is a need for firmly established characters whose motivations and personalities come across to the reader. This Daudet accomplishes with considerable vividness. The two dissenting parents, André's father and Sarah's mother, are equally well presented, with many details of local color to fill in their mildly comic roles. For Daudet was beginning, in this work, to employ the fruits of his gift for accurate observation. One of the most striking features of "La Double conversion" is its effective portrayal of the Marais section of Paris, with its special atmosphere of bustle, its narrow streets, its artisans, and its faintly exotic ambience provided by the presence of the Jewish quarter. Daudet has caught both the district and its people aptly in this long poem. The presence of a keenly observant eye is evident in every scene.

One notices, too, the dramatically successful arrangement of plot in the poem. Instead of continuous narrative, Daudet has chosen to present his story in a succession of individual scenes, each colorfully detailed in itself, and calculated at the same time to advance the story one more step. Some of the scenes are even presented in dialogue form, to enhance the dramatic quality; and at the moment when Sarah and André reveal to each other the intention to convert, the scene is handled as rapid-fire direct discourse. In short, Daudet is able to show in "La Double conversion" an instinct for both narrative and dramatic skill, with the intention of heightening to the maximum the impact of his story. There is a remarkable absence of those transition passages, idle descriptions, insignificant details, and other forms of waste motion, which tend to cause interest to flag, and which are the mark of poor storytelling. "La Double conversion" permitted Daudet to display, for the first time, the basic skills of the novelist he was on his way to becoming.   1334250

The most profoundly significant aspect of "La Double conversion," however, is to be found in its theme. Daudet was undoubtedly attracted to it, unconsciously, because it required just the qualities of uncommitted skepticism that were by that time firmly entrenched in, and basic to, his personality. The theme demanded an equally sympathetic and equally convincing portrayal both of the Catholic André and of the Jewess Sarah. Any weighting of the sympathy on one side or the other would have destroyed the effect. This perfect balancing act could not have been more congenial to Daudet's temperament: he could avoid taking sides, and, as narrator, remain throughout the detached and objective observer. And, indeed, the impartiality is scrupulously preserved throughout. The reader who approaches "La Double conversion" with some knowledge of Daudet's reputed anti-Semitism, and mindful of the violent and active race hatred of his son Léon, will be forced to admit that there is not the slightest evidence to be gleaned in this early poem of anti-Jewish bias on the part of Alphonse Daudet.[5] The reason for this is simple enough: in this story the religious affiliation of the two main characters is not the central issue. The story, to be effective, requires only that the protagonists have opposing allegiances of some kind. It could as easily have been a political or class difference as a religious one.

However, the very impartiality required in the telling leads

to a nice technical problem for the author in the ending. How
does one conclude such a tale without undermining the even
balance that has been so carefully constructed? Daudet's solution merits a final comment on "La Double conversion." Faced
with such inspiring proof of mutual affection as their double
conversion implies, André concludes that they must cast aside
theology completely and put their faith solely in love:

> "Laissons faire l'amour, mignonne,
> Et suivons l'élan qu'il nous donne . . .
> Et nous fuirons comme la peste
> La théologie et le reste . . .
> Toute la terre est amoureuse,
> Viens-t'en nous aimer quelque part."

To this flight of poetic sentiment, Sarah replies, to end the
poem: "Oui, mais ne rentrons pas trop tard!" [6] The cool and
practical-minded woman thus brings the romantic youth back
to earth, and it is an ironic smile that concludes the tale. Such
a conclusion is, at bottom, an evasion. The poet has no intention
of suggesting which faith might or should win out in the end.
Instead, characteristically, he suggests merely woman winning
out over man.

One recognizes the basic *daudétiste* conception of the relations between the sexes here. But the ironic—one might almost
say enigmatic—smile is equally characteristic of Daudet's way
of seeing the world. Confronting the need to resolve an issue,
Daudet instinctively dissolves into irony, rather than fall into
dogmatism on the one hand, or facile sentimentality on the
other. Irony was to become one of Daudet's most persistent
devices. Its function for him, as is so plain in "La Double conversion," was that of a safety valve: the means of retaining his
cherished uncommitted neutrality, a device for obtaining detachment or for concluding a discussion without a decision.
The reader is amused, and thus distracted from any reflections

about the author's failure to resolve the issue. And the author can provide a satisfactory ending without committing himself. The ironist in Daudet was essentially defensive, and expressive of one of the innermost needs of his nature.

"La Double conversion" is in no sense a great poem. But it is a very effective narrative. At the age of twenty, when it was written, Daudet showed the unmistakable talents of the story-teller. These talents he developed during the following few years principally through the medium of his *chroniques,* published at irregular intervals in the journals of the period. But even as he developed the art of the raconteur, and learned to hold the attention of an audience with his characters and incidents, Daudet was developing something equally important for his total personality as a writer: he was beginning to shape a personal vision of the world, and to create a style appropriate to that vision.

The dominant characteristic, both of that vision and of its accompanying style, during those apprentice years, can be best designated by the term "fantasy." The French word *fantaisie* conveys the idea more precisely, but the English word, in its accepted sense of whim, caprice, or fanciful invention, comes close enough to serve. With reference to Daudet, fantasy meant first and most obviously a style: gay, lighthearted and witty, bespeaking a refusal to be serious, and often a mocking intent. But underlying the style, fantasy meant a quality of the imagination, a way of perceiving and of representing reality by means of amusing and unexpected juxtapositions, or by whimsical inventions, such as the creation of animals who seem human, or by a somewhat perverse reinterpretation of traditional fairy tales and legends. Such leaps of the imagination had always, of course, the purpose of commenting thereby on a recognizable and human reality. Daudet had both a talent and a taste for this kind of invention, and it was to endure as a constant characteristic of his creativity. Even in his most realistic later works the element of fantasy, either in style or in quality of imagination, was always present.

Of course this kind of fantasy was no original invention of Daudet's. It has a long tradition in France: one finds it very prominently in Rabelais and La Fontaine, for example. Closer to Daudet, such Romantics as Hugo and Musset often displayed this gift. More significantly still, there was briefly in existence in 1861, when Daudet was at the start of his journalistic apprenticeship, a review in this vein to which he contributed called *Revue fantaisiste*.[7] Its existence, though ephemeral, attests to the popularity at the time of this kind of work. Once again Daudet was appropriating to himself what was "in the air" in the world of letters at the time. But of fantasy it can be said, as it cannot of other trends he followed, that Daudet was appropriating what was deeply sympathetic to his own nature.

It is worth distinguishing two separate veins of fantasy which Daudet tended to exploit in the course of his career as *chroniqueur*, for they represent two separate facets of his personality. There was, on the one hand, a kind of fantasy which exercised the imagination purely to entertain and beguile, the fantasy of romance. In this kind of fantasy the subject is generally love, the tone suggests rose water, satire is minimal and benign, and the central intent is to charm and to touch the sentiments. When successful, such fantasies can be most winning indeed, but they are by their very nature trivial and in constant danger of turning cloyingly saccharine. Daudet, who had a natural affinity for rose water, was not always successful in avoiding excess of sentiment. For example, the *chronique* "L'Amour-trompette," which first appeared in *Le Figaro* early in 1860, has all the lighthearted gaiety of a musical comedy, recounting the adventures of a regimental trumpeter who magically renders affectionate all who come within earshot of his trumpet. Yet the ending collapses in banal sentimentality when the trum-

peter, still standing after being "executed" by a firing squad as
a menace to public tranquillity, announces: "On ne me tue pas
aussi facilement que cela.—Je suis l'Amour." ("You can't kill
me as easily as that.—I am Love.")[8] On such a closing note the
charm of the invention slips over the edge into platitude.

A more successful example would be the fantasy called "Les
Sept pendues de Barbe-Bleue," which first appeared in the
short-lived *Revue fantaisiste* in 1861. This piece amusingly
reverses the well-known legend of Bluebeard, presenting him
as a tenderhearted victim, repeatedly, of feminine wiles and
schemes. The hanging of the wives thus becomes a satisfying
vengeance and turns the Perrault tale, known to every French-
man, into an entertaining farce. What is notable about "Les
Sept pendues de Barbe-Bleue" is that its genial gaiety is sustained wittily throughout, without any lapsing into sentimentality. There is no single moment at which the author suggests
that he takes his material seriously. For it is just such a suggestion by an author which can bring the flight of fantasy rapidly
back to earth. It can, of course, be argued quite cogently that
there is an underlying seriousness in this fantasy, if one chooses
to recognize in it Daudet's personal view of the war between
the sexes, with the sensitive man ever the prey of the calculating
woman. But that much underlying seriousness is unavoidable:
however imaginative the fantasy, it must necessarily have its
origins in the world vision of its creator. The point is one of
tone. In "L'Amour-trompette" an amusing invention is spoiled
at the end because the author chooses to introduce a seriously
intended word about love, thus shattering the fantasy. "Les
Sept pendues de Barbe-Bleue" sustains throughout the tone of
gay farce set by the original invention. Whatever serious ideas
underlie it are kept carefully below the surface.

It seems plausible to suggest that these rose water fantasies
serve the unconscious purpose, in Daudet's creative life, of
keeping certain feelings and problems at a sufficient remove

from him to render them harmless through laughter. In some fantasies the distance preserved is not adequate, and Daudet's concern obtrudes, spoiling the tone. A more revealing example of this than "L'Amour-trompette" is "Les Ames du paradis" in which the anguish of separated lovers, and the conflict between love and salvation, shine through too baldly for the fantasy to be successful. Amusement has given way to anxiety. But in the main the fantasy of romance intends only to be amusing, and its sole serious intention is the probably unconscious one of soothing the author's conflicted feelings about love.

Originality of theme hardly distinguishes these fantasies. They generally treat themes to be found already in *Les Amoureuses*. Though fantasies in this vein came intermittently from Daudet's pen during the 1860's, his success with the genre was indifferent. It was perhaps a well-considered act of self-judgment, in *Le Petit Chose*, to attribute to Daniel Eyssette a piece of just that sort, "Les Aventures d'un papillon bleu." Daudet had originally published this fantasy in *L'Evénement* as one of the *Lettres de mon moulin*, but had not considered it good enough to include in the book version of those stories. Now, for the scene of *Le Petit Chose* in which Daniel Eyssette must try to convince an audience at the Pierrotte home that he has talent as a writer, Daudet has him read this mediocre verse fantasy, thus putting an end to Daniel's literary career.[9] One way to read this chapter of the novel—the famous one entitled "Une Lecture au Passage du Saumon"—is as a sort of declaration of bankruptcy by Daudet himself, so far as this particular vein of fantasy is concerned. His apprentice years seemed to have taught him that he did not have it in him to make a career exploiting the fantasy of romance, and it is one vein which disappears all but completely from his work after 1868, when *Le Petit Chose* appeared.

The second vein of fantasy which Daudet cultivated during these apprentice years, however, played a much more enduring role in his artistic development. This was the vein of satirical fantasy, in which the intent is to comment directly and consciously upon some aspect of contemporary society. The tone was eminently Parisian, that of the boulevard wit, mocking the world around him. As with the fantasies of romance, the framework was sometimes a well-known fable or legend, the details of which were cleverly turned to topical account. But unlike the fantasies of romance, these satires were astringently pointed and knowingly sophisticated; and, in the main, the topic was not love but an issue of broader social import. It is revealing that the most notably successful of these satirical fantasies were all variations on the same obsessive theme: the conflict between imagination and reality, between art and commerce, between freedom and security in the literary life.

The earliest of these satirical fantasies is a clever adaptation of that favorite tale of childhood "Little Red Riding Hood." Called "Le Roman du Chaperon-Rouge" and published first in December 1859, the fantasy playfully portrays the heroine as the eternally young and improvident being, condemned by nature and fate to the endless repetition of the same error: she *will* take the long way to grandmother's because it is prettier, and she *will* talk to strangers along the way because it makes life more interesting. Neither reason nor reminders of the past make any impression. Each time she sets out for grandmother's she follows the same inclination toward beauty and daydreaming, and each time the ending is disastrously the same. The charm of the invention is increased when Daudet peoples the world of Little Red Riding Hood with a Polonius borrowed from Shakespeare who lectures the heroine on being reasonable, with a madman who cheerfully shares her folly, and with a pair of lovers, plus a poet, who are enticed by her enthusiasm. It is quickly evident that Daudet has used his heroine as a symbol of carefree and bohemian pleasure-seeking, the joys of the imagination in conflict with harsh reality. In the end disaster

befalls all who have accompanied her along her path, but Little
Red Riding Hood answers their complaints by pointing out
that each of them owes her a delightful day, and that, in any
case, her own fate will be even more drastic. Whereupon, she
steps defiantly into grandmother's house once more, pointing
the moral as she goes: "Il est dans ma destinée de Chaperon-
Rouge d'accepter cette mort sans me plaindre;—imitez mon
exemple, chers enfants, et ne regrettez jamais un plaisir . . .
Le bonheur n'a pas de prix; il n'y a que des sots pour le mar-
chander." ("It is part of my destiny as Red Riding Hood to accept this death without complaining;—follow my example, dear
children, and never regret a pleasure . . . Happiness is beyond
price; it is only fools who will bargain over it.") Daudet,
however, was constitutionally unable to drop the discussion
there, with the triumphant affirmation of Red Riding Hood's
way of life. "Voilà le sort des fous et des imprévoyants, de
Chaperon-Rouge et des siens. Avis au public!" ("Behold the
fate of the insane and the improvident, of Red Riding Hood
and her ilk. Let the public beware!") says Polonius, to end the
fantasy.[10] Thus the problem is neatly posed but not solved:
which is preferable, the way of the imagination or the way of
reason? The underlying seriousness of this satirical little fantasy
resides in the fact that it reflects the problem of Daudet himself. Under its inventive gaiety "Le Roman du Chaperon-
Rouge" posed the dilemma of Daudet's own future course as
an artist.

He returned to the problem, in renewed form, in perhaps the
most interesting of his satirical fantasies of this period, "Le Chien
et le loup," which appeared in Le Figaro during May 1860.
The point of departure this time was the well-known fable of
La Fontaine, with the wolf transformed into a free-lance poet
and journalist who follows his fancy but must often go hungry,
and with the dog made into a staff journalist required to furnish
daily articles on assigned topics, but enjoying a guaranteed

income. Once again the problem of freedom and imagination versus restriction and reason is graphically presented, and the arguments on both sides are lively, persuasive, and replete with satirical observations regarding the literary life. The fantasy is brought to an amusing conclusion when the wolf applies for a permanent post on the same day as the dog resigns his to turn free-lance. Characteristically, the ending is a witty evasion of the issue underlining the unconscious function of the fantasy for Daudet: a means of discussing matters of paramount concern to himself in such a way as to keep their anguish at a safe distance.

As with the fantasy of romance, so with the satirical fantasy, Daudet was airing his preoccupations while protecting his own feelings. Both "Le Roman du Chaperon-Rouge" and "Le Chien et le loup," moreover, are especially significant among the many satirical fantasies he wrote in those years because the fantasy is employed to express a major and recurring theme of Daudet's. In these two fantasies there is already implicit both "La Légende de l'homme à la cervelle d'or" and the celebrated and charming "La Chèvre de M. Seguin," from the *Lettres de mon moulin*, as well as the discussions of art and the artist which occupy so important a place in such works as *Le Petit Chose, Les Femmes d'artistes, Sapho*, and *L'Immortel*. Daudet never lost his anxious concern with the problem of preserving independence while assuring himself of a livelihood, of giving full rein to imaginative impulses while preserving full contact with reality. During his apprentice years Daudet found and developed a convenient and useful way to express this anxiety, rather than keep it suppressed within him. This device, incorporated into his permanent literary tool kit, was the use of satirical fantasy.

It is no accident that many of the fantasies, poems, and other journalistic pieces of this period were composed in the form of dialogues. For Daudet was attracted very early to the theater, and had shown from the start of his literary activity a penchant for conceiving his work as a series of scenes or situations, rather than in the form of sequential narrative. Moreover, his meridional temperament made the spoken word his most natural means of expression. The writing of dialogue came more readily to him than did descriptive or narrative prose. If we add the fact that for the Romantic generation the theater had been the battleground and the scene of victory, and therefore enjoyed both prestige and financial support from the public during Daudet's apprentice years, it is not surprising that Daudet should have been quickly drawn into active playwriting. Just as he sought in his apprenticeship to learn the crafts of poetry and of journalism, so too he sought to learn the craft of writing for the theater.

According to pattern, Daudet launched his career in the theater timidly, working first with an experienced collaborator, and scoring a quick initial success which made all his subsequent failures more difficult to bear. In 1862, while an employee in the office of the Duc de Morny, Daudet conceived the idea for a one-act play. With his characteristic lack of self-confidence and his need for encouragement, he enlisted the help of his fellow employee Ernest Lépine in hammering his idea into actable form. But collaboration was not only psychologically necessary for the insecure young author—it was also a shrewd and practical move on Daudet's part. Slightly older than Daudet, and already known among actors and directors, Lépine provided invaluable technical pointers for the novice, and was able to procure a hearing in influential quarters for their first joint effort.

Their play, *La Dernière idole*, had the good fortune to be accepted at once for production by the celebrated Odéon theater, and to be praised in reviews and continued on the boards for a successful run of several weeks. The work is a one-act drama of considerable sentimentality, in which an old man who idolizes his young wife suffers a crushing disillusionment about her fidelity, but ends by dominating his pain and achieving forgiveness. It is a thoroughly minor work, teetering constantly on the brink of tear-stained banality; yet it manages to be touching because of the genuine emotion that wells up from the character of the old man. It is worth noting, too, that this first play offers another variation of that typical Daudet theme: love is pain, usually inflicted on the gentle male by the unreliable female.

Daudet's theatrical apprenticeship included two more collaborations with Lépine and one solo effort. But the initial success of *La Dernière idole* was not destined to be repeated. *L'Oeillet blanc*, written in 1863, could not find a producer until 1865, and *Le Frère aîné*, composed in 1864, was not performed until 1867. The solo piece, *Les Absents*, had better luck in being produced the year of its composition, in 1863. But all three of these one-act plays were greeted with indifference, in the main, and did far more for Daudet's evolving competence as a writer than they did for his public reputation. He was learning the techniques of the drama with these compositions, but he was not attracting any attention.

None of the three plays merits any critical analysis as art. Yet they have interesting facets because of what they reveal of the essential Daudet in those years. Thus *Les Absents*, called a "proverb," reminds us that Daudet was very fond of Musset, and imitated him too often. Echoes of *On ne badine pas avec l'amour* are patent everywhere in *Les Absents*, a play constructed around the return of a young man to his family and fiancée after ten years away studying, and the disappointment for everyone occasioned by what the young man has turned out to be. The theme is not that of Musset, but the characters, the situations, and the tone of the dialogue derive unmistakably from him.

In *L'Oeillet blanc* Daudet gives a quite personal twist to the stock Romantic tradition. The basic plot concerns the daring

deed of chivalry performed by the hero, Le Marquis, in return-
ing to revolutionary France at the risk of his life in order to
procure a flower requested by an emigrée lady. But the play is
not an exaltation of this deed as an act of true love. A gentle
young girl, Virginie, speaks for the author and makes the play's
point: the selfish cruelty of the kind of woman who would
make such a demand of her lover. "Et cette femme t'a laissé
partir! elle n'a pas eu pitié de toi, elle ne t'a pas arrêté . . . Non,
d'un oeil souriant elle t'a regardé t'en aller à la mort. Mais quel
sang ont-elles donc dans les veines, ces créatures-là?" ("And
that woman permitted you to depart! she took no pity on you,
she did not stop you . . . No, a smile in her eye she watched
you go off to your death. Why, what kind of blood do they
have in their veins, anyway, creatures of that type?") [11] It seems
impossible not to see, in the treatment of this theme, a sort of
cri du coeur from its author. Daudet seemed simply to be reflecting his own experience, while drawing on an ostensibly
historical legend, to portray the tyranny of women over men.

As for *Le Frère aîné*, it is an improbable and cloying tale of
two brothers who loved the same woman. Completely lacking
in any dramatic action, it serves chiefly as testimony to how
little Daudet understood the nature of theater in 1864, and how
entranced he still could be by unrelieved sentimentality. *Le
Frère aîné* reveals as clearly as anything he produced in his
apprentice years the major weaknesses he had to overcome before he could rise to the level of art in his writing.

Poetry, *chroniques*, drama: these were the kinds of writing
at which Daudet tried his hand during the decade of his apprenticeship to the literary life. It would be risky to affirm that
Daudet was conscious, always, of traversing a period in which
learning and growth were more important for him than actual
achievement. There is a certain restless impatience evident in
the bewildering variety of writing he did; and his rather quick
successes as a beginner in each field gave him repeatedly the

false sense of having arrived. Yet there is some validity in the suggestion that Daudet did understand the need, in those years, to discover his personal bent, and develop his personal style. The published record makes clear, for example, that he was sufficiently self-aware to recognize, after a few years, that he was no poet, for he ceased composing in verse. He quickly discerned, also, the charm inherent in his meridional nature as a talker. He seems consciously to have set about developing and exploiting those styles of writing which allowed this meridional personality to come through, regardless of subject matter: hence the cultivation of dialogue, of letters, of private diaries, and of an intimate manner in his writing style. And if each piece of writing was, at the moment of composition, more probably a try for fame than a conscious learning device, it can at least be said that Daudet always reflected afterwards about the results produced. A conscientious effort can be traced in his apprentice years to develop more fully those veins which proved successful, and to eliminate the failures. Within those limits it is fair to say that Daudet underwent, for about a decade, a conscious apprenticeship in which he systematically learned his craft.

The volume of Daudet's output in those years is in itself as notable as its seemingly deliberate qualities of experimentation and of striving for development. It is true that Daudet was gregarious in those years, enjoyed café conversations and other such idle pleasures with fellow artists, conducted an overlong and unhappy liaison with Marie Rieu, and explored the world of sensuality with youthful zest. He shared, in short, the rather conventional bohemia of most aspiring artists of that day in Paris. But the evidence is irrefutable that he was also diligent, serious-minded, and productive. The persistent image of Daudet, perpetuated by all his biographers, as a frivolous bohemian dissipater during the years before 1868 is simply inconsistent with the unbroken stream of work he was then producing.

Much of that work has never been reprinted; it lies buried in obscure journals of the period, and, in the main, deserves its obscurity. At botttom it is indistinguishable from the reams of mediocre prose written by the long-since forgotten. But the bulk alone of his writings in those years suffices to refute the charge that they were years of aimless frivolity for Daudet. The biographers have fallen victim, in this as in other aspects of Daudet's career, to the legends perpetuated by the Daudet family. According to the "official" version, it was marriage to Julia Allard in 1867, and her influence in the direction of regular work habits, that saved Alphonse Daudet from becoming the alcoholic and bohemian failure to which his conduct in those years would have surely led. The painstaking research of such scholars as J.-H. Bornecque has at last begun to destroy this legend of a dissipated youth.

Above all, of course, Daudet's apprentice years were formative of the mature artist. He developed a personalized style emitting the warmth and exuberance of his nature, he uncovered and evolved a talent for fantasy, for satire, and for ironic observation. He found and exploited themes suited to his temperament: a personal figuration of love between the sexes, a special view of the artist's role in society, and a marked affinity for the folklore and characteristics of his native region, Provence. He acquired, by trial, error, and bitter experience, the rudiments of literary technique: how to entice and tease a reader's interest, how to arrange a narrative or organize a drama for maximum effect, how to construct a believable character with words, and finally how to exploit his natural verbal facility, while cultivating that critical judgment needed to revise and improve the first natural flow from his pen. Not the least consequence of the apprentice years was that Daudet learned the hard realities of his vocation: the need for astute management of one's talent, the fragile nature of success, the relationship between art and commerce. Daudet's was, in a material sense, one of the most successful literary careers in the nineteenth century, and it was his apprenticeship that laid the groundwork for his financial success, as for all the other elements that made up his literary personality.

By 1868 all the ingredients of character and craft were assembled in Daudet, and had become sufficiently developed to yield, in a remarkably rapid burst, *Le Petit Chose*, *Les Lettres de mon moulin*, *Tartarin de Tarascon*, *Contes du lundi*, and *L'Arlésienne*. These works, all appearing in the short span of five years, are not only his first mature successes, they are also among his most enduring contributions to literature. Thus the rather long and, at times, floundering years of apprenticeship culminated at last in the sudden flowering of an artist whose works are among those select few which constitute the permanent literary heritage of his nation.

First Successes

1 8 6 8 – 1 8 7 4

If the career of a literary artist is measured out in published volumes, Alphonse Daudet's decade of apprenticeship had yielded a beginning at least. There were now three bound volumes bearing his name: *Les Amoureuses* in 1858, *La Double conversion* in 1861, and *Le Roman du Chaperon-Rouge: Scènes et fantaisies* in 1862. But no one was more aware than Daudet himself that these volumes did not constitute literature. Each volume was but a collection of short occasional pieces held together only by the bookbinder's craft. None of the volumes could claim more than a journalistic level of quality, and none attracted the significant critical attention or popular sales that can launch a public career. The bound volumes passed as unnoticed as all the other ephemera he composed in those years. They were, for Daudet, vital pathfinders but in no sense did they constitute the first durable foundation stones in the building of a career. Before 1868 Alphonse Daudet was not yet visible as a literary figure.

Daudet's career proper begins with the first successes—those works which were composed with some conscious pretension to art, which attracted some recognition when published, and which have since maintained a continuing claim on our attention. The first of these successes, in date of publication in book form, was *Le Petit Chose* which was brought out by the firm of J. Hetzel in the first weeks of 1868. This fictionalized autobiography was Daudet's first full-length novel, his first sus-

tained, seriously intended work placed before the reading
public. It was by no means an instant best seller, and was ignored by most of the famous critics of the day, or given brief,
perfunctory notice. Yet one may speak of a first success, not
only because of the wide fame the book has subsequently
earned, but simply because its publication marked the emergence of Daudet onto the stage of the Parisian literary world,
as a writer who had to be taken seriously.

Sales of the work in 1868 may not have been spectacular but
they were respectable for a debutant, which is what Daudet
then was in the realm of the novel. A respected and successful
publisher sponsored it, and so influential a critic as Francisque
Sarcey devoted a long and laudatory article to it. In short, the
publication of *Le Petit Chose* thrust Alphonse Daudet forward
as a new young writer, who was being read and discussed
seriously for the first time. Unmistakably, *Le Petit Chose* signaled the public start of a career in letters.

The circumstances of composition are deeply revealing of
the work's meaning and intent.[1] Daudet composed the first
draft at a feverish pace, between January and April of 1866.
He had fled Paris, suddenly and without explanation to friends
or family, and had gone to the country home, near his native
city of Nîmes, of a cousin temporarily away. There, in the
isolated quiet of a deserted house, surrounded by the Provençal
atmosphere of his childhood, Daudet scribbled down, on sheets
of rough-textured wrapping paper, the poignant "Histoire d'un
enfant" which fictionalized his own growing pains. It seems
fair to conclude, from the abrupt plunge into solitude and the
atmosphere of his childhood which conditioned the work, that
Le Petit Chose was the expression of a deep moral crisis in
Daudet's life. That the crisis involved his stormy relationship
with Marie Rieu seems probable; but there is surely much more.
The need to re-examine himself, to assess both his past and his
future, controls the book's conception and its passion. The high

state of excitement and the personal involvement during the actual composition admit of no other interpretation. Daudet had gone to his cousin's house not primarily to flee Marie Rieu but to find himself. And what he produced was, as much as anything, a meditation on the making of artists. For that reason alone, the book was a fitting one with which to launch a career.

The frenetic manner of composition sprang from inner necessity, doubtless, but Daudet was, by 1866, artist enough to know that the manuscript could not be published as it emerged from the heat of inspiration. It was subjected to a very careful and painstaking revision before it was offered for serial publication in *Le Moniteur universel*, late in 1866. It is the mark of how far Daudet had progressed in the writer's art, through his long apprenticeship, that he insisted on making further stylistic revisions before permitting the work to be published as a book in 1868. This development of an artistic conscience is perhaps the most telling detail about the way *Le Petit Chose* was composed, for it marked its author thenceforth as a responsibly professional man of letters. From the historical point of view, these careful revisions emphasize the importance of this novel as the true starting point of Daudet's serious literary career.

Daudet's careful revisions happily left intact the two most impressive qualities imprinted on the book by the frenzied circumstances in which it was written: its passionate appeal to the emotions, and its intensely personal voice. No other work of Daudet's is drawn so completely from deeply personal sources. Even the second half, often criticized because it departs so drastically from the reality of Daudet's own life, is a profoundly personal statement, expressing in fantasy form the author's fears, his hesitations, his weaknesses as a man and as an artist, and conjuring up the specter of disaster to which his inherent tendencies could lead. *Le Petit Chose* is a work which, in spite of glaring faults, still captivates readers because it vibrates with the author's authentic feelings about himself. Read as emotional autobiography, *Le Petit Chose* is a very moving work, suffused with moral truthfulness about a sensitive but imperfect human being.

As a novel, however, the work is gravely flawed. For the personal conflicts that Daudet felt impelled to express in this work happened to be both potent and contradictory. The artist's control over such material, cast as fiction, was bound to be incomplete, and the novel is indeed torn asunder by the opposing themes. The Daniel Eyssette who is portrayed with such fragile charm in the first half cannot convincingly carry the weight of the sordid adventures which befall him in the second half. Perhaps no artist could have fused together successfully the vision of a rising young poet and the countervision of his submergence in early failure. Yet baldly stated the plot itself does not lack unity. Daudet was probably not mistaken in his impulse to make a novel of such a story. His failure was one of artistic control of that conception, for he betrayed its potential unity by imposing two separate visions on the two halves. Working from the reality of his own past, he could create a world peopled with familiar, comfortable characters, and could present it with an intimate tone and an ironic point of view. When he then switched to the creation of an imagined and feared future, his unconscious tendency was to alter characters, tone, and point of view. The reader of the novel thus finds himself, as the second half begins, abruptly thrust into a world in whose reality he can no longer believe. At that point the novel as art evaporates, and the reader can only salvage from the book an impression of the author's dire emotional state, and the demons which haunted him. In short, the first half of the book is both novel and autobiography; the second half is neither, and can only be read as a revealing dream-fantasy, the result of inner compulsion rather than artistic necessity.

In spite of its basic flaw, *Le Petit Chose* has gradually taken its place as a perennial favorite—one of the works for which Alphonse Daudet is now best known. The novel is therefore worth a detailed examination, in order to isolate the sources of its popularity. One may properly suspect that the secret of its popularity is also, in large measure, the secret of Daudet's popularity in general.

The book had a slow start with the public in 1868, but it quickly found its audience in the decade following the Franco-Prussian War. The comparisons with Dickens' *David Copperfield* began at that time, suggesting where one must look to uncover the true roots of its wide attractiveness. For the heart of the book's appeal is undoubtedly the portrayal of the central figure, Daniel Eyssette. He is a winning combination of sensitivity and helplessness, who calls forth the reader's protective and sympathetic interest. From the opening paragraphs Daniel appears as the unfavored child of fate: he was born on the thirteenth of May, and his birth marked the decline of the family's fortunes. Moreover, since it is Daniel who tells his story, in his own words, the sympathy evoked is the more intimately felt by the reader. Throughout the work, Daniel is warmly affectionate, decent, devoted to his family, and highly serious about his literary ambitions. His misadventures and his ultimate failure are affecting because they represent the cruel world overwhelming his innocence. Yet, telling the story in his own way, Daniel spices these sentimental events with an amused irony of manner, an air of gentle self-mockery which nicely undercuts the potential overdose of tearful emotion. The total effect is undeniably charming, and the figure of Daniel Eyssette stays in the memory.

If there is much autobiographical truth in the personality of Daniel—and there is no doubt that he has been endowed with his creator's sensitivity, passive gentleness of manner, irony, passion, and even identical surroundings and circumstances—it is nevertheless fair to say that the character acquires a life of his own, independent of Daudet. He is the naïve and weak soul to whom everything happens, from the way in which he receives his humiliating nickname, "le petit Chose" ("Little What's-his-name"), to the way in which his literary ambitions are ignominiously sidetracked into the porcelain business at the end. He is the eternal victim, the anti-hero who has dominated fiction since early in the nineteenth century—but who is here rendered winningly *sympathique* by his boyishness and his sense of humor. It is significant that Daniel never grows up: even in the midst of his sordid adventure with Irma Borel, he remains an innocent child, untouched by events. This innocence is fundamental to the book's appeal. A corrupt Daniel would merely repel the reader.

To the subtle blending of a charming protagonist with an ironic style, Daudet adds, as the last ingredient in his popular mixture, a most compelling theme. *Le Petit Chose* is, at bottom, a classic story of failure, the bourgeois tragedy of an artistic talent nipped in the bud. The average reader can identify with Daniel, because Daniel is admirably average in most respects. He is not the rebel or outcast so often presented as the prototype of the young artist. Yet he faces the world and is defeated by it: one of the most ordinary and most touching of youthful dreams. It is this very human theme which Daudet has caught in *Le Petit Chose*, and which attracted so wide an audience. More knowledgeable readers will also see in this theme something much more personally poignant: the youthful Daudet employing a fiction to exorcize, as it were, the specter of his own possible failure as a writer—the fear of succumbing to sensual and material temptations, or the anguish of possibly discovering that he has no talent. As a reflection of Daudet's personal travail in the early stages of his artistic development *Le Petit Chose* had perhaps even more appeal to the growing audience of sophisticated readers after 1870 than it had at its simpler and more generalized level as a tale of bourgeois bad luck.

But the combination of ingredients, offering something for everyone, seems to have assured its popularity in spite of all artistic weaknesses.

Since *Le Petit Chose* is Daudet's first novel, after nearly a decade of composing short pieces, the work becomes additionally interesting as the mold-setting model of his novelistic technique. This technique proved to be intimately related to the author's previous work as a short-story writer. For *Le Petit Chose* is constructed by the process of linking together a sequence of vignettes and incidents, each of which could almost stand alone. There is first the picture of the early childhood years in Nîmes, then an account of the gloomy years in Lyons, followed by the experience as *pion* in Sarlande, the first impressions of Paris, the Pierrotte family, and finally Irma Borel. To be sure, the diverse episodes are held together by common characters and a central theme. But no reader could fail to sense that Daudet composed the work by adding one scene to another, each one of which was conceived separately. The method was to become standard with Daudet: the novel by accretion.

Unlike that other short-story writer turned novelist of this period, Guy de Maupassant, Daudet was never to try his hand at another technique: that of expanding a single situation, by exploring it in detailed depth, until a whole novelistic universe is created.[2] For Daudet, controlled as he was by both habit and a particular kind of imagination, the only possible technique was creation by horizontal increments rather than by vertical exploration. Those who insisted that Daudet lacked those sustained powers of imagination which the French call *souffle*, and that he was superficial in his analysis of the human heart, have at least this much basis for their charge. Daudet was never in any of his writings an explorer in depth; he was a renderer of surfaces. And his novelistic technique demonstrates that truth. It must be added that after *Le Petit Chose* Daudet de-

veloped his novelistic technique so well that he achieved a remarkable feel of unity even in novels composed of the most
disparate elements (for example, the sprawling *Le Nabab*); and
his subtlety and penetration, albeit as an observer of surfaces,
are outstanding. If the charges of limited range and superficial-
ity are justified, they nevertheless miss the point: they accuse
Daudet of not being what he never tried to be, nor claimed to
be. In *Le Petit Chose* we can first see—from the point of view of
novelistic technique—exactly what Daudet the novelist was:
namely, a writer of keen sensitivity and a delicate ironic style,
who could use the methods of the short story to project the
broader surface of an acutely observed world.

Finally, it is important to recognize that the world of *Le
Petit Chose* is not exclusively Daudet's private one. It does
contain other characters, some of whom were already familiar
and developed types in his earlier writings. There are also in
Le Petit Chose elements of social observation and narrative
manner that derive from his apprentice years. Since these are
the very elements that later constitute the individuality of *all*
Daudet's writings, it is specifically their presence in *Le Petit
Chose* which makes this novel seem to the historian so essential
an event in Daudet's career. For this is their first manifestation
in novelistic form. Thus, for example, one finds *Le Petit Chose*
peopled not only with a typical passive and gentle hero in
Daniel Eyssette but also with Daudet's characteristic women:
the extreme incarnation of evil (Irma Borel) and the extreme
incarnation of tenderness (Camille Pierrotte). The maternal
virtues of Daniel's mother and of his brother ("ma mère
Jacques"), the artful duplicity of the fencing-master, the pervasive and passionate sense of family feeling, are all elements of
what was to emerge as Daudet's standard fictional world. So
are the observations of the volatile temper of the Meridional,
the hard-headedness of the Parisian or northerner, and the inevitable clash when the two meet. Finally, the tone of warmth

and sympathy for the ill-favored, tempered by a gentle, mocking irony, are hallmarks of the Daudet approach to the world. *Le Petit Chose*, then, as Daudet's first novel, is an exemplification of the key elements in Daudet's artistic sensibility, and the clear forecast of what was to be most peculiarly his own in his subsequent work as a writer.

It is certainly no accident that two other works of notably personal inspiration were being put together by Daudet during the same period (1866–1869) when *Le Petit Chose* was being prepared for publication. These works are *Les Lettres de mon moulin*, the famous collection of short stories, and *Tartarin de Tarascon*, the author's most successful novel of pure comedy. Inasmuch as these two books share with *Le Petit Chose* both the time of composition and common sources of inspiration, and since both these works must also be counted among Daudet's first successes and among the cornerstones of his enduring fame, it is entirely appropriate that all three publications be viewed as parts of the same effort. They can most revealingly be discussed as virtually one work.

Les Lettres de mon moulin appeared in book form in 1869, issued by the same publisher, J. Hetzel, who had published *Le Petit Chose* the year before. Both works had their origins in 1866, and both reflect the profound influence of Daudet's native Provence, as does—to an even greater degree—*Tartarin de Tarascon*. And although *Tartarin* was finally published as a book only in 1872, its origins go back even further than the other two works, to the time of Daudet's trip to Algeria in the winter of 1861–62. Both the narrative and the central character evolved from that date through several very different versions. The serialized version published in 1869, and composed largely that same year, constitutes virtually the text we now know. It was not importantly altered for the book edition three years later. Thus what these three early successes have in common is that they were composed overlappingly during the same three-year span (1866–1869), reflect heavily the author's preoccupation with his native region, and are principally inspired by intimate and personal associations. Taken as a group, then, they offer a portrait of the young artist and his maturing talent in the period immediately preceding the Franco-Prussian War.

Just as *Le Petit Chose* can be read as an effort on Daudet's part to come to terms with himself as an individual and as an artist, so *Les Lettres de mon moulin* appears—in significant measure—to be an assessment of himself as a product of Provence. Though the stories purport to have been written in an abandoned windmill near Fontvieille, Daudet actually did the bulk of the writing in and around Paris.[3] The insistence on the frame of the mill setting suggests the author's determination to project a world seen through Provençal eyes. And that he was still much concerned with self can be seen in the recurrent themes of the stories: the Provençal character, the ravages of love, and, above all, the plight of the artist.

The archetypal story, incorporating two of the three themes and strongly implying the third, is certainly the piece (not really a "story" at all) called "Le Poète Mistral." In it we find evoked, affectionately, the meridional character, customs, and language as embodied in the great poet Frédéric Mistral; and above all, we find Daudet expressing a reverence for the seriousness of art. Mistral's painstaking care in polishing each line of the Provençal verse which so few will be able to appreciate completely wins Daudet's admiration. He is put in mind of the statement of artistic integrity offered by his favorite bedside author, Montaigne, whom he quotes: "Souvienne-vous de celuy à qui, comme on demandoit à quoy faire il se peinoit si fort en un art qui ne pouvoit venir à la cognoissance de guère des gens, 'J'en ay assez de peu, répondit-il. J'en ay assez d'un. J'en ay assez de pas un.' " ("Be mindful of that man who, when he was asked for what purpose he toiled so hard at an art which could not come to the knowledge of very many people, replied: 'I have enough even if there be few. I have enough if there be just one. I have enough if there be not a single one.' ") [4]

Daudet's admiration was profoundly personal. It was a credo he wished to make his own. One should not be deceived by the bantering tone of these stories and the fact that they were originally published as occasional journalism. By this time, his apprenticeship served, Daudet consciously strove for art. When he prepared the stories for literary permanence, in book form, he carefully edited out those journalistic touches and topical references that would lose their point with time.[5] For example, the original opening paragraph of "La Chèvre de M. Seguin" was completely recast to eliminate references to Monselet and Henri de Pène, two popular *chroniqueurs* whose names—as Daudet clearly sensed—would soon mean nothing to the reading public. The frivolous opening paragraph and a final sentence of commentary in the newspaper version of "L'Arlésienne" were eliminated in order to give this dramatic tale the stark impact of the barest possible narration. A number of the original newspaper pieces were scrapped entirely, as unworthy. In the only notebook that survives, recording Daudet's work on these stories, we find not only much rewriting (of sentences, paragraphs, and whole stories), but even a good deal of experimentation with possible tables of contents for the book, in search of the most effective order of presentation.[6] The evidence is overwhelming that, in these stories, Daudet tried to apply the standards of artistic integrity which he so admired, and wrote about, in "Le Poète Mistral." And that maintenance of artistic integrity was an immediate and personal problem to him is attested not only by the whole of *Le Petit Chose*, composed in the same years, but in other stories of *Les Lettres de mon moulin* besides "Le Poète Mistral": such as "L'Homme à la cervelle d'or," "Le Portefeuille de Bixiou," and, perhaps above all, "La Chèvre de M. Seguin," that delightful parable of the artist torn between freedom and security.

This matter of artistic integrity quite naturally compels consideration of the serious moral problem that has enveloped *Les Lettres de mon moulin* since it was first suggested, in 1883, that Paul Arène was actually the author of these vignettes. Virtually no one today takes the extreme position that *Les Lettres* is wholly the work of Arène. Yet the matter has never been satisfactorily cleared up: how much of it is the work of Daudet, and how much of Arène? In the face of this continuing controversy, it must appear dubious indeed to assert that Daudet was seriously concerned with artistic integrity in *Les Lettres de mon moulin*. However, what scholarship has been able to uncover about this controversy (in the absence of unambiguous statements from Daudet and Arène themselves) is, in fact, sufficient to show that the reality of a Daudet-Arène collaboration does not really invalidate the claim to artistic integrity on Daudet's part.[7]

It should be said, first off, that documentary certainty about this matter seems permanently out of reach, since there is no trace of any original manuscript for a good deal more than half the stories. The only extant manuscript concerns a limited number of stories written in 1868 and being readied for book publication in 1869.[8] This manuscript shows no trace of Paul Arène's collaboration, but both writers have publicly admitted the collaboration, and both have affirmed that Arène's role was essentially minor. Unfortunately, the two accounts do not accord on the details. The result has been doubt, confusion, and occasionally rather angry charges and countercharges.

Yet one may safely fall back on a piece of deductive reasoning, firmly based on the known facts: Daudet worked in some form of collaboration all his artistic life, from the day he sought the help and advice of his older brother Ernest, at the age of sixteen, until the day he died in 1897, when he was working on a play with Léon Hennique. In all these collaborations we know that Daudet supplied the ideas and even a first draft of the composition. What he asked of a collaborator was advice, criticism, but above all a sympathetic hearing and moral support, without which he could not function. What he could never do, and was never known to do, was to collaborate in the working out of someone else's ideas. It is evident that his need for collaborators, and his way of collaborating, were deeply rooted in his character.

It seems logical to suppose, therefore—and it is consistent with all known facts—that Daudet's collaboration with Paul Arène, on *Les Lettres de mon moulin,* was of exactly the same sort. Arène's role, probably confined to 1866 when the first dozen stories were written, could only have consisted of suggestions and criticisms of a minor nature. The conception, the style—in short, all the fundamental and unique qualities—must belong to Daudet. To be sure, a particular turn of phrase, here and there, may well have been suggested by Arène. We shall never know the precise, detailed truth of the matter. But the artistic essence of the book is surely Daudet's and there is nothing truly inconsistent or hypocritical about his concern for the maximum of artistic integrity. He could sign them in good conscience, knowing that to the extent that they were works of art, they represented Daudet's art and no one else's.

But even more central to *Les Lettres* than the theme of artistic integrity is the theme of the Provençal character. The stories are dotted with the language and the landscape, the behavior and the customs of the Midi, skillfully and deliberately evoked for a Parisian audience. Daudet set out to capture the tone of Provence, in all its variety, as a sort of exotic treat for the boulevards—and a nostalgic exploration of his own roots for himself. Though not all the material of these stories is Provençal in origin (the actual visit recorded by Daudet in "Les Vieux," for example, took place in Chartres and was transplanted in the fictionalized version to a village near Fontvieille), Daudet has turned almost all of it into vignettes of his native region. Even the pieces on Corsica ("Le Phare des sanguinaires," "L'Agonie de la *Sémillante*") and on Algeria ("A Milianah") stress the meridional temperament and speech habits of the local natives. The atmosphere and the cast of characters in *Les Lettres de mon moulin* are almost wholly southern.

Unlike *Le Petit Chose*, however, which is rather frankly autobiographical, *Les Lettres* is only indirectly personal. Recounting the pride of Maître Cornille, the weakness of Le Révérend Père Gaucher, the deviousness of Tistet Védène, and the sufferings of Jan who could not forget his Arlésienne, Daudet was enumerating aspects of the Provençal character which an informed reader might well feel to be a reflection of the author's own personality. But it is indirect. Wherever Daudet is present in the stories—as in the "Avant-Propos" and in "Installation," for example—he is present as a Parisian, observing with interest, sympathy, often a touch of malice or irony, more often amusement. But always observing. What is occurring in *Les Lettres*, and what was not occurring in *Le Petit Chose*, is that Daudet is learning to draw on himself for the genuinely felt emotion, while still managing to objectify that emotion. He sought ways to separate the emotion from himself, so he could control it, and give it an artistic rendering attached to an invented character or situation. The individual stories of *Les Lettres de mon moulin*, at their best, are more successful as art than *Le Petit Chose* precisely because they draw on much the same matter (Daudet himself) but find what T. S. Eliot calls an "objective correlative" through which to express that matter. The superior control of tone and emotion in *Les Lettres* results from this unconscious objectifying of self—a process which was also soon to produce his most sustained effort at comedy, *Tartarin de Tarascon*.

The casting of himself as observer is, of course, not merely an artistic device, but also an unconscious protective mechanism, by which Daudet placed himself at a safer distance from his emotions. *Le Petit Chose*, composed at white heat and in the first person, had only a gently ironic style to fall back on as protection. In *Les Lettres* Daudet employed a bolder, more satirical irony to achieve this distance (as in "L'Elixir du Révérend Père Gaucher," or "La Mule du Pape"), and above all, he cast himself as the outsider, the observer in most of the stories. This is nowhere more evident than in those tales touching on the suffering of love, of which the prototype is "L'Arlésienne." In all of these stories the situation involved—so characteristic of Daudet's imagination and his view of love—is that of the gentle male suffering at the hands of some unscrupulous but irresistible female. In "L'Arlésienne" the author hears the story from a local resident, after having been struck by the grim outward appearance of the farmhouse in which the tragedy had occurred. In "La Diligence de Beaucaire" the author also gets the story indirectly, while traveling on a stagecoach. In "Les Deux Auberges" the author wanders by chance into the inn and collects the story. As the observer (the framework of the collection, it will be noted, casts the author in this role from the start) Daudet is able to present these stories movingly while remaining shielded himself from the kind of involvement —and pain—that would result from writing more personally, as he had done in *Le Petit Chose*.

Though Daudet is actually present in these stories as observer only, it is not an insignificant presence. The tone of the whole collection is set by the narrator's voice, the familiar style of the letter writer, addressing the entertaining fruits of his observations to a knowing Parisian public. By the device of this frame, Daudet is able to give to each story its appropriate tone: the right note of amused and sly irony in "L'Elixir du Révérend Père Gaucher," the proper warmth and enthusiasm for the Provençal landscape in "Installation," the immediacy of his personal sense of horror as a witness in "Le Phare des Sanguinaires," and the pleasant jocular irony which successfully counters the inherent sentimentality of "Le Secret de

Maître Cornille." Thus the observer in each story controls it, and in the course of the whole collection this observer takes on a distinct character, emerging as a persona in his own right who gives the book its spirit and its unity. Much of the success of the volume can be traced to this persona. It is as though the reader were listening to the lively raconteur in person. The familiarity and sparkle of the style attain a spoken effect, what Daudet himself called "littérature debout." [9] It has a natural spontaneity which is that of casual conversation, and which has created for this collection of stories the reputation of being "sunny," "gay," and "charming." It comes as a surprise, perhaps, to many readers to be told that some three quarters of these stories are actually grim or at least pathetic. Only a few of the stories are frankly funny. But the impact of the style has colored the reputation of the whole book, and the impression it has left on generations of readers.

Les Lettres de mon moulin is, then, as much a personal testament as *Le Petit Chose*, both because the author is himself the presence that holds the parts together and gives the collection its character, and because the subject matter, though objectified, is ultimately an exploration of those regional traits and attitudes, the Provençal character, which made Daudet what he was. Because the approach was objectified, the work is somewhat more successful as art than *Le Petit Chose*. But basically the two books are very much of a piece.

The composition of *Les Aventures prodigieuses de Tartarin de Tarascon* can now be regarded, surely, as the third volume of a trilogy: a sustained example, in full-length novel form, of what Daudet had been doing in the individual tales of *Les Lettres*. Tartarin has come to be regarded as a type, a literary creation embodying the character of the Midi within himself: the talkative, wildly imaginative, and slightly ridiculous essence of Provence. But Daudet was just as much talking about himself as about any universal type through Tartarin, and as in *Les*

Lettres and *Le Petit Chose,* the underlying impulse in the composition is the need to explore the self and its roots.

It is significant that the now celebrated character of Tartarin started out very differently as a type in the author's mind. Originally Tartarin was simply the caricatured portrait of a cousin of the author's with a mania for hunting. He began his life in letters in 1863, in "Chapatin le Tueur de lions," an amusing *chronique* compounded of the personality of the cousin and reminiscences of a recent trip to Algeria. Many of the same incidents as appear in the later novel are recounted here, but the short *chronique* is curiously flat reading, and attracted no attention on its original appearance. The reason is that Daudet confined his narrative to a portrait of his cousin, exaggerated for comic effect. The impression created is principally that of a writer straining for laughs. What is missing is the author's personal identification with the material, a sense of being intimately part of what he is describing. The work is flat because a dimension is lacking, the dimension of self-involvement. When Daudet returned to this material in 1869, with *Le Petit Chose* and *Les Lettres* behind him, he had a whole new manner with which to bring it to life—a sparkle and spontaneity which came from his appropriating the work to himself, and which made of his creation not an observed phenomenon but an objective correlative of his inner being. It is true that in 1869 he called his character not Chapatin but Barbarin. He had still not hit on the happy invention of Tartarin, and did not do so until serial publication of the work brought protests and threats from a family named Barbarin in the town of Tarascon. But that is the only important difference between the version serialized in 1869 and the version published in book form in 1872. The true key to Tartarin's success is the difference between the versions of 1863 and 1869—the difference between a casual observation and a creation drawn from the life blood of its creator.

The points of contact between the personality of Daudet

and that of his comic creation, Tartarin de Tarascon, are surprisingly numerous, once one comes to think about it. Since the
two are on the surface at opposite poles, however, the resem-
blance has never received the attention of critics, and seems to
have gone unnoticed by Daudet himself. The first identity one
notes is that of indecisiveness. Comically dramatized in the
amusing interior dialogue of Tartarin-Quichotte and Tartarin-
Sancho, the indecisiveness of Tartarin, torn between heroic
ambitions and cowardly fears, is but the fundamental ambivalence of Daudet, inflated to comic proportions. Daudet was
fully aware of the duality of his nature, as his notebooks show,
and he was often distressed by it. It showed up in his career in
numerous ways: his hesitations over choice of styles or subject
matter; his insecurities about his own values and even about
persevering in the life of the man of letters; his long travail
over his relationship to the French Academy. Like Tartarin,
Daudet had the heroic ambition to achieve greatness as a writ-
ter, but was assailed by doubts and fears that undermined the
forceful determination and single-mindedness required for such
achievement. It was this ambivalence in his own nature which
he caricatured so pointedly in his Tartarin, and which he seemed able to see, in this exteriorized form, as essentially ludicrous.

When Tartarin, having been shamed into embarking for Algeria, promptly forgets the lions and subsides into amorous
dalliance with Baïa, we recognize another aspect of his character, and one we can also associate with Daudet. Tartarin has
been deflected from his heroic ideal by fleshly temptation. Was
not this temptation a snare with which Daudet had actively
fought? One thinks at once of the Irma Borel sections of *Le
Petit Chose*, in which Daudet's struggle is recorded. When the
Tartarin-Baïa section was composed, in 1869, Daudet had but
recently been able to end a long, painful, and degrading liaison,
and had made a respectable marriage to a woman who was herself a writer and who helped rather than hindered his ambitions.

It is perhaps on that account that the Irma Borel episodes, written before the marriage, are grim, whereas the Baïa episodes are absurdly comic. Daudet could more readily afford to laugh about such things in 1869. It seems significant that nothing even remotely resembling the Baïa sequence is included in the "Chapatin" version of 1863. In any case, the trait of fleshly temptation in Tartarin, it can hardly be doubted, is drawn from the creator's own life.

Tartarin's Don Quixote-like ability to see Baïa as an exotic flower, rather than the Marseilles prostitute she was, as well as his capacity for endowing everything he touched with grandeur and panache—in short, his unbridled imagination, is another trait basic to his comic essence. In this instance we are dealing not with a trait Daudet had, but with one which he feared in himself, and which he suppressed ruthlessly. Fearing to be taken in, duped, or merely ridiculous, Daudet lived all his life in mortal dread of the potential of his imagination. He considered himself subject to the hot-headed exaggerations of the meridional temperament, and his career is in ample measure a struggle to remain a cool, detached, independent realist—to subdue, that is, the southerner within. In Tartarin, Daudet seemed to be giving the trait full expression, but inflated to comic proportions, as though to exorcise it. Casting himself as the ironic observer throughout the novel, Daudet made of Tartarin the scapegoat of his own fears, and of his irony the shield and the self-comfort which have been its classic uses in literature.

Finally, one must mention Tartarin's habit of exuberant talkativeness. Daudet is at pains to point out that Tartarin is less a conscious liar than a victim of his own exuberance. He speaks out of an overspilling imagination, and is soon so carried away by his own words that the line between reality and imagination vanishes. Now, the testimony is general, from all who knew him, that Daudet was a gifted talker, a conversationalist who could charm and persuade easily. If he was far from being a Tartarin, he certainly believed his conversational gifts to be a meridional inheritance, and he may well have feared a tendency to overdramatize events in conversation—and ultimately to fall victim to this tendency himself. The novel *Numa Roumestan,* concerning a political figure who is precisely that kind of unwittingly irresponsible talker, touches on the same problem in more serious vein, and shows that it was an abiding concern with Daudet. In this trait, too, one senses that Tartarin represents an escape valve in comedy for a characteristic his creator feared in himself.

The indecisiveness, the sensuality, the hyperimaginativeness, the garrulity—these traits form the central armature of Tartarin's comic personality, and all seem to be drawn, in some rather direct fashion, from the innermost characteristics of Daudet himself. In an oblique but very real sense, then, Daudet was writing about himself in creating Tartarin, almost as much as in creating Daniel Eyssette. There is, at the very least, as much of Daudet in Tartarin as there is of Flaubert in Emma Bovary—and for largely similar reasons. In Daudet's comic novel, as in Flaubert's realistic one, the central protagonist is the butt of the author's raillery, marking his effort to root out of himself the very traits he ridicules. And in this sense, *Tartarin de Tarascon* belongs with *Le Petit Chose* and with *Les Lettres de mon moulin* as creations of profoundly personal inspiration and significance.

Just how personal a creation Tartarin was became irrefutably evident when Daudet wrote the sequels, *Tartarin sur les Alpes* (1885) and *Port-Tarascon* (1890). The transformations in the character correspond so fully with the changes in Daudet himself that there can be no doubt of the subjective source of his inspiration. His cousin Reynaud, the prototype of the early Chapatin, had long since been forgotten. But it would be a mistake to isolate the personal identification in *Tartarin de*

Tarascon, as though that sufficed to explain the success of the work. *Tartarin de Tarascon* is a work of comic genius, not because it is concealed autobiography, but rather because the hero is an authentic literary creation, who lives on in the reader's memory after the book has been read. Daudet has achieved the creation because the ironic stance he adopted as the narrator gave him sufficient distance from his creation to bring it to life. *Tartarin* succeeds where *Le Petit Chose* does not, because the balance of personal involvement and distance is just right. The result is sustained comic invention of great originality, filtered through a mocking, detached, and thoroughly charming observer. Much of the effectiveness of *Tartarin* can be traced to the narrative technique, also employed in many stories of *Les Lettres de mon moulin,* in which one has the impression of listening to a spirited, witty, and brilliant conversationalist. It is more of that *littérature debout* in which the personal charm and manner of the narrator plays a major part in our enjoyment. The combination of a truly inspired comic figure such as Tartarin, enough imagination to invent a sequence of hilarious incidents, and the sparkle and spontaneity of a familiar style makes of this work a unique creation in the history of French humor.

The exact originality of *Tartarin* is worth trying to define. Daudet was right in describing it (in *Histoire de mes livres,* written nearly fifteen years after the book was published) with the Provençal word *galéjade:* a burst of mocking laughter. It lies outside the great tradition of French comedy—the tradition of Molière, Voltaire, Stendhal, Flaubert, Anatole France—which employs a delicious sense of the ludicrous in the service of some profound moral principle, or of a social commentary with far-reaching implications. *Tartarin* is undoubtedly too trivial to bear the weight of any serious ideas. Beneath its surface one finds significant indicators of Daudet's personality, as I have suggested. And some have made a case for *Tartarin* as a penetrating analysis of the meridional temperament generally. But it is hard to take even this claim seriously. The work satirizes certain foibles of a relatively minor kind. It does not pretend to vaster import, and cannot be made to support any.

On the other hand, *Tartarin* is at an equal remove from the typically genial humor of the English, in which the central figure is comic but lovable, and in which the world appears as an innocuously, winningly amusing spectacle. Daudet has often been glibly compared to Dickens, but the resemblances between *Pickwick Papers*, that typically English specimen of fun, and *Tartarin de Tarascon* are really quite superficial. Daudet's tone and intentions are too satirical, and Tartarin is too absurd a figure, and too much the object of mockery, for any meaningful comparisons with the gentle, slightly silly, but eminently human figure of Mr. Pickwick. The nearest approach to a parallel with *Tartarin* must be sought, rather, in certain of the broader farces of Molière like *Les Fourberies de Scapin*, and in selected parts of Rabelais, particularly early chapters of *Pantagruel* and of *Gargantua*, in which the laughter is hearty, based on absurd situations, but without serious undercurrents. The truth is that *Tartarin* is laughter for its own pure sake, and for those who would ask no more of it than it can offer, it is a remarkably inventive and sustained piece of delightful entertainment, unique in its period in France, and with few genuine parallels in Western literature as a whole.

The trilogy of *Le Petit Chose*, *Les Lettres de mon moulin*, and *Tartarin de Tarascon* marks a clear stage in Daudet's maturation, both as writer and as human being. Composed between 1866 and 1869, the three works show a writer turning inward into himself for raw material, and discovering the means of rendering this material effectively, in his first genuine successes. They represent the culmination of years of apprentice learning, with some of the very same material now turned to much more polished account. They are youthful works, in both outlook and manner: boyish zest for life, gaiety and exuberance, spontaneity and innocence, keen but unseasoned emotions, vividness but no great depth. Technically, the three works mark a significant progression. Starting with almost pure autobiography in *Le Petit Chose*, Daudet evolves until, by a process of objectification and the adoption of a stance of ironic distance, he is able to write of himself with detachment. The ambivalent drives in Daudet's nature—a warm intimacy demanding affection, and a fear of betrayal demanding independence and a careful show of objectivity—are thus reflected in his art. In *Le Petit Chose* we may see the intimacy setting the work in motion, then abruptly giving way to fear as the last part of the book founders in an unconvincing invention chiefly designed to conceal the intimacy. But in the best stories of *Les Lettres*, and in *Tartarin de Tarascon*, we can see the conflicting drives in a sort of happy balance, producing remarkably effective expressions of the Daudet of that moment. The combination of personal inspiration and ironic distance worked.

But the equilibrium was, by the force of things, not able to endure. The person who was the source of the inspiration was himself changing and maturing. The changes necessarily gave rise to new and different materials, and created unprecedented demands on the device of ironic distance. Nor are these changes simply the result of the impact of the Franco-Prussian War on Daudet, though that impact was very great indeed. Rather it was the normal consequence of time and experience, hastened but not created by the shock of 1870-71. For during those years Daudet was, after all, emerging from youth into adulthood. His view of life, once casual and gay, was growing more serious as his tastes and ambitions matured. He took on responsibilities, regular habits, and lofty aims. He married in 1867, had a son in 1868, and began to feel the solid pressures of providing for a family, and defining his place in the world of grown-up men. By the time of his thirtieth birthday, in 1870, he was no longer preoccupied with himself exclusively, but was seeing that self in relation to much wider horizons. The outbreak of war was a shock—but one for which his inner evolution had prepared him. Although he wrote, in 1870, to his cousin Timoléon Ambroy, "c'est un nouvel instinct qui m'est poussé, l'instinct patriotique" ("this is a new instinct which has cropped out in me, the patriotic instinct"),[10] the growth was not nearly so sudden as he claimed. Daudet had been finding and accepting values outside himself for years before 1870, including the "patriotic instinct" he displayed while traveling with Alfred Delvau in Germany in 1865.[11] But the war, and the civil war which followed, undoubtedly made the changes crystallize dramatically: Daudet was expanding his self, enlarging his private universe, turning outward.

Artistically, this maturation posed problems, however, for one of his particular combination of psychological traits. The self on which he had hitherto learned to draw for his artistic substance was now radically changed. The technique by which he had been able to balance his self-involvement with irony no longer worked: the equation had been unhinged. Accordingly, the years from 1869, after *Tartarin* was completed, until 1874, when he completed a new full-length novel—the first since *Tartarin*—were tortured years of renewed searching for a balance. The work he produced in those five years was voluminous, astonishingly varied, but only rarely of top quality. It was virtually a new apprenticeship, in search of a new career. And in 1872 his confusion and desperation (after the public failure of his play *L'Arlésienne*) grew so intense that he seriously questioned the reality of his literary talent, and contemplated taking a bureaucratic post, abandoning literature. It was his wife Julia who, in that extremity, reinforced his faltering ego and persuaded him to continue writing. Thus, less than five years after he had apparently reached the gates of success, Daudet found himself confronted with the specter of failure.

There can be no doubt that this five-year crisis in his career, from which he was to emerge a successful novelist of realism, was a poignant personal drama for Daudet, in which he suffered painfully. Faced with a self that was now infinitely broader and more complex, and with a world that had become equally so for him, he was obliged once again to flounder about as he had done during his apprentice years, in search of creative renewal. His travail is reflected in the many kinds and styles of writing he essayed between 1869 and 1874, restlessly seeking the key to a new artistic equilibrium.

These diversified efforts are divided between drama and the journalistic vignette or short story. The theatrical works were especially blighted by his now badly shaken confidence in his creative powers. For example, *Le Sacrifice*, produced in 1869, was an ill-conceived and hastily written attempt, after the collapse of his collaboration with Ernest Lépine (their *Le Frère aîné* had failed miserably in 1867), to prove that he could succeed in the theater on his own. The basic plot was without dramatic force: a young artist sacrifices his career for the happiness of his family. Clearly, Daudet was seeking in this play to express the same preoccupations as had animated *Le Petit Chose*, but without finding a viable form for the ideas. The motivation of the characters is often unbelievable, and the spiritless action progresses through a somniferous bath of sentimentality, right down to an improbable and sticky happy ending. *Le Sacrifice* has perhaps but one source of interest for the student of Daudet's career: in the hero's father, Le Père Jourdeuil, Daudet has created his first full-length portrait of a *raté*, the artistic failure, boastfully living out his days on the imagined triumphs of his youth. This character type was to figure prominently in many later works, beginning with the famous Delobelle of *Fromont jeune et Risler aîné* whose refrain was: "Je n'ai pas le droit de renoncer au théâtre" ("I haven't the right to give up the theater"). It is of interest to note how early the possibilities of the type had attracted Daudet. And it is difficult not to relate his interest in the type, manifesting itself at the same time as the composition of *Le Petit Chose*, to his own deep-rooted fear of failure.

Lise Tavernier, his next play, is a good deal worse. He wrote it during the war period, and it had the briefest of runs in January 1872. Equally sentimental by comparison with *Le Sacrifice*—it concerns the tribulations of an unfrocked nun!—*Lise Tavernier* borders on the incoherent because of the melodramatic twists and turns of the main plot, the general atmosphere of intrigue, the murky motivation, and the bewildering profusion of characters and subplots. Its chief significance lies in the fact that its quick failure seems to have impressed on Daudet the virtues of a simple, strong plot line in a drama.

His next play, *L'Arlésienne*, an expansion of one of the stories in *Les Lettres de mon moulin*, reflected this lesson. The play's substance also suggests that, still trying for his first real triumph in the theater, Daudet was now turning back to the materials of his first successes in an effort to recapture the magic formula. *L'Arlésienne* was a failure with the public in 1872, but it was a sensitive, persuasive play—undoubtedly Daudet's best work for the theater. The public vindicated the author subsequently, acclaiming the play when it was revived in 1885; and it has since become a staple in the repertory of French theater.

The strength of *L'Arlésienne* is its tragic inevitability: few characters, only one basic situation, and the action grinding slowly to a relentless conclusion. The original story was stark, denuded of detail. Fleshed out for the stage, it has the same simple grandeur. Daudet has eliminated the father, and given the hero's mother a strong and moving role in the action. Moreover, as counterpoint to the cruel woman of Arles (who is cleverly made a constant but unseen presence throughout the play) Daudet has created a simple and sweet young girl, Vivette, thus completing the triangle typical of all Daudet's trage- dies of love: the heartless woman, the passive weakling, and the tender "other woman." Finally, to round out fully the central theme of love and its effects, Daudet has introduced into the play version old Balthazar, as an example of one who success- fully but painfully resisted passion, and the hero's younger brother, dubbed "L'Innocent," whose simple-mindedness, it is suggested, is traceable to his not having had a fair share of his mother's affection. Clearly, there is much personal projection in the character of the hero—now called Frédéri instead of Jan —and part of the play's power may be said to be the note of personal involvement which renders so real and poignant the passion of Frédéri. Daudet was not altogether wrong in suggest- ing that *L'Arlésienne* was simply the reverse side of the same coin as *Tartarin de Tarascon:* what might be called "le Midi tragique" and "le Midi comique." The atmosphere and charac- ters of both works were obviously very close to him, and the works depicted two possibilities in his own nature.[12]

Daudet's playwriting activities during this crisis seem casual and desultory when compared to the feverish pace at which he produced short stories, studies, and vignettes between 1869 and 1874. In large part this activity was, of course, a financial necessity. But, in part, it was also the reaction of a man of thirty who, confronted by war and possible death, suddenly asks himself what he has accomplished with his life. A broken leg prevented Daudet from serving at the outbreak of the war in 1870, but with Paris under siege he joined the National Guard later in the year. We know from his notebooks that the war impelled him to re-examine his life and his values. And it is a fact that beginning in February 1871 (while the war was still on), and extending to December 1873, Daudet published a series of nearly one hundred short pieces of prose in the journals of the period. It is this massive effort which appears as a new apprenticeship, and a casting about for a new equilibrium in the drives that then beset him and conditioned his art.

The first pieces, in 1871, concerned observations of his own regarding the behavior of his compatriots under siege in Paris. Some were actual incidents, recorded in a vivid and nervous style, others were invented stories, comic or pathetic, illustrating some aspect of life in trying circumstances. An initial grouping of these writings was published in book form in 1871, as *Lettres à un absent*—many of the pieces had been composed in the form of letters from an observer in Paris to an unnamed Parisian, absent in the provinces. Soon, however, while the pace of writing continued at the rate of one item every ten days or so, the pieces began to change in both content and form. He returned to earlier Provençal themes, resurrected and recast old material from youthful *chroniques*, then experimented with impressionistic writing: descriptions of places, evocations of character types, and vignettes of observed life. Slowly he moved into a whole new range of sensibility: the careful observation of the urban scene around him, and its objective, precise rendering in prose. He showed an interest in a wide range of personalities, some public figures, some obscure individuals he had observed, some invented. Artists in particular attracted his attention, and the poor. But the significant fact is that though he continued to find material in himself or in others with whom he could identify, he was now finding it possible, virtually for the first time, to create from materials that were purely observed, outside himself, and having no visible connection with him. He was learning to get outside himself more, and to render the objective world around him. He was pursuing to its logical consequence the direction he had begun to take in his earlier trilogy of first successes. From concern with self alone, he had advanced to a concern with self objectified through an external medium. Now he was going beyond that and concerning himself with externals unconnected with self in any obvious way.

These pieces were largely composed under pressure of a contract, and as other journalists have done before him, Daudet took his material wherever he could find it. Much of it was trivial, and deserved oblivion. But a creditable amount of it was worth salvaging for the dignity of book covers. Besides *Lettres à un absent*, published in 1871, Daudet drew three other volumes from this outpouring of journalism. First, a collection of short stories published in 1873 as *Contes du lundi*, employing a rubric under which a whole series had appeared every Monday morning in one journal for more than six months; then in 1874, two volumes: wartime and patriotic pieces collected under the title *Robert Helmont: Etudes et paysages*, and a group of fictional variations on the single theme of artists and their women, *Femmes d'artistes*. Both *Lettres à un absent* and *Robert Helmont* were composed chiefly of pieces too topical to endure, and were thus never reprinted. Neither was *Femmes d'artistes*, for Daudet came to recognize that it had an artificial and strained air, as a result of his failure to conceal in each succeeding story the obvious sameness of plot and theme. He later reshuffled all this book material, scrapping much of it with a ruthless self-criticism which one must admire, and grouping the best of the stories from all collections into just two definitive collections of his short stories: *Les Lettres de mon moulin*, considerably augmented over the first edition of 1869, and *Contes du lundi*, substantially altered and enlarged from the text first issued in 1873.

Thus, of the stories and vignettes Daudet published in such profusion between early 1871 and late 1873, perhaps one quarter were never printed in book form and were quickly forgotten. And of the remainder which were put in books, only a relative handful were finally deemed worthy of representing the permanent "literary baggage" of their author. Yet this handful has among it such gems as "La Dernière classe" and "Le Siège de Berlin," which have given Daudet a reputation as one of the masters of the French short story. Out of the mass of material scribbled so feverishly to meet deadlines, there has come down to us a small but valuable literary legacy.

What now seems most significant about the stories and plays written between 1869 and 1874 is the change they reveal in the personality and the artistic vision of Daudet himself. The change is, fundamentally, that produced by growing up, and it had both gain and loss in it for Daudet's art. The great gain was the expansion of his scope. In those years he moved out of his enclosed egocentric world enough to begin to grapple meaningfully with a whole range of serious matters outside his immediate self: family, profession, country, social class. These had previously been concerns, or subjects, of his only insofar as they provided a reflection of his inner self. The great loss was the quality of spontaneous gaiety, and of warm intimacy, which one finds in the best of *Les Lettres de mon moulin* and in *Tartarin*. These qualities, belonging as they do to youth, were to vanish in this more mature, more serious Daudet who emerged after the Franco-Prussian War. He did not, of course, lose his sense of humor, or his warmth. But the spontaneity and the natural gaiety died, as his humor became more satirical, more calculated, and more purposeful; and the simplicity and directness went out of his warmth, as it became more the result of artifice, a controlled personalization of style, a mannerism.

When, in 1873, Daudet was casting about for a new subject of some scope on which to work, he hit on the idea of a story that would reflect everyday life in the Marais district of Paris, with its small shops and poor working-class people. The very idea of the subject is enough to suggest how far Daudet had come along the path away from his inner self to the objective world outside. His first thought was to cast the story in the form of a play. Failing to find a satisfactory dramatic form for the material, he abruptly changed his plan and began turning it into a novel. When the story appeared in 1874, under the title *Fromont jeune et Risler aîné*, he found he had scored his first really major public success. Sales were rapid, and higher than for anything he had ever published previously. Almost overnight, Daudet found his future was assured financially. What is also clear is that, for some years to come at least, his future was also assured artistically. With this novel he had found his new direction. He was to be a novelist of realism.

The Novels of Realism

1 8 7 4 – 1 8 81

Alphonse Daudet's path to literary realism was not only natural in that it marked an artistic coming of age. It was equally natural in that it developed logically out of traits deeply rooted in his fundamental nature. He had always been keenly observant, a habit which had much to do with impelling him toward a career in letters. He developed very early the urge to record—in memory or in notebooks—the significant details of what he had seen on any given day. And there seems no reason not to credit the common assumption that his near-sightedness itself was a stimulus to observation, having forced him very early to look more intently at the world than people of normal vision do. Further, Daudet possessed a capacity for unflagging fascination with the world around him, and especially with people. It was part of his natural enthusiasm for life that he was seldom bored, and always found something to occupy his attention in every encounter or circumstance. Lastly, however much Daudet had a need to feel liked, his nature craved equally the right to privacy and a sense of uncommitted independence. Just as his early stance of mocking irony had supplied the distance needed to deal artistically with himself and his meridional heritage, the stance of objectivity now offered him a comparable emotional haven for dealing with the world around him. If at this juncture of his career realism had not already existed, Daudet would have had to invent it.

It is, of course, a significant additional factor that realism did already exist, and that Daudet had already encountered it head-on by 1874. It is not merely that Daudet was an admirer and a keen student of Balzac—though he was that, and his work shows the clear traces of it. Nor is it that by then the novels of Flaubert and the Goncourt brothers, to say nothing of those of the formally labeled *école réaliste* (Champfleury, Duranty, and so forth), had firmly established the literary theory of realism. The meaningful encounter had come in 1872, when Daudet met, and was received as a member of, that small group of ardent realists who used to meet regularly to talk about literature: Flaubert, Turgenev, Edmond de Goncourt, and Zola. It was in these meetings, no doubt, that Daudet heard much of the theory of realism in the novel expounded and defended by active and dedicated practitioners.

Yet this is by no means to suggest—as some have—that Daudet was thereby simply an imitator, an opportunistic borrower of other people's ideas. It was surely as much affinity for their ideas as any need to borrow them that attracted Daudet to this group. And it is an incontestable fact that his realism was so personal, in its quality, as to remain instantly identifiable, and completely distinct from the work of any of his friends or contemporaries. Whatever Daudet may have learned from his friends he obviously made very much his own. Nevertheless, one need not shrink from the probable fact that Daudet *was* influenced. It was both his great strength and his weakness that he was essentially a passive personality, open to suggestion and influence. It was his gift that he was acutely sensitive, alive to all the currents of thought and feeling around him, and able to express and reflect them effectively. It was his misfortune that, in his career, he often responded too readily, because of this keen sensitivity, to unwise influences, and lacked the kind of deep convictions and inner drive needed to counter such influences. Both triumphs and disasters in Daudet's long career always owed something, at least, to the author's extraordinary receptivity to environmental forces.

Daudet's triumphant emergence as a novelist of realism, then, was produced by the lucky confluence of the stage he had reached in his personal artistic development with the rising fortunes of the champions of literary realism. It is important to bear in mind, however, that Daudet's embrace of realism in 1874 did not by any means imply an abrupt jettisoning of the ironic sensibility he had displayed in 1868. It was a gradual evolution that had occurred, and the unique quality of Daudet's realism resulted from the heavy carry-over of his past into his new approach. Just how much continuity there was in Daudet's evolution from ironist to realist can be seen in a comparison of *Fromont jeune et Risler aîné* with *Le Petit Chose*.

To an astonishing degree these two novels share fundamental elements: a dominant theme in which integrity and idealism fall prey to evil; a constellation of characters among whom the good are weak and the evil are strong-willed; and a stylistic manner intended to seize on and engage the reader's emotions. The resemblances go well beyond these generalities, too: each novel tells virtually the same basic story, except that in *Le Petit Chose* the younger brother (Daniel Eyssette) holds center stage while his older brother (Jacques) hovers protectively on the periphery; whereas in *Fromont jeune et Risler aîné* it is the older brother (Guillaume Risler) who is the central victim, while the younger brother (Frantz) plays a secondary role. Sidonie Chèbe, the scheming and ambitious product of the Marais, is really but a more fully detailed and more plausible version of the Irma Borel of *Le Petit Chose*. It is noteworthy that both incarnations of female wickedness end the same way: performing on stage in the degrading atmosphere of tawdry showplaces. The silent and gentle Désirée plays the same part in *Fromont jeune* as is played by the long-suffering and inarticulate Mlle. Pierrotte in *Le Petit Chose*. And the pretentious bohemianism of Delobelle is a fully realized creation, expanded from the café intellectuals satirized in *Le Petit Chose* and employed for the same purpose: to dramatize the difference between integrity of character and fakery. Finally, it can be observed that both works are built on an identical set of values and similar motivations: the preservation of a family's unity and honor, and a concern for personal integrity.

There can, then, be no doubt that *Le Petit Chose* and *Fromont jeune et Risler aîné* are products of the same general cast of mind, the same imagination, and the same sensibility. Nevertheless, the two works are more different than they are alike, and it is the differences—all the more visible once one has recognized the resemblances—which are significant, and which mark the new direction in Daudet's art in 1874.

The key difference is undoubtedly in the consciously chosen setting and purpose. However similar may be the theme and the characters (and these are probably unconscious similarities), the plot circumstances, the milieu, and the artistic objectives of the author are all different in *Fromont jeune et Risler aîné* from what they are in *Le Petit Chose*. Daudet has himself stated, in print, that he intended to write something that would deliberately contrast with his earlier "provincial" material (he was thinking of his play *L'Arlésienne*, at that time in rehearsal), a work for Parisians and about Paris, "une oeuvre plus près d'eux, de leur vie de tous les jours, s'agitant dans leur atmosphère" ("a work closer to them, to their daily lives, unfolding in their own atmosphere").[1] Quite naturally, he chose to depict the quarter of the Marais in which he was then living. His aim was to construct a situation in which the commercial life of the neighborhood would provide the main background and motivation of the characters. Business ethics and family rivalry were to shape the action. The Parisian was to recognize his own daily existence in the details of the work: its descriptions, characters, and events. Such a conception is a far cry indeed from the highly personal universe which Daudet had depicted in *Le Petit Chose*. He was turning resolutely away from his private self, the exotic atmosphere of the Midi, and the life of the artist, which had been his chief materials before. He was looking outward, seeking to render the life of others less immediate to his own experience. And he wished to portray an ordinary, everyday, popular form of life. He was, in short, adopting the optics and the aesthetics of realism.

A necessary corollary for Daudet in his adoption of the realist's viewpoint was a changed attitude to the world of commerce and to bourgeois values generally. For Daniel Eyssette the partnership with his father-in-law in the porcelain business represented defeat: the end of his artistic aspirations, the descent into the banality of commerce. Pierrotte is sympathetically portrayed as a man of shrewd ability and integrity, but the whole novel exudes the feeling that these virtues are admired by Daudet only from a safe distance. In *Fromont jeune et Risler aîné*, however, Daudet has put the virtues of commerce at the very center of the good life. What was a consolation prize, in defeat, for Daniel Eyssette has become a life's ambition realized for the elder Risler: full partnership in a respected business firm. No doubt, this reflects the maturity of the responsible family man in Daudet—his personal values had undergone some change. But it reflects also his changed aesthetics: his need now to enter, with full sympathy, into the mentality of the new world he was describing. In this, of course, Daudet differed temperamentally from Flaubert who could only write about the bourgeoisie from a scornful distance. Still, it is probably true that for all his effort to enter sympathetically into the commercial world, there remains something a bit forced—"convenue et romanesque" ("conventional and storybooklike") Daudet himself called it[2]—about the plot of *Fromont jeune*. It was, after all, his first attempt at this kind of objectified portrayal. One feels a certain artificiality in the insistence on Risler's reverence for the firm's reputation. The realistic stance was to become rather more natural to Daudet in later novels. *Fromont jeune* marks a resolute, if not yet truly skillful, turn away from the attitude to the commercial world displayed in *Le Petit Chose*.

A further difference between *Le Petit Chose* and *Fromont jeune*, closely related to this changed attitude to the world of commerce, is that of tone. *Fromont jeune* is an oppressively serious and solemn novel. Daudet treats the principal characters and their milieu with great earnestness. There is no tendency to mock, nor even a faint flicker of irony, in the manner of their presentation. Only the episodes involving the actor Delobelle show that the ironist of *Le Petit Chose* is still active. For the rest, there is no lightening of the tone. The petty concerns of these bourgeois personalities, which one might have expected Daudet to depict with malicious gaiety, emerge instead as gravely significant. The full force of Daudet's pessimistic view of man hangs heavily over the novel. Now, the events and the theme of *Le Petit Chose* are in fact no less somber. But the ironic presentation allows one to think of *Le Petit Chose* as a work of gaiety, whereas *Fromont jeune* seems rather a work of unrelenting realism. It is as though Daudet's personality had undergone a change, as though his outlook had altered. And indeed, this telltale matter of tone, in comparing the two novels, does seem to suggest that something of the young Daudet's sunniness and wit had been subdued by his marriage, the Franco-Prussian War, and the process of maturing. Though he had by no means lost his sense of humor, he was taking the world a good deal more seriously.

Even the ironist in Daudet seemed to spy darkened hues in *Fromont jeune*. The portrait of Delobelle is perhaps the most delicious morsel in the novel, a sharply observed and tellingly depicted figure of the *raté* type. This character has quite justly joined the gallery of immortal literary types, like Tartarin, Falstaff, or Don Quixote. With a sure instinct Daudet has epitomized the full essence of his character by seizing on his constant refrain: "Je n'ai pas le droit de renoncer au théâtre."

All the pretentiousness as well as the egotism and the delusionary madness of the character can be deduced from this one revealing trait. Daudet's fine comic touch in the use of this Balzacian device of portrayal via the characteristic utterance is precisely that displayed in *Tartarin de Tarascon*, in many stories of *Les Lettres de mon moulin*, and in certain characterizations in *Le Petit Chose*, such as those of Jacques Eyssette, M. Pierrotte, and Irma Borel's African maid. But in the character of Delobelle there is a grim note. He is not merely the butt of laughter, he is an object of blame. Daudet is at pains to show us that Delobelle's behavior directly causes suffering to others. We may laugh at him, but the laughter is bitter, for the social consequences of the personality are bitter. In the portrayal of Delobelle we can see especially well that the gaiety had gone out of Daudet's ironic vision. The sparkling tone of his early successes was now gone forever.

A final difference to be noted between the two novels is that of structure. *Le Petit Chose* is, by its autobiographical nature, a chronologically linear composition, with few characters and little in the way of intricate plotting, dramatic confrontations, surprises, or purposeful proportioning of incident. Written hastily, *Le Petit Chose* is almost purely a work of instinct. But *Fromont jeune et Risler aîné* is a much more consciously shaped structure, in which there is visible evidence of Daudet's striving for artistic control and effects. The book does not begin at the beginning, for example. Instead, Daudet employs the device of the mass scene to accomplish the exposition. The wedding of Sidonie Chèbe to the elder Risler provides the occasion when all the principal characters of the plot can properly come together, for a revealingly significant event. Daudet makes the most of it. The remainder of part one then goes back in time to fill in the essential background of each main character introduced. Thus the opening chapter, probably an outgrowth of the original conception of the work as a play, plunges the reader at once into the middle of the action, at a tense moment, when the main characters and the main forces that will shape the plot are in plain view. It is an effective device for winning prompt attention from the reader, and one to which Daudet was to have regular recourse thereafter.

The novel has four parts or Books, of almost equal length, and so arranged that each Book ends on a pointedly dramatic and suspenseful note. In this symmetrical shaping one can perhaps again see the influence of theatrical thinking on Daudet's sense of composition. After the dramatic opening of the first chapter, Book One tells in flashback the story of Sidonie Chèbe's youth, and brings the reader expectantly to the threshold of her infamous triumph. Book Two recounts Sidonie's deepening inroads into the firm's solvency and her assault on Risler's honor. A letter to Frantz Risler ends Book Two on a note of hope, which evaporates when Frantz falls victim to Sidonie's seductiveness in Book Three. Book Four provides a resolution of the events in which Sidonie's downfall is balanced by her carefully prepared vengeance which destroys Risler. Interwoven in this sequence of events are the subplots involving Delobelle the actor and his hapless family, including the daughter Désirée who attempts suicide; the Fromont family and the pathetic rascality of Georges; Planus the cashier; and Sidonie's father, M. Chèbe. The subplots are carefully juxtaposed against the events of the main plot so as to provide contrast at suitable moments. And the complexity of characters, representing various social classes and types, is intended to round out the portrayal of the Marais quarter in all its aspects. Compared to the simple lines of *Le Petit Chose*, then, *Fromont jeune et Risler aîné* is a deliberately complicated and intricate architectural feat. This difference in structure signifies Daudet's entrance into novel-writing, not as a form of self-expression, but as a serious artistic discipline, whose rules he intended to discover and conscientiously apply.

The art of *Fromont jeune* is highly conscious, and the results are extraordinarily powerful. The emotions of the story are undeniably compelling. The fact that so many readers wrote to Daudet while the book was appearing serially, pleading with him not to let Désirée die, is only the most dramatic proof that the novel is effective. Sidonie is a memorable example of the destructively ambitious woman, and Delobelle, as we have seen, is a triumphant specimen of character portrayal. The plot is tense and well managed, and the Marais comes convincingly alive as a milieu in the pages of this novel. Perhaps most interesting of all is the impression Daudet has conveyed of the destructive power latent in the very existence of cities, and of such commercial enclaves as the Marais. Paris itself becomes a leading protagonist in Daudet's story, a principal force in reducing his characters to despair. Of Désirée's suicide, Daudet notes:

A Paris, surtout dans les quartiers ouvriers, les maisons sont trop hautes, les rues trop étroites, l'air trop troublé pour qu'on aperçoive le ciel. Il se perd dans la fumée des fabriques et le brouillard qui monte des toits humides; et puis la vie est tellement dure pour la plupart de ces gens-là, que si l'idée d'une Providence se mêlait à leurs misères, ce serait pour lui montrer le poing et la maudire. Voilà pourquoi il y a tant de suicides à Paris.

(In Paris, especially in the working-class sections, the houses are too high, the streets too narrow, the air too murky for one to notice the sky. It gets lost in the smoke from the factories and the fog that rises from the damp roofs; and then life is so hard for most of those people, that if the concept of Providence mingled with their miseries, it would only be as something to shake your fist at and curse. That is why there are so many suicides in Paris.) [3]

And to sum up this aspect of Daudet's theme, there is the book's ending, in which the faithful old cashier, Planus, having seen the dead body of Risler who had hanged himself, catches a glimpse of the city stirring into life in the early morning hours: "La vie recommençait . . . Machine, en avant! Et tant pis pour qui reste en route! . . . Alors le vieux Planus eut un mouvement

d'indignation terrible:—Ah! coquine . . . coquine . . . criait-il
en brandissant son poing; et l'on ne savait pas si c'était à la
femme ou à la ville qu'il parlait." ("Life was starting up again
. . . Machine, forward march! and too bad for those who fall
by the wayside! . . . Thereupon old Planus made a frightful
gesture of indignation: Ah, the hussy . . . the hussy . . . he
shouted, brandishing his fist; and one did not know whether
it was the woman or the city he was addressing.")[4]

The closing scene is likely to recall Balzac's device at the
end of *Le Père Goriot* in which Rastignac's ambiguous cry of
defiance—"A nous deux maintenant!"—can also be read as a
reference both to a woman and to Paris. Daudet, who made no
secret of his admiration for Balzac, was surely conscious of the
Balzacian echo in his ending but he made the scene very much
his own.[5] The indignation of Planus against the city is justified by all the unhappy events of the novel, which culminate in
Risler's grisly suicide. Yet just as Planus leaves uncertain for the
reader whether Sidonie is more to blame than Paris, so the
author himself is plainly ambivalent in the presentation of his
novel's urban setting. On the one hand, he dwells with warmly
affectionate detail on his descriptions of the Marais quarter and
the bustling life that abounds in its narrow streets. On the other,
he underlines when he can the baleful pressures exerted by the
crowded city on the helpless poor. Daudet, a transplanted
Meridional, was becoming a novelist of the Paris he both loved
and resented, and his ambivalent feelings about the city were
to become a running theme in all his work after *Fromont jeune*.
The closing scene of this novel, in its ambiguity, epitomizes the
way in which Daudet would make the Balzacian theme of the
city characteristically personal to himself.

The attention Daudet devoted to the city of Paris in *Fromont
jeune* provided the occasion for what is perhaps the most
notable of the new stylistic mannerisms he developed in his
move toward realism. In this novel the description of physical

settings is not only more elaborately detailed and objective than anything Daudet had ever attempted before, but it is also conscientiously researched. In the first chapter, for example, the wedding banquet is evoked with minute details of the table arrangements, decorative plants, and food at Véfour's; and when the newlyweds go to their apartment, Daudet traces their path as though he were composing his sentences with a map of Paris before him: "On traversa les Halles, la rue de Rambuteau pleine de voitures de maraîchers; puis, vers le bout de la rue des Francs-Bourgeois, on tourna le coin des Archives pour entrer dans la rue de Braque" ("They crossed the Market district along the Rue de Rambuteau, full of the trucks of market gardeners; then, towards the end of the Rue des Francs-Bourgeois, they turned the corner into the Rue des Archives in order to enter the Rue de Braque").[6] That was the kind of precise and factual sentence which Daudet had not had occasion to write before, but which is found throughout *Fromont jeune.*

In the same way Daudet's accounts of the way Désirée and her mother make ornaments from exotic birds and flies, or of the work Sidonie does with artificial pearls, or of the operations of the paper factory display a range of information which could only have come from careful inquiry and note-taking. Throughout *Fromont jeune* the reader senses the presence of a narrator who has obviously walked the streets of Paris, notebook in hand, compiling documentation.[7] The "document humain," which was the hallmark of the Naturalist novel à la Zola, entered Daudet's career with *Fromont jeune*, and heavily influenced the content and structure of his sentences.

In *Fromont jeune et Risler aîné* Daudet also, for the first time, made heavy and conscious use of certain narrative devices which, as he was well aware, had proved valuable tools for his fellow realists, particularly Flaubert. Thus, resort to the device of *style indirect libre*, free indirect discourse, a favorite invention of Flaubert's, abounds in *Fromont jeune* from the start. In his previous work, it is rare. Its purpose is to impress on his readers, without artificial transitions or elaborate analytical passages, the quality of mind of his characters. On the first page Daudet tells us that Risler goes through his wedding day feeling like a man in a dream. Then abruptly, without any explanatory linking phrase, we are placed directly inside Risler's dream by the shift from third-person narration to first-person, and we experience what he does: "Maintenant voici les voitures de gala . . . Puis l'entrée à l'église, deux par deux . . . L'orgue, le suisse, le sermon du curé . . . Et le grand coup d'orgue de la fin, plus solennel à cause de la porte de l'église large ouverte . . . les exclamations du quartier . . . 'Le marié n'est pas beau, mais la mariée est crânement gentille . . .' C'est cela qui vous rend fier quand on est le marié." ("Now here come the special carriages . . . Then the entrance into the church, by twos . . . The organ, the uniformed officer, the priest's sermon . . . And the great burst of organ music at the end, sounding even more solemn because the church portals are wide open . . . the admiring cries from the neighborhood . . . 'The groom isn't handsome, but the bride is darned pretty . . .' That's what makes you proud when you are the groom.")[8] Repeatedly, Daudet plunges the reader in this fashion, without preliminaries, into the thoughts of his characters. He had discovered a valuable tool, and though he rarely displayed any genuine originality in the use of this device, he was astute enough to recognize its great contribution to realism in conveying a vivid sense of immediacy.

A second technique which Daudet began to cultivate for the first time noticeably in *Fromont jeune* is that of what might be called narrative impressionism. To spare the reader the lumbering, carefully detailed passages of description which impede action, and to give a feeling of swift pace, Daudet frequently handled descriptions, or some kinds of action, in a

nervous, almost telegraphic prose style which conveyed an
impression rather than a precise picture, and suggested a whole
spectrum of activity or feeling not actually described. By the
omission of normal connectives, and by the careful choice of
words—usually verbs, sometimes adjectives or nouns—arranged
in a series, Daudet found he could compress a great deal into
a single sentence, as in the following example which describes
how Sidonie's father, perpetually unemployed, would spend his
afternoons: "Et le mari s'en allait, prenait le boulevard, flânait
aux boutiques, attendait l'autobus, passait la moitié de la journée
dehors pour deux brioches de trois sous qu'il rapportait tri-
omphalement en s'épongeant le front." ("And the husband
would go off, would walk down the boulevard, browse among
the shops, wait around for the bus, and so spend half the day
outdoors just to get a couple of three-cent buns which he would
then bring home triumphantly, wiping the sweat from his fore-
head.") [9] The suggestively pictorial phrases and the sentence
rhythm convey a remarkably full notion of M. Chèbe's movements and even of his character with a minimum of words. It
was a style Daudet quickly made his own, beginning with this
novel, for he recognized the pace and vividness it could inject
into those necessary passages of drab description and routine
action which the theory of the realistic novel required.

While developing new techniques Daudet did not abandon
wholesale the techniques he had learned earlier. *Fromont jeune*
gives a generous display of the author's ironic wit, not only in
the famous portrait of the broken-down actor Delobelle, but
also in the impotent posturing of M. Chèbe, and in the vices of
old age exemplified by the venerable ancestor of the Fromont
family, M. Gardinois. There is rich evidence here also of Daudet's fine ear for speech and sharp eye for the telling detail or
mannerism. And, in spite of the great objectivity at which he
aimed, Daudet did not forego the infusion of warmth and
personal involvement in his narrative tone which had virtually

become his trademark. There are passages in this novel in which formal narrative diction disappears, and one has the feeling not of written prose but of a transcript of the author talking out loud. An example among many would be the passage which launches Book Two, a description, but personalized, calculated to charm the reader as well as convey an atmosphere, with its deliberately colloquial turns of phrase and its conversational rhythm:

Midi. Le Marais déjeune.

Aux lourdes vibrations des *angélus* de Saint-Paul, de Saint-Gervais, de Saint-Denis-du-Saint-Sacrement, se mêle,—montant des cours,—le tintement grêle des cloches de fabrique. Chacun de ces carillons a sa physionomie bien distincte. Il en est de tristes et de gais, d'alertes et d'endormis. Il y a des cloches riches, heureuses, tintant pour des centaines d'ouvriers; des cloches pauvres, timides, qui semblent se cacher derrière les autres et se faire toutes petites, comme si elles avaient peur que la faillite les entende. Et puis les menteuses, les effrontées, celles qui sonnent pour le dehors, pour la rue, pour faire croire qu'on est une maison considérable et qu'on occupe beaucoup de monde.

Dieu merci, la cloche de l'usine Fromont n'est pas une de celles-là. C'est une bonne vieille cloche, un peu fêlée, connue dans le Marais depuis quarante ans, et qui n'a jamais chômé que les dimanches et les jours d'émeute.

(Noon. The Marais district is at lunch.

Mingled with the ponderous vibrations of the angelus being rung at the Churches of Saint Paul, Saint Gervais, and Saint Denis of the Holy Sacrament, one hears—rising from the courtyards—the frail ringing of the factory bells. Each one of these carillons has its own quite distinctive character. There are sad ones and gay ones, bright ones and sleepy ones. There are rich, happy bells ringing out for hundreds of working men; poor, timid bells which seem to hide behind the others and to make themselves as small as they can, as though they were afraid that bankruptcy might hear them. And then there are the deceitful, shameless bells, those that ring for exterior show, for the street, to make people believe that this is a firm of substance which employs a lot of people.

Thank God, the bell of the Fromont factory is not one of that last kind. It's a good old bell, a bit cracked, well-known in the

Marais for forty years, and it has never been idle except for Sundays and days when there was rioting in the streets.) [10]

It must be noted, however, that Daudet's engaging warmth of tone did get out of control at certain points in *Fromont jeune et Risler aîné*, deteriorating into a direct emotional appeal to the reader, without subtlety, and frankly intended to produce a facile tug at the heartstrings. For example, when Sidonie takes Frantz Risler's written declaration of love and coldly informs him that she proposes to use it as blackmail against him, the author concludes the scene with the comment: "Et il ne la tua pas!" ("And he did not kill her!")[11] And in the two chapters at the end of Book Three, which recount the attempted suicide and then the death of the crippled Désirée Delobelle, Daudet's manner becomes excessively saccharine, with tearful asides and deliberate underlining of the pathos throughout.[12] Those are the passages which particularly appealed to the public in 1874 but which make rather painful going for the modern reader unaccustomed to such naked sentimentality. Those pages must be judged among the weaknesses of this otherwise powerful and moving novel, an example of Daudet's sometimes unreliable taste leading him to abuse one of his skills. Much the same can be said of the passage concerning "le petit homme bleu," the spirit who reminds men of their debts, which introduces Book Four, the point in the novel when the theme of fiscal integrity comes to the fore.[13] The invention of this spirit was a case of Daudet's drawing on one of his previous skills—his talent for delightful fantasy—to bring some liveliness and imagination to a theme which, he sensed, lacked dramatic force. Unfortunately the device fails, for pure fantasy in a realistic novel has a way of sounding arch and affected, rather than charming.

The flaws of *Fromont jeune et Risler aîné* are few, though they are damaging. The strengths, however, are a good deal more impressive, and the book deserves both the fame it achieved with its popular audience in 1874 and the relative popularity it has enjoyed among the reading public since. It is far from the best of Daudet's novels, but it retains compelling qualities which make it a superior achievement.[14] What makes it especially significant in this study, however, is that it marks one of the few clear stages in Daudet's career, a key turning point in his development, when he regrouped his skills, consciously cultivated new ones, and, in the writing of this novel, set the mold for the great bulk of all his work that was to follow.

Whatever the strengths and weaknesses of *Fromont jeune et Risler aîné* may appear to be now, the work was acclaimed in 1874, sold very well, and was crowned by the French Academy. It was both a popular success and, on the whole, a critical success as well. It made Daudet, suddenly, a national figure with a mass public. The financial benefits were enough to give Daudet his first genuine sense of security. Yet, artistically, his insecurity remained as strong as ever. Self-assurance was never really to be part of Daudet's make-up, even when he enjoyed the status of one of the world's best-known novelists. It is completely in character that following the great success of *Fromont jeune* Daudet's chief dilemma concerned the choice of a subject for his next novel. But the mold of realism had been set. Whatever his hesitations over a choice of subject, Daudet no longer hesitated over its nature: he was now an observer, whose artistic goal was the objective and accurate rendering of the society which surrounded him. For the next decade Daudet was to be a novelist of Parisian life and manners. The subtitle he gave *Fromont jeune*, "Moeurs parisiennes," was not merely a description of one novel, it was a program for the future.[15]

In 1874, with *Fromont jeune* successfully launched, Daudet began to construct another novel of Parisian life around two figures of the Second Empire of whom he had personal knowledge, and about whom he had earlier written two short journalistic pieces: the notorious Duc de Morny, and the less well-known François Bravay, a pathetic Meridional who came to Paris with a newly made fortune from which he was rapidly separated.[16] It is noteworthy that the material which now occupied Daudet was all observed reality. Daudet was later wont to confess—not without a touch of pride, one feels—that his was not the kind of imagination that could invent characters and plot out of nothing. His starting point had to be something he had observed at first hand: he wrote "d'après nature," "from nature," as he himself put it.[17] This lack of creative imagination —in that special sense—was undoubtedly one more reason that it was so natural for Daudet to embrace realism. Realism as a literary theory accorded well with his writer's equipment, and provided him with an aesthetic rationale for his writing methods.

However, in 1874 the Morny and Bravay material proved intractable, and another real-life incident from his experience abruptly displaced it in his thoughts and took shape as a possible novel. This was the story of a youth whom Daudet had befriended at his country home in Champrosay. Daudet had been struck by the youth's sensitivity, and was deeply moved to learn that his toilsome life as a factory worker had been imposed on him by his mother's lover who had refused to pay for a decent education for the boy. Eventually, Daudet learned, the boy fell ill and died, abandoned completely by his mother, who did not even come to see him as he lay dying in a charity hospital.[18]

An author can be known by the material he chooses to treat. It reveals much about the direction of Daudet's art at this point that he found this incident appealing, and suitable for a novel. Its fundamental sentimentality is evident, whatever its other potentials. It seems plain that Daudet was especially responsive to the touching pathos in this story. Perhaps it was the strong public reaction to the Désirée Delobelle episodes in *Fromont jeune* that helped Daudet to gravitate to that kind of subject again. It is clear from his own comments that he was deeply gratified and flattered to find that he could so powerfully affect the public. Almost naïvely, Daudet noted in the *Fromont jeune* article of *Histoire de mes livres:* "pendant sa publication, je sentis pour la première fois autour de mon oeuvre l'intérêt sérieux de la grande foule. Claire et Désirée avaient des amis, on me reprochait la mort de Risler, des lettres intercédaient pour la petite boiteuse. La vie n'a rien de meilleur que ce lever de la popularité, cette première communication du lecteur avec l'auteur" ("during its publication, I felt for the first time in connection with my work the serious interest of the mass audience. Claire and Désirée had friends, I was reproached for the death of Risler, letters interceded on behalf of the little crippled girl. Life holds nothing better than this upsurge of popularity, this first communication between reader and author").[19] The raw material which became the novel *Jack* obviously afforded Daudet the chance to repeat this facile triumph confirming the establishment of a trend in his work.

It is a matter of record that this element of pathos was to be an integral part of the raw material in everything he wrote thereafter. At the end of his career, with his creative powers in serious decline, it became almost the only viable element, as witness *Soutien de famille*. This weakness for pathos sentimentally presented was, without question, the most serious and pervasive flaw in Daudet's novelistic imagination. In his best work it is well hidden but it is never absent. Its definitive crystallization as part of his creative imagination can be dated from the public enthusiasm for *Fromont jeune et Risler aîné*, though it had manifested itself fleetingly as early as the poems of *Les Amoureuses*.

Jack is certainly a flawed work, and chiefly because of this strain of pathos and sentimentality. Yet it is a curiously interesting work, and important as evidence of Daudet's advancing mastery of novelistic technique, and of the continuing vigor of the frenzy that had gone into *Le Petit Chose*. The longest novel Daudet ever wrote, it was nevertheless the easiest, requiring less time per page, and fewer revisions, than any other work. Begun very late in 1874, it was completed by October 1875. The sureness and confidence with which the work was composed can be seen in the flowing, vivid style and the relatively smooth plot construction, by comparison with the awkwardnesses of tone and artificialities of transition which had marked *Fromont jeune et Risler aîné*. The flush of success, no doubt, helps to account for this easy craftsmanship, as does the fact that Daudet was then in unusually good health and good spirits. Shortly after *Jack* was finished, Daudet's health began to trouble him. A particularly alarming crisis in 1878, marked by extreme pain and the spitting of blood, ushered in a time of almost continuous suffering, during which he would hardly ever know respite from bodily torture, and would require drugs constantly to sustain himself. *Jack* was the last work Daudet composed in serenity of mind and body, and this shows in its easy-reading quality, if not in its theme which was excessively grim and pessimistic. It was indeed a "livre de pitié, de colère et d'ironie" ("book of compassion, anger, and irony") as Daudet called it in his dedication to Flaubert. And this description points to another of the work's virtues besides its technical smoothness: its patently authentic and committed passion. No reader of the work can fail to sense Daudet's genuine and personal concern with the social waste and injustice represented by the story of this young boy.

But passion is a dangerous virtue in art, and *Jack* is a perfect example of the ways in which passion uncontrolled can disfigure art. The sentimentality of the author, combined with the sentimentality implicit in his material, ignite passion but lead to excesses which undermine the reader's willingness to believe. Thus the central misfortunes which Jack suffers—being compelled to live and work in the demoralizing atmosphere of the ironworks at Indret, and being denied the solace of marriage with the girl he loves, Cécile—are both flimsily motivated. These events seem willed into being by Daudet, rather than brought about by an implacable destiny. If it seems understandable that d'Argenton might be possessively jealous enough to demand the departure of his mistress' son, it is entirely arbitrary that he should insist on apprenticing the frail boy to an iron foundry rather than to something more suitable to his physique and temperament. And the secretive and mysterious attitude of Cécile in the matter of her illegitimacy, driving her to refuse to marry Jack, is a most unpersuasive contrivance. In these two major plot developments, as well as in certain lesser features of the book, the reader senses too plainly that Daudet allowed his passion rather than the inner logic of the characters and situations to dictate his inventions.

This artificiality of plot spills over into the characterization as well. Certainly Jack himself seems too docile and too unspirited to be a believably natural young boy. He seems rather the too-perfect embodiment of filial piety, a type demanded by the theme. Jack thus emerges as colorless, puppetlike, and without individuality. Similarly, the figure of his mother suffers from the needs of the book's theme. Ida de Barancy is flighty, irresponsible, and selfish, all of which is quite believable. But it is necessary that she love devotedly and faithfully an impecunious fraud like d'Argenton, and that she permit her money to be squandered and her son to be degraded without protest, as though these acts were unrelated to her own selfish interests. If Jack is an unbelievable character, Ida de Barancy is a believable character whose actions belie her personality. But the most artificial character of all is undoubtedly Dr. Rivals, who is so much the embodiment of wisdom and generosity that he seems not to have a human heartbeat, but to exist as a sort of Platonic ideal. One feels that Dr. Rivals is no character but a concept, an allegorical figure in a morality play.

To these artificialities must be added the flaw of extraneous episodes in the structure. However much Daudet's technique had improved in smoothing out transitions and carrying the reader persuasively where he wishes to go by means of stylistic charm, he could scarcely conceal the fact that a certain number of episodes over which he dwelled both skillfully and lovingly were quite superfluous. Thus the three chapters of Part One which describe the atmosphere of the Gymnase Moronval, and tell the story of the pathetic prince of Dahomey, give a fascinating glimpse into one of the more exotic corners of Paris, but do not importantly advance the main action. Similarly, the delightful description of Bélisaire's wedding in Part Three, evoking so vividly the simple joys of the poor in Ménilmontant, is an inorganic interlude which delays the story from a structural point of view. Since Daudet has chosen a chronological presentation of Jack's life to make his point, such episodic interruptions tend to prevent the building up of a cumulative impact such as the chronological presentation is designed to achieve. The reader senses—and probably not mistakenly—that such episodes represent a kind of literary hors d'oeuvre: excellent pieces of observation and evocative reporting, but at bottom unrelated to the matter at hand.

It is a fair guess that this novel is so long because Daudet did not exercise the kind of stern artistic discipline that would have made it shorter. Years later he sought, perhaps, to justify himself against this criticism when he argued, in his account of *Jack* in *Histoire de mes livres*, that he did not wish to be like those writers who "se consument stérilement pendant des années sur un même ouvrage, paralysent leurs qualités réelles et en arrivent à produire ce que j'appelle de la 'littérature de sourd', dont les beautés, les finesses ne sont plus comprises que d'eux seuls" ("waste themselves unproductively for years over the same work, paralyze their authentic qualities and as a result manage to produce what I call 'deaf man's writing,' the beauties and subtleties of which are grasped by no one but themselves").[20]

These words seem passing strange when it is recalled that the novel in question had been dedicated to Flaubert! Yet it is Flaubert who must be allowed the final word on the matter, so far as *Jack* is concerned. "Un peu trop de papier, mon fils" ("a bit too much paper, my son"), he is reported to have said to its author.[21]

These faults noted, one must in fairness return to its good qualities which are more substantial still than the previously noted dexterity of its style and the authenticity of its emotions. For one thing, the novel overcomes its artificialities enough to be a genuinely moving experience even for the modern reader. Daudet is extraordinarily effective especially in depicting the brutalizing power which overwhelms the sensitive, frail boy apprenticed to an ironworks. Part Two of the novel is one of the earliest and one of the most effective outcries in fiction against child labor and the dehumanizing consequences of industrialization. It is interesting that much of the impact of those parts in the book was achieved by direct observation. Daudet, for the first time, deliberately adopted the methods of his fellow realists and made a special field trip to Indret, notebook in hand, to document the episodes from reality. Yet the most effective and memorable passage which utilizes the factory locale does not depend on the documentation but is an impressive feat of the imagination. As the book ends, Jack undergoes delirium in his final illness, and in a feverish dream imagines himself trying to reach Cécile and his mother through a forest of monstrous, gaping-mouthed machines waiting to devour him. Nothing could render more dramatically for the reader the emotional consequences of Jack's apprenticeship than the vivid account Daudet gives us of his hallucinatory vision. The full and terrible pathos of Jack's story is caught indelibly in this dream sequence, one of Daudet's most original and most perceptive pieces of writing.[22]

One must also count among the memorable excellences of

Jack the creation of Amaury d'Argenton, surely the most fully realized of all Daudet's attempts to portray the artistic fraud. The figure of d'Argenton towers above even that of the very successful Delobelle, for d'Argenton is somewhat more consciously fraudulent and evil, without losing any of his capacity for self-delusion. He has greater complexity, more human traits; he is closer to our experience of the *raté* type, less innocently cruel than the simple-minded Delobelle. And it is also true that the person of d'Argenton provided a focus in *Jack* for Daudet's great talent as a satirist and ironist. Some of the novel's finest pages describe the fatuousness of d'Argenton declaiming his poems publicly, or self-importantly running a literary journal. As in earlier works, so in *Jack*, Daudet displayed a most penetrating insight into the shadow milieu of the arts, the domain of the fraud and the failure. It was one of his special, and perhaps unique, talents to be able to understand and portray this milieu with so much skill.

A final excellence worth noting is the memorable, delightful quality to be found in isolated episodes, particularly in the early depiction of the Gymnase Moronval and, much later in the book, the development of the character of Bélisaire, his marriage, and the remarkable wedding sequence which is so alive with the quality of daily life in the working-class quarters of Paris. It is, of course, the practiced hand of the great short story writer which is manifest in these two episodes. Though the episodes are inorganic, so far as the novel's structure is concerned, each is a gem of vivid description, and unforgettable in precisely the same way as the best of the *Lettres de mon moulin* or the *Contes du lundi*. For all its faults, *Jack* is yet rich with evidence that Daudet had within him the qualities of a very gifted artist.

With *Jack* published and out of his system, Daudet now turned back to the novel previously begun, focusing on the characters of the Duc de Morny and of the hapless François

Bravay, the "nabob" who flashed briefly across the Parisian scene during the the Second Empire. In these two figures, as Daudet perceived, could be symbolized both the public and the private decay of morality which stamped the last decade of the reign of Napoleon III. Strangely enough, however, in his initial gropings to find a suitable framework for this material Daudet apparently did briefly consider an optimistic pattern, in which his protagonist, resembling the Duc de Morny, would have his rakish conduct moderated by a wise friend and counselor. What Daudet had in mind, of course, was a renewal of Fénelon, but with a modern Telemachus guiding rather than guided by the experienced Mentor. Fortunately, this conception did not crystallize beyond the author's preliminary notebooks, for it seems likely that the dramatic power of the material could never have emerged in such a vein.[23] Instead, Daudet chose to return to the reality he had himself witnessed, and to cast the material as a grim portrait of decadence in the Paris of the Second Empire. What is worth retaining, however, from this earliest conception of *Le Nabab*, is the first glimpse it gives us of the didactic tendency which was later to emerge much more forcefully in Daudet's creative impulses. During the writing of *Le Nabab* it proved to be only a brief flirtation with an idea soon abandoned. But the impulse would be heard from again, more insistently.

When the finished work appeared, in 1877, it bore the same subtitle as *Fromont jeune:* "Moeurs parisiennes." But this time, more than in any other Daudet novel, the true hero—or villain—was Paris. There is, of course, considerable truth in those critical estimates which see *Le Nabab* primarily as a historical novel, portraying the atmosphere of the reign of Napoleon III. *Le Nabab* is a vast canvas, the broadest cross section of society Daudet ever tried to encompass. He has distributed his characters over the whole social spectrum, covering the governing nobility, the financial tycoons, the professional classes, the art world, white collar clerks, and the humble working classes. The novel is set in the year 1864, and is at explicit pains to suggest to the reader a tableau of corruption in a doomed regime. Nevertheless, it is Paris in its eternal character, rather than in its particular atmosphere of the Second Empire, that dominates the work and provides it with its theme. For *Le Nabab* is, above all else, a study of the corrosive power to destroy, morally and physically, which is wielded by the modern city over its inhabitants. The theme which was barely adumbrated in *Fromont jeune* now comes to full statement.

It is interesting to discover, however, that this theme of urban destructiveness was not central to Daudet's conception of his novel at the outset. What initially aroused his literary instincts, as his preliminary notes show, was rather the theme of social corruption, as exemplified in the pathetic history of two individuals, the Duc de Morny and François Bravay, who had acquired and cynically exploited great power, in public and in private, only to be deserted just as cynically by everyone the moment their power faded. It was only after the armature of the plot had been constructed around the interrelated activities of these two figures that the theme of the city rose to the surface to dominate the whole. Somewhere between conception and execution, Daudet's point of view toward his protagonists, now named the Duc de Mora and Bernard Jansoulet, underwent a transformation; instead of being the prime movers in the action they became the chief victims. Even the quack doctor, Jenkins, whom Daudet originally invented as a symbol of pervasive corruption and as a convenient link among the various characters, never quite becomes the villain of the piece, for in the end we learn that he is himself enslaved to an uncontrollable passion for Félicia Ruys, and hence merely another pathetic victim. For the first time, moreover, Daudet composed, in *Le Nabab*, a novel which does not have a female protagonist, like Irma Borel or Sidonie Chèbe or Ida de Barancy, who is the source of destruction and evil. One can only conclude that in this instance Paris became Daudet's *femme fatale*, and left no room for the creation of any rival villain. The title of the novel may be *Le Nabab*, but the last words of the book make it clear that the title role has been assigned to a victim, not a hero. The work is completely dominated by the power of Paris to control, corrupt, mutilate, or destroy. And the death of Jansoulet, awesome though it be in its circumstances, is described on the last page with Paris pointedly at center stage, as "une des plus grandes, des plus cruelles injustices que Paris ait jamais commises" ("one of the greatest, cruelest injustices which Paris has ever committed").

Ultimately, then, *Le Nabab* emerged from the long travail of composition with a new and impressive complexity but still in the same vein as *Fromont jeune et Risler aîné*. Shaped by the same compassionate concern for those who are destroyed by the forces of modern life, *Le Nabab* is a novel of realism which does not shrink from the precise and detailed observation of ugliness and evil, but which adopts a point of view constantly sympathetic to the victims. There is rigorous objectivity in the author's refusal to see urban life, or human character, as any better than in fact it is. Yet the image is softened by the clear emotional participation of the author, who is visibly touched by what the human scene offers to his gaze. The mixture of tones, coldly observant and yet pitying, betrays the ambivalence of the author toward his material. In *Le Nabab*, as in *Fromont jeune* and *Jack* before it, this ambivalence undeniably diminishes the novel's power.

Yet it is true that *Le Nabab* retains overwhelming power, and is in the opinion of some Daudet's most forceful creation. Its impact certainly exceeds that of *Fromont jeune* and *Jack* because of its scope alone. In *Le Nabab* Daudet has caught the essence of a whole society, rather than just one milieu within it. He has explored political life at its top levels, and private existence in its obscurest forms, within the same novel—and found them ultimately equal in vanity and sterility. He has shown that the complexity of the modern metropolis overwhelms not just a segment but all layers of its social being. The texture of the novel is as rich as its scope is broad. Vivid characters, intense and dramatically revealing scenes, convincingly created and varied backgrounds, all add to the build-up in the novel of a sense of reality caught *sur le vif*, like a series of candid snapshots, and the feel of inevitability about man's fate in the life of the city. *Le Nabab* is a massive effort on Daudet's part to see his world whole, though refracted, of course, through his personal prism.

Corruption, of values and of morals, is the pervasive presence in Daudet's Paris. To this end, he has astutely built his narrative around two opposite but representative cases: the well-born Duc de Mora, already entrenched in a position of power; and the obscure, newly rich Bernard Jansoulet, an outsider who comes to Paris seeking power. Both are corrupted and destroyed, both corrupt and destroy others. The death scenes of both men summarize memorably the meaning of the composition as a whole. For both death is a moment of implacable truth, when the self-serving indifference of those around them is openly, cruelly revealed, and the vanity of their careers is exposed to their own view. Both scenes are done with trenchant irony, and constitute high points in the structure of the novel, and in its emotional impact on the reader. Perhaps more effective still is the famous chapter, called "Drames parisiens," which describes some of the radiating consequences of death and corruption in high places.[24] Notable for its understatement, and its rhythmic, elegiac prose, this chapter has rightly become an anthology piece, for it combines beauty and simplicity of style with overwhelming emotional force. It describes the dignity with which a lesser victim of Paris, M. de Monpavon, recognizes the collapse of his false world, and commits suicide: cold, corrupt, selfish, but proper to the end. His walk to death takes him past others similarly afflicted by events, similarly bent on self-destruction. The whole chapter becomes a symbolic condensation of all the strands running through the book, a summary of the inevitable fate of all who are touched in their different ways by the contagion of the metropolis.

For the modern reader, nevertheless, *Le Nabab* must be put down as an impressive failure. However much one feels the power of the theme, and however successful one finds individual scenes, the truth is that this sprawling novel is overextended. Its diverse elements do not quite cohere, and it fails thereby to persuade. There are too many separate plots interwoven: the Duc de Mora and his entourage, Jansoulet and his family, the banker Hémerlingue, Jenkins and his medical practice, Félicia Ruys, Passajon and his diary, the Joyeuse family, and the photographer-playwright André Maranne. The weaving is intricate, clever, at times impressively skillful; but Daudet's loom is not broad enough to hold all the elements together. Technically it is not a unit but a patchwork of parts. The error of *Fromont jeune* is repeated and multiplied in *Le Nabab*. The reader is forced too often into an awareness of contrivance and coincidence called into play to rescue the author's plot. It is not merely that in spreading his base Daudet failed to go deeply enough. Rendering surfaces was in any case Daudet's forte. It was rather that he chose too unwieldy a surface for the limits of his art. His subject was major, even imposing; his effort was meritorious; but his talent was simply not equal to the task. It was Daudet's try at writing an *Education sentimentale*, and it proved he was no Flaubert. *Le Nabab* is in that sense an honorable failure. And it was a failure whose lesson, as we shall see, Daudet was wise enough to learn.

One of the subsidiary effects of Daudet's having spread himself too thin—constituting another of the book's weaknesses—is that many of the characters, and especially the title figure,

Jansoulet, are too shadowy to be credible. Jansoulet, for example, is vividly portrayed as a naïve victim of a rapacious and cruel society. There is some hint of his lust for power, and his longing for respectability and acceptance, which make him vulnerable as a stranger to the Parisian jungle. But the qualities in him which earned him his fortune, the shrewdness and the hardness in him, are but vaguely suggested and rest on no substantial basis. We learn too little of his early years to comprehend Jansoulet as a complete human being. In the end he seems more a tool for constructing the plot than flesh and blood. Since Jansoulet is drawn from life, the failure of the character to come alive for the reader points to a failure of art on Daudet's part. It can perhaps be argued in his defense that Daudet knew his model too superficially, and, in the vast canvas he was painting, could not supply enough detail through his imagination to succeed in making Jansoulet seem real on the basis of this superficial acquaintance. By contrast, the Duc de Mora and M. de Monpavon do come off somewhat better, perhaps because these were men whom Daudet understood more fully. But few of the other characters emerge with much vitality, being, like Jansoulet, one-dimensional and a bit mechanical: plot devices rather than people. Characterization is perhaps the most glaring of the novel's weaknesses.

A final flaw in *Le Nabab*, and one which had by then become a characteristic—not to say a vice—of the author, was the excessive sentimentality, the gross appeal to the tearful emotions. The particular area in which Daudet exploited this vein in *Le Nabab*, the Joyeuse family (we are not even spared in the name!), represents an unusually weak invention, both because the link between this family and the main figures of the plot is tenuous and artificial, and because the family itself and its activities have no very convincing reality. M. Joyeuse, who somehow bravely conceals his jobless state from his family for so long, is simply incredible even at the most practical level of realism. His bevy of giggling daughters grow rapidly tiresome. What compounds the error in these saccharine inventions is that Daudet adopts an over-emotional, personalized style for these scenes, so that the modern reader tends to turn away in embarrassment.

Such a passage as the following shows the abuse Daudet was capable of, in seeking to reach the emotions of his readers. Describing in chapter XVII the Joyeuse family's preparations for a Sunday outing to celebrate the forthcoming marriage of Elise Joyeuse to André Maranne, Daudet pauses to consider the whole matter of Sunday in Paris.

Dimanche de Paris, dimanche des travailleurs et des humbles, je t'ai souvent maudit sans raison, j'ai versé des flots d'encre injurieuse sur tes joies bruyantes et débordantes . . . mais aujourd'hui, abjurant mes erreurs, je t'exalte et je te bénis pour tout ce que tu donnes de joie, de soulagement au labeur courageux et honnête, pour le rire des enfants qui t'acclament, la fierté des mères heureuses d'habiller leurs petits en ton honneur, pour la dignité que tu conserves aux logis des plus pauvres, la nippe glorieuse mise de côté pour toi au fond de la vieille commode écloppée; je te bénis surtout à cause de tout le bonheur que tu apportais en surcroît ce matin-là dans la grande maison neuve au bout de l'ancien faubourg.

(Parisian Sunday, Sunday of workers and of the humble, I have often cursed you unreasonably, I have poured out streams of abusive ink against your noisy and overflowing joys . . . but today, abjuring my errors, I exalt you and I bless you for all the joy and respite you bring to courageous and honest toil, for the laughter of children who welcome you with their shouts, the pride of mothers happy to dress their little ones in your honor, for the dignity which you preserve in the dwellings of the poor, the resplendent garment put aside for you at the bottom of the rickety old chest of drawers; I bless you above all because of all the happiness which you brought in such abundance that morning into the huge brand new house at the far end of the old suburb.) [25]

The cloying and tasteless tone, the facile emotion, are unfortunately quite typical of the manner in which Daudet deals with every scene involving the Joyeuse family in *Le Nabab*.

No other novel of Daudet's is so heavily larded with this kind of sentimentality—he was thereafter to exercise heroic restraint over these personal outbursts. The quality of his imagination, of course, could not change; the kind of person or situation he would choose to depict had to continue to have a foundation in pathos; but his tone and manner would be rather more disciplined in his work after *Le Nabab*. In 1877 he still seemed to feel, however, that the kind of personal hyper-emotionalism first displayed in the scenes about Désirée Delobelle in *Fromont jeune* was an important ingredient in his public success. Perhaps under the influence of Edmond de Goncourt, Zola, and Flaubert, who criticized these purple passages severely, Daudet slowly checked and modified this lamentable tendency after *Le Nabab*.[26]

It is certainly to Daudet's credit that the failures and the successes of *Le Nabab* seemed to be clear to him, and to leave a continuing mark on his work thereafter. His next novel, for example, *Les Rois en exil* (1879), offers clear evidence that Daudet was attempting to profit by and advance from the lessons of *Le Nabab*. Recognizing that both public interest and his own best native talent had been engaged by his choice of characters and events that were historical and publicly known, Daudet chose now to deal with a case history of deposed royalty, at a time when the Parisian public was gossiping about a number of such recent affairs. But recognizing also that *Le Nabab* had been too ambitiously vast in scope, he narrowed his sights and produced in *Les Rois en exil* a much more limited and tightly knit drama. This choice of subject confirmed Daudet's continuing preoccupation with the image of Paris as destroyer of human values and his irresistible impulse toward the pathetic. Both were aspects of the success of *Le Nabab*. But no gross error of taste, such as his creation and stylistic handling of the Joyeuse family, intrudes into *Les Rois en exil*. That lesson too had been learned.

Les Rois en exil was, then, another in the series of novels of realism, exploring in well-observed detail aspects of Parisian life and, like *Le Nabab*, concentrating especially on the cruel and destructive potential of the city. The milieu of deposed royalty living in a strange city was sufficiently novel to be fascinating to author and public alike, yet it was a real and immediate topic for the Paris of 1879. Daudet made a touchingly human drama out of the plight of a royal family thrown on the mercy of a heartless city. And the novel contains a few scenes of impressive skill and enduring impact: the brilliant account in chapters five and six of the dubious business enterprise of J. Tom Lévis, and his way of preying on the gullible and the unfortunate; the fantastic and yet amusing story of the early life of Elysée Méraut, with its monarchist passions cultivated in a hothouse atmosphere almost completely divorced from reality; and the famous chapter nine, describing with delicious irony a prize-giving session at the French Academy. The culmination of the story's drama, the scene in which the proud Queen, Frédérique, tremblingly brings herself to the humiliation of asking Méraut to pawn the crown jewels, only to find that the jewels are paste because the King has got to them first, is a tour de force of artful theatrical timing and a most affecting and memorable climax. There is no doubt that Daudet, in spite of the illness which became frighteningly acute during the writing of *Les Rois en exil*, and led him to fear he might not live to finish it,[27] displayed his customary skill and talent in this book, and demonstrated that, at his best, he was a very great artist indeed.

Yet *Les Rois en exil* is decidedly a minor work. It is not merely that the excellent parts are balanced by too many weak ones, robbing the work of power. That is, after all, in greater or lesser degree, the truth about virtually everything Daudet wrote. That was his great tragedy as a creative artist. Some of his works, however, are able to endure as powerful creations in spite of their weaknesses and failures. *Le Nabab* is an example. The gravest and most damaging fault with *Les Rois en exil* lies in the total conception. Daudet was seduced here into treating a trivial theme, touching perhaps, but marginal and insignificant in any larger sense. Perhaps the tremendous effort of *Le Nabab* had left him exhausted and capable only of turning his attention to minor matters. Whatever the explanation, *Les Rois en exil* is a work lacking in creative energy, conceived in a minor mode, and its scattered excellences are not enough to give it significance. For the modern reader, this novel can have little to say except for its spotty proof that whatever greatness Daudet possessed was at least not dead in 1879, but merely dormant.

If the work is lacking in aesthetic significance, it has some interest at least as a stage in Daudet's artistic evolution. For one thing, it illustrates the persistence of Daudet's attachment to pathos, even unto the choice of subject. But there is a particularly instructive example of the danger in pathos in this novel: the scene in which Elysée Méraut himself wounds the young prince whom he has been educating for Queen Frédérique. The scene was meant to be a *clou*, a "star attraction," one of the decisively powerful scenes in the novel. The appropriate ingredients are indeed present: Elysée is growing more and more confident in his work as tutor; Frédérique, proud and distant, is almost on the point of admitting that she is in love with Elysée; the young prince, Zara, gives every sign of growing into a strong and successful monarch. Suddenly, the cruel irony of fate intervenes, and all hope is shattered as the prince lies wounded, perhaps dying, on the ground and Elysée kneels beside him, groaning that he is himself the guilty person. Unfortunately, it is not the cruel irony of fate at all, but an accident that has occurred, by fiat of the author, and the reader cannot help sensing that. Accidents do happen in life, and can be thoroughly grim, even bitterly ironic. But in art such accidents are reduced to pure contrivance, for they do not arise out of any inner necessity in the characters or the situation. They could as easily *not* happen, had the author so willed. Daudet's notebooks show that he constructed this scene on a real-life incident in which a friend of his had accidentally wounded his own son.[28] Daudet's error was to be entranced by the pathos of the situation. He tried to transplant life unchanged into art, asking chance to play the role of fate. However moving in real life, such accidents amount only to trickery in literature.

Other Daudet hallmarks to be found in *Les Rois en exil* are especially prominent among the characters created: the weak male stereotype, represented by the King; the *femme fatale* who exploits him (Séphora Leemans); and the woman of strength, intense maternal devotion, and pride (Frédérique). This last figure, a type not fully developed earlier, but outlined in the Mme. Weber of *Jack* and in Félicia Ruys of *Le Nabab*, receives its first starring, full-length role in *Les Rois en exil*. Thereafter, of course, she becomes a basic and constant type in Daudet's fictional world. It can perhaps be suggested that the model for this type of figure was probably Daudet's wife, Julia.

Another element of *Les Rois en exil* which seems especially typical of Daudet's fictional world is the intricate and artful chicanery worked out by J. Tom Lévis. Daudet had long been fascinated by such complex and clever swindles or *tripotages*. He was of course ambivalent about such things: always fearful of being swindled himself, but admiring of the imagination which creates them. Individual scenes exist in *Le Petit Chose*, *Tartarin de Tarascon*, *Fromont jeune*, and *Le Nabab* which demonstrate Daudet's entrancement with such scheming. He uses swindle as a plot device, indeed, with such regularity as to suggest some sort of fixation on his part. Finally, in *Les Rois en exil* he finds a way to make swindle an important and central plot device, carrying a great portion of the book's main action.

The reader, moreover, cannot help but be aware in this book of the author's ambivalence on this subject. While Lévis is reprehensible and King Christian II is a contemptible weakling, the details of the elaborate swindle by which the royal fortune is to be completely extracted from the King are recounted with undisguised admiration, almost with relish. By the manipulation of tone, Daudet makes it possible for the reader to detest Lévis, pity the King, and savor the swindle all at the same time.

One final significant but elusive trait deserves to retain our attention in *Les Rois en exil*, first because it bears so meaningfully on the rest of Daudet's career, and secondly because the trait emerges more saliently in connection with *Les Rois en exil* than anywhere else. That is the matter of Daudet's personal, political, and moral opinions as expressed through his fiction. Critics and commentators of 1879 seized on the chapter describing the mystic monarchism in which Elysée Méraut grew up, and chided Daudet for ridiculing the beliefs of his own family, and insulting the memory of his devotedly royalist father. But other critics, concentrating on the sympathetic treatment of Queen Frédérique and her ideals, accused Daudet of insulting the Republic by writing so plain a defense of monarchism! Soon an ingenious resolution of these contradictory interpretations was proposed, in the form of a rumor that Daudet had first planned the novel just after the Franco-Prussian War and before the Third Republic became a reality in 1875. At that time his intentions were supposed to have been to write a defense of monarchic principles. But by the time he got around to composing the work, the political winds had changed, Daudet's father had died, and Daudet found it prudent to beat a hasty retreat. The novel was thus supposed to betray Daudet's political opportunism and insincerity, to say nothing of his presumable artistic sloppiness in failing to hide the traces of his changing opinions.[29]

These petty quarrels of yesteryear are no longer of any

moment, but for the present-day student of Daudet's career, this entire incident poses two important questions: How is it possible that a book should be open to such contradictory interpretations on so basic a point as the political spirit in which it was written? And, assuming the scurrilous rumor to have no foundation in fact (and it appears, indeed, to have none that diligent research has been able to turn up), why should Daudet have been the object of such malicious character assassination?

As to the first question, it may be useful to recall that *Le Nabab* occasioned similar contradictory opinions, some feeling that Daudet was guilty of reprehensible behavior for satirizing a man in whose employ he had willingly served (Morny) and a man whose bounty he had enjoyed (François Bravay, in whose house Daudet had once dined); others claiming that Daudet had drawn indulgent and even sympathetic portraits of a political figure of monumental irresponsibility (Morny) and of a shady opportunist who had sought to corrupt Paris with his ill-got wealth (Bravay). It is also a matter of record that some residents of the Midi considered the novel *Tartarin de Tarascon* to be an attack on the region, while others considered it to be an amiable celebration of the regional character and happily claimed Daudet as a Provençal patriot.

The pattern is clear: not only do Daudet's critics seem to refract Daudet's work through the prism of their own prejudices (hence the contradictions) but Daudet's work itself lends the opportunity for it. Presumably no one has ever read Flaubert's *Madame Bovary* as a celebration of life in the provinces! The point would seem to be that Daudet manages to write on both sides of such questions at once. The reason is simply that Daudet himself is without firm convictions on these matters. It was not in his nature to be partisan, and particularly not about politics, which interested him not at all. Indeed his whole being, as we have seen in his earliest writings, resisted clear and unequivocal commitments on any subject. This fundamental psychological tendency to avoid taking a stand expresses itself in his fiction by means of an unconscious balance in his presentation of all controversial issues. Nowhere does this avoidance of firm positions emerge more clearly than in *Les Rois en exil,* in which he manages to show both the inherent dignity and the frequent absurdity of monarchic principles. Biased readers could find in it what they wished to find. Yet the novel is neither defense nor attack, but a human drama compounded of the characteristics to be found in royalty and in the politics of monarchism. The steadfast refusal of Daudet to take sides made possible—perhaps inevitable—contradictory interpretations.

The second question is somewhat harder to answer. It was Daudet's nature to want very much to be liked. Some of the weakness of his art we have already ascribed to this trait. He would not knowingly arouse the hostility of others, yet it is a fact that, from the mid-1870's on, Daudet was the object of considerable personal vilification. The rumor about the composition of *Les Rois en exil* was typical in that it accused Daudet of insincerity, turncoatism, two-facedness, and opportunism. Daudet himself was inclined to dismiss such attacks (though he smarted under them, as any reader of his notebooks can see) as the result of pettiness and envy because of his public success as a writer. But this seems to be only part of the story. The hostility he aroused was not consciously provoked but very possibly the result of that very inability to commit himself which has been described above. Refusing to take a stand, out of deep psychological need, Daudet projected without realizing it an image of elusiveness and remoteness which can be exasperating to many. It can easily be misinterpreted as deviousness and lack of forthrightness. He wanted to be liked, but he could give no one his allegiance. Through this inner conflict in himself he aroused the animosity of others.

The virulence of this animosity can be documented in the

repeated public attempts that were made, without let-up, to discredit Daudet during the last twenty years of his life and for long after—indeed down to the present. The efforts to prove for instance that Daudet did not write *Les Lettres de mon moulin* still persist as the most notable example of the implacable hostility Daudet aroused without wishing it. In its day, *Les Rois en exil* was one of the first of his novels to beget public attack. *Le Nabab* had done so also though at first it provoked more gossip than attack. Following *Les Rois en exil*, however, it was a rare volume that Daudet published that did not incite innuendo, personal criticism, or even slander. This caused Daudet a great deal of suffering, and became one of the chief reasons he took to deploring the life of the man of letters in his later years.

In sum, one must say of *Les Rois en exil* that it contains enough of the typical ingredients to be a fully accredited Daudet product, but except for certain interesting emphases, it added nothing original or lustrous to the story of his evolving career. Indeed, the lack of creative energy which marks the book's conception suggests that Daudet was then suffering from a sort of writer's fatigue, and that *Les Rois en exil* was composed purely on the momentum of previous performances, like a reflex action. During the writing of *Les Rois* Daudet was apparently marking time, awaiting new inspiration and a new upsurge of creative energy.

When inspiration came, it was not exactly new, and it was surprisingly personal for an author who had made a firm turn toward objective realism half a dozen years before. Under the working title *Nord et Midi*, Daudet began to construct a new novel, in 1880, exploring the contrast between the meridional character and that of the Parisian. The contrast had struck Daudet forcibly and personally when he came to Paris as a young man in 1857. His marriage to Julia Allard had made his own household an intimate living example of the contrast. And he had touched on the matter, gingerly, in various of his works, most notably in *Le Petit Chose* and *Le Nabab*. Now, for reasons that can never be adequately known, he set out to make a full-scale exploration of the subject in a novel which reached publication in 1881 as *Numa Roumestan,* with the subtitle "Moeurs parisiennes."

Besides the return to more personal sources of inspiration, *Numa Roumestan* offers another change in Daudet that demands notice. For instead of the pathetic situation which attracted Daudet to the writing of the first four novels of realism, this novel has its origins in an idea—one might even properly call it, as Paul Bourget did, a thesis.[30] Daudet's starting point in this novel was his notion that the passionate and inflated imagination of the southern temperament was both opposite and incomprehensible to the cool and rational reserve of the northern temperament. Wherever these two temperaments met, thought Daudet, whether privately in a family or publicly in national politics, there must inevitably be drama: clashes, misunderstandings, suffering. He therefore imagined a southern politician married to a Parisian woman, and composed a novel as a sort of demonstration of his hypothesis. The difference to be seen here is vital. From *Fromont jeune* to *Les Rois en exil* Daudet had begun with human beings observed in an emotionally moving situation. In *Numa Roumestan* the root is also observation—but of a psychological generality rather than of a situation. The starting point of the composition was not people but an idea. The purpose of the writing was not purely to engage the reader's emotions with precise observation of reality and a powerful human drama, but additionally to persuade the reader of the truth of a thesis. Daudet was, then, showing in *Numa Roumestan* the beginnings of a new outlook about the art of the novel, a turning away from objective realism toward both a more personal and a more didactic approach. *Numa Roumestan* marks a stage of transition in Daudet's career.

There is nonetheless every reason to classify *Numa Roume-stan* as one of Daudet's novels of realism. However much he may have turned with personal relish to the analysis of the meridional temperament once again, he objectified his creation to a remarkable degree in the character of Numa, who is compounded primarily of observed types with but very little of Daudet in his make-up. The novel records very detailed observations of the backstage life of politicians, and renders the color and bustle of southern scenes, as well as the intrigues of Parisian ministerial circles, with completely objective fidelity. There is even the pathetic situation, tucked away in a subplot, to remind the reader that it is still the author of *Jack* and *Le Nabab* who is wielding the pen here. The story of Hortense Le Quesnoy, her blind love for the ridiculous Valmajour and her death from tuberculosis, is obviously in the same vein as the story of Désirée Delobelle, Cécile Rivals, and others of that stripe. There is, perhaps, less attention paid to those in humble circumstances than in earlier realistic novels—one more sign of transition—but in the main *Numa Roumestan* is a novel of contemporary manners which can rightly take its place with the four earlier novels of realism.

Numa Roumestan is one of Daudet's more effective novels because, for all its objective realism, the work springs so intimately from Daudet's own life. In general, Daudet's most successful creations are those which draw heavily from his own personal experience, and the temptation is great to see in the marriage of Numa and Rosalie a transposition of Daudet's own marriage. The character of Bompard, and the numerous scenes of boisterous satire in the novel, also reflect the return of the persona of the Daudet of old. Vivid characters, zestful satire, and a penetrating glimpse into the private life of a public figure: these are the qualities that make this novel live. And it will be noted that they add up to the very best qualities discernible in the two basic modes of Daudet's art: satire and realism. Perhaps it is this blend of his best qualities that made Daudet feel he had written his most fully realized work in *Numa Roumestan*, the one that fulfilled his intentions most completely.[31] Few would agree that it is his best novel—in the long run it lacks dramatic power—but one can comprehend why it should have taken its place in Daudet's affections as his favorite. It is surely the novel which most fully represents the variety of his outstanding talents.

The clearest indication of the novel's weakness, however, is the fact that while it is a novel about the life of a politician, it is strangely not at all a political novel. The reader is given elaborate and detailed knowledge of everything about Numa—except his political ideas. One never has any notion of what Numa, his party, or his opponents stand for in the political arena. It is possible that Daudet wished thereby to underscore the ideological void of French political life. However, a more convincing explanation of this curious anomaly is simply that Daudet had no interest in politics.[32] It is something of a tour de force, no doubt, that Daudet's novel can exist at all, in such an ideological vacuum. But there can be no question but that this missing dimension reduces the novel's scope and robs it of a tenseness and force that it might otherwise have conveyed. Numa is diminished by being portrayed without ideas or political commitments—he seems pale, less real, and hence less believable. Nevertheless, it would be a rare reader who would not be caught up in the passions and the human problems of the book. As the story of a man struggling with his own weaknesses and with the alien nature of a different temperament, *Numa Roumestan* is a successful novel. It still has the power to fascinate the reader, to grip the imagination, to involve one in its atmosphere and events. It falls somewhat short of being a masterpiece, but it is a most impressive performance.

The most significant observation to be made about the period of Daudet's novels of realism (1874–1881) is that it is the period in which he attained wide fame and an international reputation. By 1881, when *Numa Roumestan* came out, hinting at a new artistic direction for its author, Daudet was one of France's and the world's leading novelists. The flaws so visible today, the limitations and the gaucheries, above all the sentimentality, were not nearly so glaring to the readers of 1881. In the France of that year only Émile Zola was held to have greater power as a novelist of realism, and only the recently deceased Flaubert was recognized to be a greater master of style and form. In less than ten years Daudet had gone from an interesting minor writer on regional themes to the heights of international celebrity as a literary interpreter of the contemporary world.

From the vantage point of the twentieth century, this trajectory of Daudet's fame seems perverse. *Les Lettres de mon moulin* and *Tartarin de Tarascon* are surely superior works of art to any of the five novels of realism, and even *Le Petit Chose* is more charmingly affecting, with all its faults, than the works which brought him glory. Yet the contemporary judgment was not really so wrongheaded. Sensitive and gifted as he was, Daudet turned to realism instinctively, at a time when the public longed to see itself faithfully reflected in what it read; and Daudet performed the task well. He proved a penetrating observer, a revealer of the soul of Paris which the ungifted Parisian could but dimly sense. In spite of the lapses of taste and errors of judgment introduced into his novels here and there, Daudet mastered the technique of the novel of realism rapidly and brilliantly. His novels were never indisputable masterpieces as a whole, but each contained numerous passages which the public was quite right to recognize as the product of authentic though imperfect genius. At his best Daudet was one of the most gifted of the realists, and his work of those years merited its fame. Even today the historian of literature would single out Daudet's work in that era as among the handful that still possess vitality enough to survive. Most of the

hundreds of novels published in the same years have been de-
servedly forgotten and are now unreadable. Moreover, the
success of those years naturally brought with it the "rediscov-
ery" of the early Daudet. *Tartarin, Les Lettres,* and *Le Petit
Chose* were all frequently reprinted between 1875 and 1880,
and their wide public fame dates from the reprintings. Daudet's
great prominence, by 1880, was therefore not the pure product
of his realism, but the rounded recognition his entire career was
by then receiving.

But Daudet did not simply become a successful caterer to
public taste in the years from 1874 to 1881. Rather he became
a fully developed, highly skilled professional man of letters.
It was a period of tremendous growth and remarkable fertility.
Not only did he produce five long novels in eight years, but he
helped turn three of his novels into plays during the same
period, wrote a considerable amount of occasional journalism,
and conducted a weekly column of drama criticism from 1874
to 1880, missing or farming out amazingly few of the weekly
contributions.[33] He had developed systematic work habits and
discipline, mastered the problems of career management (Daudet earned a formidable reputation as a shrewd negotiator and
exploiter of his literary property for maximum gain), and
learned to be a serious student of his delicate art. If he lost some
of the spontaneity and frivolity of his youth, he acquired a keen
insight into human character, a sharp eye for the significant
detail, and a fluid, well-controlled technique for articulating his
insights and observations. Nor had he quite lost his ironic flair,
and his gay wit, flashes of which appear throughout his novels
of realism. The fact is that between 1874 and 1881 Daudet had
come of age as a serious writer and a skilled novelist. He had
learned his craft.

But as *Numa Roumestan* plainly suggests, the years of objectivity were giving way, by the end of this period, to the need
to re-examine himself and his Provençal origins, and to assert

values and discover meaning in life. Where formerly he had been irresistibly drawn to situations because they were pathetic rather than meaningful, by 1881 Daudet seemed more inclined to espouse causes, as a result of his reinforced self-confidence. He was tending to find in ideas as much as in people the springboard for his creativity. These are, to be sure, matters of degree and of emphasis. The appeal of the purely pathetic, and the method of objective observation, had become integral parts of Daudet's thinking by 1881. They could not disappear or be displaced. But the emphases were plainly shifting, and these two aspects of his art ceased to dominate and direct his work quite so fully after the publication of *Numa Roumestan*.

The Erosion of Objectivity

1 8 8 1 – 1 8 9 0

The posture of objectivity, so scrupulously maintained in Daudet's novels of realism, had served him well by 1881, answering his psychological needs and furthering his development as a literary artist at the same time. He had been able thereby to escape somewhat from the prison of self-doubt and to transcend the limits of self-absorption. His scope as a novelist broadened immeasurably and his powers of observation were sharpened. But above all, in the posture of objectivity he found the means of achieving truly memorable creations without doing violence to his personal distaste for public commitment. For an artist of Daudet's ambivalence and deep personal anxieties, objectivity offered perhaps the only viable path to the attainment of the fullest artistic maturity of which he was capable. For Daudet, the principles of realism had been a godsend and a necessity.

The way in which *Numa Roumestan* was conceived, however, starting from a notion of Daudet's about the opposition between the northern and southern temperaments in France, suggested that by 1881 objectivity had begun to outlive its usefulness for the author. The very success of the device, creating a new self-assurance in the author, undermined his psychological need of it. He began to be more willing to assert his opinions and to be publicly identified with them. In *Numa Roumestan* one could begin to sense the art of advocacy blending with the art of observation. He was further pushed in the direction of stating positions and espousing causes by the natural force of things. He was now famous, and over forty. Responsibility and leadership were thrust upon him, both in private and in public, reluctant though he was to accept. Within the family, for example, he was the head of a household and father of two sons, the elder of whom, being teenaged, now stirred in Daudet a sense of the paternal duty to take an active role in the boy's education, to influence his moral outlook, and to help shape his awakening intellect. Publicly he was now a prominent man of letters, besieged for interviews, opinions, and advice. Being a man who was notably cordial and helpful, because he was always eager to please, Daudet readily conquered his fear of commitment, at this time of his life, and slipped gradually into the role of statesman, counselor, and source of wisdom in the republic of letters. Coupled with his success-inspired self-confidence, this new role impelled Daudet far along the path of abandonment of objectivity in his work and his attitudes.

It is additionally true that because he had passed his fortieth birthday, a man of Daudet's temperament was bound to feel the need of personal stock-taking. The erosion of his stance of objectivity inclined him not only toward didacticism but also back toward his earlier subjectivity. This tendency was powerfully reinforced by Daudet's onslaught of illness, the as-yet-undiagnosed third stage of syphilis which was ultimately to inflict unremitting pain on him till his dying day. In 1878 he had suffered the first violent attack. Sulphur baths failed to provide relief in 1880. Daudet began to have, guiltily, the feeling that this suffering was retribution for his past; for without knowing its precise nature, he associated it with his bohemian youth when—as he now felt—he had profligately abused his body.[1] Sensing a decisive transformation in his life, and fearing that he might never know robust health again—indeed, that he might soon die—Daudet naturally became more preoccupied with himself, his achievements, and his responsibilities to his family. His novels of this period can therefore be expected to reflect, directly or indirectly, those intensely private concerns.

It is probable that a final factor in Daudet's turn away from strict objectivity as an artistic method was simply his restless and sensitive nature. The method of objectivity had given him discipline and artistic control, but he soon chafed under the regime and began to find its potentialities too limited. Daudet himself expressed these dissatisfactions with the novel of objective observation when explaining how he came to conceive the idea (never executed) of writing a novel about the life of Napoleon: "Mon Dieu, oui. Pour le jour où le Roman de moeurs me fatiguerait par l'étroitesse et le convenu de son cadre, où j'éprouverais le besoin de m'espacer plus loin et plus haut, j'avais rêvé cela." ("My God, yes. Looking toward the day when the novel of manners might weary me by the narrowness and the conventionality of its framework, when I might experience the need to spread myself farther and higher, I had dreamed of that.")[2] Though these words were written in 1887, it is more than coincidence that Daudet was here discussing his state of mind when composing *Numa Roumestan* in 1880. His urge to "explain" Napoleon as a product of the Midi, in a new kind of novel, reveals the direction his creative processes were taking. His secret insecurities were stirring again, gently guiding him to new modes of expression, and away from his established pattern once more.

What appeared as only a vague hint of a new approach in *Numa Roumestan* emerged full-blown and unmistakable in his next novel, *L'Evangéliste*, published in 1883. As the title is meant to suggest, *L'Evangéliste* is an attack against religious fanaticism, and in particular against that kind of zeal which is turned to imposing conversion on the young and innocent. As in *Numa Roumestan*, however, Daudet was moved by more than a purely theoretical hypothesis about the nature of religious fanaticism. The passion of denunciation which animates the novel has specifically personal roots, just as did the north-south opposition which formed the basis of *Numa Roumestan*. The reality on which Daudet based *L'Evangéliste* he had observed uncomfortably close to home: a woman who was tutoring his son, Léon, had seen her daughter seduced by a fanatical religious sect, and converted to a renunciation of the world and a repudiation of her own mother.[3] Daudet, who had firmly opposed giving his sons a strict religious upbringing (he was as uncomfortable with religious commitment as with any other kind of commitment, even though he was no atheist), perhaps saw some vindication of his stand in the suffering of Léon's tutor. At the very least, he saw in the story an exemplary illustration of the anxiety he himself felt as a parent about the education of his children. *L'Evangéliste* was therefore a thesis novel in which Daudet had a definable personal stake: not only compassion for someone close to his household, but fear for himself and his own family.

It is perhaps the uncontrolled intensity of personal feeling which, in the end, made *L'Evangéliste* one of Daudet's weakest novels. The shrillness and the sermonizing obtrude, and deform too many of the characters and incidents. Much of the novel is hard to credit, based though it be on reality. The weakness is especially visible in the character of Eline Ebsen, who is the young girl victim of Mme. Autheman's fanatical sect. She is portrayed as simple and impressionable, but at no point does the reader enter her mentality sufficiently to comprehend what attracted her to the religion or why she was able to abandon her warm intimacy with her mother so quickly and so completely. One never believes in her reality, as a result. Her mother, Mme. Ebsen, is weakened as a creation by being too idealized: pious, devoted, and kind, she seems a heavily one-sided image of maternal suffering, a symbol rather than a human being. By the same token, Daudet is unable to avoid facile sentimentality in the situations and incidents he invents to develop his thesis. Eline and her mother, for example, are shown to be happy, warm-hearted people before the conversion, and the neighboring family of Lorie-Dufresne and his motherless children become the objects of their solicitude, introducing hopes for permanent happiness all around. This whole structure, characters and situation, are too obviously manufactured with an eye to making the conversion more heart-rending. Throughout the novel, invention is thus deadeningly controlled by the needs of the thesis demonstration and by cloying schemes to win the emotional assent of the reader. The work is undermined as fiction because it skirts so dangerously close to pamphleteering.

Yet the theme is potentially explosive, and the novel possesses certain extraordinarily masterful elements. Outstanding is the portrayal of Mme. Autheman, a demonic type who is an imposing variant of Daudet's favorite character, the destructive female. She is shown to be selfish, coldly ambitious, and unrelenting, driven by destructive impulses quite unrelated to the religious fervor she claims, but psychologically sound and persuasive. Mme. Autheman is as frighteningly successful a creation in her way as Sidonie Chèbe or Séphora Leemans. Similarly, the account of M. Autheman's suicide is unforgettable because of Daudet's power of empathy for the suffering of unrequited love. Although Autheman is at first portrayed almost in terms of caricature—ugly, physically deformed, and a moral weakling—the reader is made to overcome his revulsion when Daudet displays the best of his art to enter into the feelings of a suffering soul aching for love and crushed by a cruel and insensitive woman. When Autheman throws himself out of a window, the reader is powerfully affected because he has been made to share with great immediacy in the anguish of the victim.

L'Evangéliste has also a formal distinction which merits notice. Ever since *Le Nabab*, with its sprawling plot and subplots, Daudet had been exercising a growing restraint in the formal conception of his work. *Les Rois en exil* had a much reduced scale, and *Numa Roumestan*, while more complex in the breadth of social patterns that it tried to encompass, did not become overburdened with too many inorganic subplots. *L'Evangéliste* is notable for its apparently conscious, scrupulous, and disciplined sobriety of structure. The story is tightly woven, the characters are relatively few, there are no subplots artificially encrusted upon the main situation, and the writing is spare and direct. These characteristics, marking a heightened concern for artistic form on Daudet's part, were the products of his experience with the novel of realism, the application of lessons learned. For although Daudet was now embarked on a retreat from objectivity, he had by no means abandoned the skills acquired during his preceding phase. In *L'Evangéliste*, and in all his works thereafter, he continued to display the discernment of the sharp observer, the artful technique of the storyteller, and the devices of plotting, characterization, and structure which the novels of realism had taught him. And in *L'Evangéliste* he succeeded for the first time in pruning irrelevancies and sharpening focus so noticeably as to constitute, in his career, a new direction in the formal aesthetics of the novel. Daudet seemed to be announcing, with *L'Evangéliste*, his dedication to the ideal of the short, tightly plotted, dramatic novel, in preference to the vast panorama.

This ideal Daudet came closest to attaining in the novel which followed, the celebrated *Sapho*, published in 1884. *Sapho* has taken its place as the Daudet novel which is best known to the general public both in France and abroad. Its subject matter has a potential for sensationalist exploitation which no doubt accounts for the tremendous international popularity it has enjoyed to the present day. For the novel concerns a case of what the French call *collage,* or unwed cohabitation, and more explicitly the case of a young man's sexual bondage to an unloved mistress. Daudet's handling of the subject is in no wise pornographic, nor even mildly titillating, but its reputation as an especially "French" French novel will not die. If one can ignore its reputation, however, one can find in *Sapho* a superior work of art and, surely, Daudet's finest achievement in realistic fiction.

It is suggestive that *Sapho* was written so speedily and smoothly, in about one year. Daudet certainly found it one of the easiest books to write that he had ever done, doubtless because what it dealt with, *collage* in the bohemian world of artists, was largely drawn from personal experience and was a matter of intense private concern to the author. Although there are no clear records on the subject, it seems likely also that during the writing of *Sapho* Daudet was favored with a let-up in his illness and hence a considerable spell of freedom from pain. The result is a work conceived with clarity, composed with admirable directness and economy, and written with pungency and vivid realism.

It seems incontestable that in the corrosive relationship between Jean Gaussin and Fanny Legrand which forms the heart of the book Daudet transposed his own long and painful liaison with Marie Rieu. External details are altered—there is no suggestion, for example, that Jean Gaussin is himself a budding artist—but the psychological truth is drawn from Daudet's own life. In *Sapho* we have, indeed, the most detailed portrayal Daudet ever composed of his view of the relations between the sexes. This view dominates the relationships he created in all his novels, and its main lines have therefore been pointed out before: the weak-willed, gentle, and sensitive male; the domineering, coldly inconsiderate female; and usually a passive and tenderhearted young girl who timidly completes an unbalanced triangle. In *Sapho* this kind of triangle is not merely one among other situations in the book but is the very subject of the book itself. The novel undertakes as its purpose a precise dissection and analysis of the ingredients which compose such a relationship. But the bond between Jean Gaussin and his Sapho, Fanny Legrand, is identified now explicitly not as love but as the pull of the flesh, as sensuality. *Sapho* is an analysis of the vice of lust, and an effort to show how a decent young man can be enslaved and destroyed by it. The book thus powerfully illuminates, by its concentration on the one theme, one of the central and most insistent motifs in all of Daudet's novels, man as the victim of woman. For Daudet, the vulnerable secret of man is his sensuality, rather than his capacity for love. When faced with the choice between violent sensual delight and tender affection, man as Daudet sees him is too weak to choose wisely. *Sapho* is not only a confession, it is Daudet's personal summation of man's nature and his fate in this world. Implicit in all his other works, Daudet's view is here stated explicitly, and is as rigorously demonstrated as a geometrical theorem.

In this respect, *Sapho* continues the didactic trend begun with *Numa Roumestan*. There is no doubt that it was conceived as a thesis novel, and the famous dedication "pour mes fils quand ils auront vingt ans" ("for my sons when they reach the age of twenty") frankly acknowledges the conscious intent of the author, seeking to teach wisdom to his sons, and hoping to keep them from his own mistakes. The book is as much a preachment in intent as *L'Evangéliste*—yet it is a great deal more affecting. There is some basis for a complaint against moralizing in *Sapho*, to be sure—most notably the passage in which Jean Gaussin's Provençal aunt cries out against the corrupting influence of Paris.[4] Here was a favorite theme of Daudet's, and he pressed his point at this juncture somewhat clumsily and artificially. Yet for most of its length the novel is totally engrossing, and remains free of any taint of the sermon.

The explanation for the effectiveness of *Sapho* in spite of the moral thesis which so clearly inspires it would seem to be that Daudet's theoretical purpose was overwhelmed by the nature of the material, and what comes through in the book, primarily, is the author's profound personal emotion as he re-creates a segment of his own youth. As with Baron Autheman in *L'Evangéliste*, so with Jean Gaussin in *Sapho*, Daudet enters so fully, and with such empathy, into the character's feelings that the reader is made to experience them with keen immediacy. Although Jean Gaussin is of that breed of passive and dull anti-heroes popular in French fiction since Balzac, his feelings, his sensuality, and his fleshly enslavement are made powerfully vivid through Daudet's words. Fanny Legrand is a most successfully created character, moreover, and the kind of animal magnetism that she could exert over a weak and sensual male is almost tangibly rendered in the book. The fact is that, in the actual composing, much of the preaching was forgotten in favor of a concerted effort to render the quality of this relationship with precision. Most of the text is devoted to detailing the manifestations of the potent but neurotic bond between the two main characters. So that, in spite of occasional intrusions of preaching, or artificialities in plot or characterization, what comes most powerfully across to the reader, what dominates the whole work, is the psychological truth of the quality and feel of the relationship.

Daudet conveys this more profoundly and more fully than perhaps he himself realized. It is precisely the rendering of this truth that gives the novel its greatness and its impact. One might say that Daudet set out to preach a moral lesson but ended by baring his soul. *Sapho* thus represents one more demonstration of the fact that where Daudet reaches most directly into his inner being for the source of his art, his work proves to be most effective. Those works of his, like *Sapho*, *Les Lettres de mon moulin*, *Tartarin de Tarascon*, and *Le Petit Chose*, that well up out of his own most deeply felt experiences are certainly the ones which are most satisfying to the reader, and the most likely to endure.

Though the fine analysis of the relationship between Jean Gaussin and Fanny Legrand dominates the entire novel, *Sapho* has other admirable characteristics which bear mentioning. The central theme, implicit in the main liaison, is borne out amply by the other irregular relationships which are interwoven with it. These subsidiary relationships ring varied changes on the theme of the destructive effects of *collage*, and thus reinforce the novel's impact. They are closely integrated into the subject, and help to give the novel a satisfyingly dense yet unified structure. Further, these relationships taken together give to the novel a documentary value, composing as they do a lively portrait of the artistic bohemia of that day. *Sapho* is not only a novel of psychological realism, it is a most convincing and objective rendering of a particular milieu as well, in the earlier manner of *Fromont jeune et Risler aîné*.

Finally, it is worth calling attention to the delicacy and tact with which the novel is written. So much of it takes place in the bedroom that Daudet could easily have yielded to the temptation to indulge the prurient with coarse language and explicit detail; or he might conversely have retreated into pale prudery. But Daudet has managed this problem with taste and skill; without sacrifice of vigor or realism he has managed to avoid any offensive crudeness. In this respect *Sapho* is a triumph of controlled art.

With all its fine qualities, *Sapho* is nevertheless not quite that complete masterpiece of irreproachable perfection for which the admirers of Daudet always longed in vain. Not only is it occasionally preachy in tone, but it has a strong streak of facile sentimentality to boot. This is especially glaring in those sequences that involve Jean's return to his Provençal home, and his project—never realized—to escape his bondage by marrying the sweet and gentle Irène. Though perhaps necessary to bring out fully Jean's weakness and his enslavement to Sapho, these sequences are handled so mechanically, and the secondary characters are so wooden, that no reader can believe in them. The ending also is unsatisfying. To have Sapho be the one who breaks off the relationship is consistent enough with the nature of the characters. But Daudet was clearly striving too hard for effect in having the break come under the melodramatic circumstances of a last-minute decision by Fanny Legrand not to accompany Jean on his consular mission. And Fanny's clear-eyed but sentimental analysis of their relationship in her final letter seems frankly out of character. Her generosity and her perspicacity here are contradicted by all that precedes. No, *Sapho* is no unflawed masterpiece. But its best elements make of it an authentic and moving *cri du coeur*, and as such it will live.

The next project which began to tempt Daudet was a novel centering on the French Academy. He had had his satirical fun with the topic previously: in some references inserted in *Le Petit Chose* and *Jack* in passing, in a short story of *Femmes d'artistes* called "Confidences d'un habit à palmes vertes," and in the celebrated ninth chapter of *Les Rois en exil*, which describes with elaborate irony a public prize-giving session of the august body. When, after such a record of attacks on the Academy, he was urged to be a candidate for election himself, in 1883, he responded with characteristic ambivalence by making inquiries about procedures, without committing himself. However, his inquiries discouraged him. In particular the obligatory visits to each academician to solicit his vote horrified Daudet, for it required more deference to others and more allegiance to a public institution than his need for independence could allow.[5] As a sort of unconscious compensation for this disappointing experience, Daudet began in 1883 to amuse himself by noting the antics and activities of acquaintances who were academicians, watching the politics which went into each election when a vacancy occurred, and concluding before long that the whole milieu offered a chance for a novel of scathing social satire. In this phase of his career it was natural enough that he should gravitate to a subject which offered a didactic intent and an outlet for moral indignation. And it was equally characteristic of this phase that the subject should have some intimately personal relevance. By late 1884 the novel about the French Academy was already taking shape in his imagination.

The project was abruptly sidetracked, however, when Daudet received a financially attractive offer from a publisher who wished him to revive Tartarin. Daudet has stated quite forthrightly that it was the money that prompted him to write *Tartarin sur les Alpes*.[6] He reasoned that he was menacingly, perhaps incurably, ill and that he owed to his family the fullest possible commercial exploitation of his talent while there was yet time. This was an opportunity he felt he could not afford to miss. It is astonishing, under the circumstances, to find that *Tartarin sur les Alpes*, published in 1885 and therefore composed with almost the same speed as *Sapho*, and prompted by no more noble motive than material gain, should have turned out to be a very funny book, and, except for the perhaps disappointing transformation of the hero, a worthy sequel to the original *Aventures prodigieuses de Tartarin de Tarascon*. What is even more interesting and improbable about this novel is that, in spite of the circumstances of its composition and the nature of its genre, it should have fitted so completely into the pattern of Daudet's preoccupations in those years. For *Tartarin sur les Alpes* shares with the other works of this period—no doubt unconsciously—both the tendency to preach and the impulse to turn inward for his inspiration.

At the conscious level, *Tartarin sur les Alpes* was intended to be a satire of the mountain-climbing craze, then enjoying one of its periodic recrudescences as a popular sport among European tourists. Alpine clubs were being formed everywhere in the 1880's, and the Swiss government was vigorously promoting the craze in its advertising of tourist attractions. Daudet had recently visited Switzerland, and had acquired a somewhat cynical view of the whole business. He therefore employed his commission to revive Tartarin in order to mount an attack on mountaineering fraudulence and exploitation. The tone was gay, and the events fanciful, but no reader of the book could fail to note the pointed barbs which turned up in every chapter, satirizing the Swiss tourist industry.

But the conscious preaching, built into the original conception, is only part of the story. Other satirical elements crept irresistibly into the work as Daudet went along. His two ridiculously pedantic historians, Astier-Réhu and Schwanthaler, provide comedy with a strangely tart tone. Echoes of the satirical novel on the French Academy he was preparing—Astier-Réhu was destined for a key role in it—seemed to intrude into *Tartarin sur les Alpes* because they obsessed the mind of the author. The inclusion of Nihilist émigrés from Russia in the farcical doings of this novel also marks the extent to which serious and disturbing public matters then current in France managed to force their way into this work. Finally, the presence in the group climbing Mont Blanc of the young Swedish pessimist, imbued with the ideas of Schopenhauer and Hartmann, is another reflection of the temper of the times, out of place but irresistible to Daudet. The early 1880's marked the peak of Schopenhauer's influence in European thought, the moment of his greatest public vogue.[7] It was a time of widespread pessimism, and in Schopenhauer a whole generation had suddenly discovered its malaise articulated. But this was more than a public issue for Daudet—it was also deeply personal. His older son, Léon, now a young man of sixteen, had lately been confronting his father with the ideas of Schopenhauer, and Daudet had in some alarm been seeking adequate replies to his son's arguments. The famous verbal duel between the Swedish student and Tartarin in the thirteenth chapter of *Tartarin sur les Alpes,* in which Tartarin tries to dissuade the youth from suicide, is but a transposition of the earnest discussions Daudet had been having with his own son.

This very scene between Tartarin and the Swedish youth points up better than anything else in the book the extent to which *Tartarin sur les Alpes* was an unwittingly personalized work. For it is not just the echo of Daudet's problem with his own son which is noteworthy here, but even more the character, manner, and role we find assigned to Tartarin himself. In the early Tartarin novel the "hero" was the object of laughter, an embodiment of all that is inflated and ridiculous in the southern temperament. But in his new incarnation of 1885 Tartarin has mellowed, and become less ludicrous; if he is still comical and fatuous, our laughter has been made less mocking, more friendly and benign. What has happened, in part, is that Tartarin has been dislodged as the principal object of Daudet's satire. Our sympathies, indeed, are thrown *toward* Tartarin because so much of the satire is aimed at the envious citizens of Tarascon, led by Costecalde, who seek to undermine his fame and reputation. More interesting still is that Tartarin has become a lovable and sympathetic figure: it is not too much to say that now Daudet is identifying himself with his hero. It is, for example, Tartarin who speaks for common sense—that is, for Daudet himself—in the debate over suicide with the young Swede. This is a remarkable transformation. In the course of fifteen years Daudet had shifted his own attitude toward Tartarin from amused and ironic observation to one of affection, admiration, and—by the end of this novel—personal identification with him.

This startling change in Tartarin's character, which makes

him far less a comic figure, is compensated for by the presence in this novel of Bompard, who now supplies the irresponsible exaggerations and the hilarious ineptitudes which were the source of so much of the fun in the earlier Tartarin novel. Bompard is, of course, borrowed from the cast of *Numa Roumestan*: a sign that Daudet's creative juices were beginning to run dry and that the invention of new characters was becoming increasingly difficult. But the instinct to include Bompard in this novel was right, for in him Daudet could find again the gaiety and the fantasy the novel was meant to have, and which he was obviously not prepared to express any longer through Tartarin.

And the gaiety and fantasy *are* there. The comic invention of *Tartarin sur les Alpes* is well sustained, solidly constructed, and satisfying throughout. The book marks a return of the sparkling and witty imagination of Daudet's youth, almost as though Daudet had found in the opportunity to write a sequel about Tartarin a longed-for flight from the somber world of his maturity, and a respite from his personal sufferings. The laughter of this novel contrasts so forcibly with the grim pessimism of all his other novels of this period that it takes on some of the air of a suspension in time, or a figurative clearing in the woods which one comes upon unexpectedly. It may well, indeed, have been a sort of temporary relaxation for the author. Yet no sensitive reader could overlook the extent to which Daudet's usual gloomily serious world managed to intrude itself so insistently and at so many points throughout the novel. *Tartarin de Tarascon* is all sunshine and unrestrained, full-throated laughter. But *Tartarin sur les Alpes*, touched with the weight of the author's mature years, has its laughter coarsened with purposeful and harsh satire, and its sunshine partly clouded over with the solemn woes of a pessimistic age. It is still hilariously entertaining reading, but it bears the stigmata of its particular moment in time and in Daudet's career.

If *Tartarin sur les Alpes* was a sort of holiday, it did not last long. In 1885 Daudet's physical suffering began to grow acute and insistent, and it had by then become quite clear that neither his friend Charcot, who was perhaps the most celebrated specialist in Europe on neurological diseases, nor anyone else would be able to cure him. Victor Hugo's death that year, marked by a day of national mourning and an elaborate public funeral, provided for Daudet a most painful and humiliating reminder of the advanced state of his own ill health. For at the funeral, in full public view, Daudet found his muscular control so poor that he could not hold a pen untremblingly to sign his name.[8] He was now suffering pronouncedly from locomotor ataxia, a sickness of muscles and joints associated with the third phase of syphilis, which renders all motion painful and difficult, and which now threatened Daudet's physical ability to continue as a writer.

He was finding it, moreover, quite difficult to get back to work on his French Academy novel. His son Léon was increasingly difficult for him to handle. A brooding adolescent, Léon showed an urge to write, which his father wished to discourage; and he was increasingly sullen about the medical studies on which his family had embarked him. After the birth of their third child, a daughter, in 1886, relations between Daudet and his wife underwent serious strain for reasons about which one can only speculate. For some time afterwards, as Julia Daudet revealed in a letter to Edmond de Goncourt, Alphonse moved his study out to a small workshop in the garden of their home at Champrosay, and no longer worked in close collaboration with his wife, at the same desk, as had long been their custom.[9] The year 1887 was particularly hard on Daudet, bringing repeated disappointments and bitternesses of a personal and professional kind. The play version of his favorite novel, *Numa Roumestan*, was indifferently received by the public that year. He had a falling out with various friends, such as Edouard Drumont, to add to the isolation he already felt because of his difficulties with his wife and his son. And when the affair of the "manifeste des cinq" broke, in the late summer, it was a crowning blow to a succession of embittering events.

The "manifeste des cinq," an open letter signed by five young writers protesting against Zola's latest novel, *La Terre*, was an unsavory business. Their criticisms of Zola were in bad taste and gratuitously insulting. Their proclaimed disaffection from Naturalism was fatuous, since they had been in no sense Zola disciples before that. It is probable that the gesture was primarily intended to be an attention-getter for the ambitious young writers. It attracted ripostes in the same vein from defenders of Zola, who lost no time in insinuating that the publication of the manifesto had been instigated, out of pure envy, by Edmond de Goncourt and by Alphonse Daudet. Goncourt and Daudet were quick to deny the charge, but the suspicion remained, since some of the manifesto's five signers were known to be part of Goncourt's literary circle, and since the coolness that had lately developed on the part of Goncourt and Daudet toward Zola was a matter of general public knowledge. The truth of the matter will doubtless never be known, inasmuch as the principals in the affair have left contradictory and singularly uncandid accounts of what happened.[10] But Daudet's involvement could in reality have been no more than remotely marginal, even according to the most ill-disposed accounts. His bitterness at being so directly accused of this low perfidy was therefore sincere and not without cause.

Certainly Daudet experienced this unseemly squabble over the "Manifeste des cinq" as the last straw in a particularly trying period of his life. The extreme acerbity with which the petty vanities of the world of letters are discussed in the novel *L'Immortel* can only be read as the end result of the accumulated tribulations of 1887.

Daudet, of course, was not completely idle from the moment

in 1885 when he completed *Tartarin sur les Alpes* to the point in 1887 when he began to get a final version of *L'Immortel* down on paper. Besides writing the play version of *Numa Roumestan* already mentioned, he had written a new group of reminiscences about his early career, for various journals, and was at this time collecting and revising for book publication all he had written in this vein. The pieces appeared in two volumes, in 1888, entitled *Trente ans de Paris* and *Souvenirs d'un homme de lettres*. Still readable, and sometimes quite charming, these reminiscences are nevertheless trivial and superficial. They add little either to our essential knowledge of Daudet, or to his stature as an artist, though they attest to his public-pleasing skill as a journalist.

In 1886 Daudet also published a short tale for children called *La Belle-Nivernaise*, which enjoyed some popularity at the time. It was a curious exercise, composed in a sort of rhythmic prose in which almost every sentence formed a paragraph unto itself. The story is saccharine, sentimental, and moralistic, quite unworthy of Daudet at his best. A publisher suggested the idea, and Daudet seems to have composed it rapidly, by dictating it to a young man with literary ambitions, Hugues Le Roux, whom Daudet wished to help. Le Roux then tidied up the text for the author, smoothing out some of the rough spots, and received in exchange a handsome share of the royalties.[11] The incident is typical of the way in which Daudet, at the height of his fame, used to take an interest in young writers and seek ways to help them (while helping himself, to be sure) without making them feel they were the objects of charity. As for the composition itself, *La Belle-Nivernaise* is chiefly of interest in showing the newest dimension of his artistic bent during this vehemently didactic phase of his career. If Daudet accepted the commission to compose a children's story—and it must be remembered that as a famous and best-selling author he was besieged with proposed commissions most of which he rejected

—it is because he was increasingly preoccupied with his role as a parent and because he was approaching his work more and more from the vantage point and with the optics of a man observing and addressing a younger generation rather than his contemporaries. *La Belle-Nivernaise* is dedicated to his younger son, Lucien, and its non-too-subtle theme is that the affection of the family circle is the highest good available to a child. *La Belle-Nivernaise* is hardly to be taken seriously as art, but it offers one significant index to Daudet's more obsessive concerns in 1886.

It is in *L'Immortel*, published in 1888, that we find these particular concerns, as well as the consequences of Daudet's varied harrassments of 1887, most dramatically reflected. *L'Immortel* is a harsh and bitter novel, the most unrelievedly grim portrait of Parisian life he ever composed. To that extent, the novel was distinctly uncharacteristic of its author. Oddly enough, however, the Parisian public of 1888 showed no surprise at this abrupt change in Daudet. Instead, *L'Immortel* was gleefully received as a deliciously wicked scandal sheet, and provided that season's favorite drawing-room sport: fixing the presumed "real" names to its fictional characters. The assumption was automatic, in that kind of audience, that the novel was an act of vengeance by a rejected candidate for the French Academy.

It is only with the perspective of time that it is possible to take a different view of *L'Immortel* from the gossipy opinions which dominated the public in 1888. Obviously, much of the venom in the book had to do with Daudet's recent personal frustrations, all unconnected with the French Academy. The Academy served only as a convenient symbol of official and institutionalized values in the literary world with which Daudet was then disgusted. His limited dealings with the Academy dated back five years to 1883, and had, in any case, given little cause for rancor. The fact is that Daudet had no vengeance to seek in attacking the Academy, but was using it as a pretext to vent his spleen over a more general dissatisfaction with his lot as a writer.

Moreover it was generally overlooked that the Academy is far from the sole focus of the novel's attention. Sharing the spotlight with Astier-Réhu and the academic circle is his son, the unscrupulous young architect Paul Astier, and all his associates who symbolize for Daudet the unprincipled rising generation, of which he despaired. Thus the true focus of the novel is more fully represented by the entire Astier-Réhu family, encompassing as it does both the academic milieu and the new youth, and symbolizing what was for Daudet the worst aspect of the contemporary scene, the collapse of the family ideal. Daudet expresses his theme at the end of the penultimate chapter, in a scene which groups father, mother, and son together at a bitter moment in their relationships: "Tableau de famille, en effet; mais de la famille moderne, atteinte de la longue fêlure qui court du haut en bas de la société européenne, l'attaque dans ses principes de hiérarchie, d'autorité; fêlure plus saisissante ici, à l'Institut, sous la majestueuse coupole, où se jugent et se récompensent les vertus domestiques et traditionnelles." ("A family portrait, to be sure; but of the modern family, wounded by the long fracture that runs from top to bottom in European society, and that attacks the family in its principles of hierarchy and authority; a fracture that is more startling here, at the Institute, under the majestic cupola, where domestic and traditional virtues are judged and rewarded.")[12] L'Immortel was an expression of dark despair by a writer who, far from seeking a petty vengeance, was testifying to a vision of the world in which his own generation had lost its values to vanity and materialism, and the generation which followed, infected by Darwinian notions of the survival of the fittest, was turning out to be fiercely insensitive.

L'Immortel grew understandably enough out of the confluence of circumstances and preoccupations which attended its composition. The French Academy as a study in pompous pedantry, and as a milieu of petty intrigue, had fallen under Daudet's pen on numerous occasions, and since 1883 he had decided to make it the center of a novel of manners, not so much out of any pique but simply because he needed a new subject for a novel. During the time that he collected material, and while the conception was growing to maturity in his mind, Daudet underwent a series of shifts in outlook. Illness and family troubles oppressed him, literary quarrels and personal squabbles upset his equanimity. Perhaps under the additional spur of the volumes of memoirs he was preparing to publish, Daudet was driven by these pressures to review his life and his career, and he found it sadly wanting. The final redaction of *L'Immortel* was thus affected by a moody crisis which had been building up in Daudet—for causes unrelated to the novel's subject—all during the work's gestation period. The depression and anger Daudet felt about the world around him colored the writing of this novel, which might otherwise have been, to judge by the material, another somewhat preachy and personally oriented novel of realism such as he had been writing since 1881.

What made *L'Immortel* unique in execution was that its pessimism was so completely pervasive and unrelieved. For the first time Daudet composed a novel without a single main character whose virtues were admirable or who could represent simple decency or who could even command the reader's pity. All the important figures in the book are shown to be either evil or contemptible. There is not even the usual pathetic situation in which good is overwhelmed by evil; for the world of this novel is devoid of good, as though Daudet's imagination had suddenly become a place of darkness without light. Only the sculptor Védrine and his family are exceptions to this bleak image of Parisian society. But Daudet's point in this seems precisely to be that they stand outside it and are not a part of it. Indeed, Védrine himself seems not only outside Parisian society but even organically outside the novel. He seems merely a device, a tool by which Daudet can work himself into the edges of the novel in the role of detached observer. Védrine turns up everywhere, knows everyone, but plays not the slightest role in any of the action, influences no one, and maintains a strict, if highly ironic aloofness. His only concern is his art and his family. The novel could have been written without Védrine, who contributes nothing to it except the point of view of the author. Védrine is, of course, Daudet himself, and it is through this character that Daudet has provided an explicit personal reference in this novel, paralleling the self-involvement we have seen in all the other novels of this period, beginning with *Numa Roumestan*. Védrine's aloofness, his devotion to art, his affection for his family, are Daudet's personal commentary on the ugly and vain intellectual world of Paris which forms the true subject of the novel.

L'Immortel is a fascinatingly unique creation in Daudet's career, for the reasons suggested, but it has been largely ignored and neglected since its brief *succès de scandale* in 1888. It is now one of the least-read of Daudet's works, and for the perfectly understandable reason that it is a poor novel as art, shrill, preachy, and topical. The uncontrolled anger in which the composition is bathed undoubtedly wrenched characters and action out of focus. Astier-Réhu is simply too stupid to be a believable historian; Freydet is too naïve to be a believable candidate; Paul Astier is a bit too cynical; Fage, the hunchbacked book dealer, is a bit too grotesque. Structural unity also suffers as Daudet tries to weave together the milieu of the academicians themselves, the atmosphere of the influential academic salons, the provincial world of Freydet, the circles of the opportunistic rising generation exemplified by Paul Astier, and the calm world of the sculptor Védrine. The reader feels the artificiality of these juxtapositions, and of such outworn narrative devices as Freydet's letters to his sister, in spite of all Daudet's accumulated skills as a craftsman and a persuasive stylist. It is not the harshness of its theme that makes *L'Immortel* a failure, but the fact that its passionate fury serves a didactic rather than an artistic end. In his eagerness to denounce the decay of the family, and the loss of integrity in the arts, Daudet has distorted the reality of his characters, and forced an unconvincing unity on material that is too bulky and too disparate to be fused together.

That is not to say, of course, that *L'Immortel* lacks all distinction. As with other Daudet works which are, as a whole, failures, *L'Immortel* has gloriously successful moments. The fifth chapter, which describes the gala dinner of an academic salon, and the eighth chapter, which recounts the funeral of Loisillon, secretary of the Academy, are in Daudet's finest satirical vein, pungently witty and with a sharp eye for the telling detail. These two chapters deserve to be better known as individual pieces of fine writing. But woven as they are so tightly into the fabric of this inadequate novel, they seem doomed to obscurity for they do not lend themselves readily to removal from their context. One other fine chapter, the last one, is even less likely to receive its due for it is tied even more closely to the total context. Nevertheless, few readers of *L'Immortel* would deny that this final chapter, presenting the disillusionment and suicide of Astier-Réhu, is a moment of majestic power and poignant emotion. As the final commentary on the ironic title and the dominant theme, the last chapter of *L'Immortel* is indeed unforgettable. But it is a largely unrewarding path that leads to it.

L'Immortel was in some sense a purgative for Daudet. In it he seemed to release the tension built up by a long accumulation of resentments and frustrations. Its particular tone of unrelieved harshness was never to recur in his work. Enough momentum was left over at the end, to be sure, to carry Daudet into his first original play (that is, one not constructed by the dramatization of one of his own novels) since *L'Arlésienne*. This was *La Lutte pour la vie*, a work produced with scant success in 1889, continuing the career of Paul Astier after his cynical marriage to the Duchesse Padovani. In it Daudet seemed to be settling his personal account with the matter broached in *L'Immortel*, the question of the new youth of which he was grimly aware. He shows Paul Astier continuing his hard, ambitious, and unprincipled path, making his way in what he regards as a Darwinian struggle for life (hence the title), until in the rather melodramatic ending, he is shot dead by a contemporary who lives by the same code. Thus Daudet composed his own uneasy portrait of the new generation, more famously analyzed in Dostoyevsky's *Crime and Punishment*, and, during the same year as *La Lutte pour la vie*, in Paul Bourget's *Le Disciple*. Daudet's ending is, of course, the significant clue to the fact that *La Lutte pour la vie* was only the last feeble gasp of the passion that animated *L'Immortel*. For Paul Astier pays for his crimes in the play, as the evildoers do not in the novel. And in his preface Daudet defends the play's ending by insisting on his firm belief that "tout se paie" ("everything must be paid for,") no one ever really "gets away" with anything, in the long run. His outlook had begun to shift slightly. If the world was perhaps still full of evil for him, he was now willing to see the evil as at least relieved by inevitable retribution. *La Lutte pour la vie* drained off the last of the poisons which had produced *L'Immortel*, and announced a new, more benign, outlook in the author toward his world, and a new conception of his role as an artist. The full dimensions of this new outlook are to be seen clearly in a transitional novel, *Port-Tarascon*, published in 1890.

Port-Tarascon completes the Tartarin trilogy, but it is the palest of the three and reflects a serious decline in Daudet's capacity for comic invention. *Port-Tarascon* is a sadly uninspired work, and, in its lack of genuine gaiety, no doubt expresses the somber conditions of work now imposed on Daudet by his failing health. Like *Tartarin sur les Alpes*, *Port-Tarascon* was certainly written for money, and at the instigation of a publisher. But it may also have represented for Daudet an unsuccessful effort to escape into laughter from the acute physical suffering he was then undergoing.

By 1890 Daudet knew his disease was definitely not curable, and the pain in all his arm and leg joints had become so constant that he could no longer function without heavy doses of chloral. There is no doubt that he feared the spread of the disease to his brain, as his notebooks reveal. Partly to distract himself from this dread, partly because it was so much a part of his introspective nature, Daudet began to record, in a separate notebook which he proposed to keep secret from his wife, his own thoughts and impressions about his illness, as well as his precise observations of his physical deterioration. He considered making a book of these notations—perhaps even a novel. He had already assigned to it a title, *La Doulou*, the Provençal word for pain which seemed to him more expressive than "La Douleur," and which suggests a natural impulse in him to return to his roots at this time.

It was during the time that he was recording his own suffering that he also worked on *Port-Tarascon*. Far from being an escape, however, *Port-Tarascon* merely picked up the infection of Daudet's paramount preoccupations in 1890. The whole work has a surprisingly gloomy cast: Tartarin has become old and has lost even his fake bravado, the events he gets involved in are often cruel and painful rather than funny, and in the end Tartarin dies a broken and disillusioned man. Daudet seems not even to have the heart for spirited satire, such as he demonstrated in *Tartarin sur les Alpes*. The novel sounds tired, subdued, lacking in creative energy, and expressive of a saddened sympathy for the human condition.

There is not enough substance in *Port-Tarascon* to support any serious critical evaluation. At the most it is a curiosity for the student of Daudet's career, who recognizes in the transformed figure of Tartarin that Daudet had now gone all the way in his tendency to identify himself with his hero. It belongs in the development of Daudet's career since *Numa Roumestan*, showing as it does a highly personal source of inspiration at its psychological roots, and giving vent frequently to an urge to sermonize, moralize, and instruct regarding man's folly, and in particular regarding the meridional tendency to exaggerate reality. But the satiric verve which made *Tartarin sur les Alpes* a successful creation from the very same tendencies is lacking in *Port-Tarascon*. This work falls flat.

What is new in *Port-Tarascon*, what marks it as a transitional work, is precisely this absence of satiric verve, and its replacement by a tone of gentle, melancholy, indulgent pity for human foibles. Tartarin, in particular, embodies this tone. In governing the fantastic transplanted colony, he displays a benign and understanding wisdom suggestive of a man who has gone beyond passionate involvement in the affairs of men, who feels detached yet anxious to help lighten the burden. This is of course a far cry from the previous incarnations of Tartarin. But, more important, it is a new tone and outlook for Daudet himself, since it is clear throughout the novel that Tartarin and Daudet are one. If there are echoes of the bitterness of *L'Immortel* still resounding in *Port-Tarascon*—the abject and perfidious behavior attributed to characters like Costecalde and Excourbaniès, for example, bespeaks a more contemptuous than comic outlook on human nature—the book is nevertheless dominated by this new, tolerant, and long-suffering Tartarin, whose former extravagances have all subsided. No doubt Daudet's own awareness that Tartarin's boisterous laughter had modulated to a smiling and indulgent amusement with human weakness led him to call *Port-Tarascon* a *"livre d'humour."* He had in mind, no doubt, the genial and non-aggressive style of comedy generally attributed to the English, and designated by the word "humor" for which the French were wont to acknowledge they had no equivalent. Since this distinction between English humor and French comedy had been a lively subject of critical discussion in the 1880's, Daudet naturally enough seized on the distinction to define for himself the tone he had tried to impart to his novel, and the outlook he wished it to express.[13]

This tone and this outlook were highly conscious matters with Daudet, and seemed closely tied to his own feelings about his art after the publication of *L'Immortel.* For Daudet seems to have recognized, as most of the public and the critics had not, that in *L'Immortel* he had unleashed a quite unprecedented and uncontrolled flow of venom. That was neither the impression he wished the public to have of him, nor a conception of himself that he could live with. *L'Immortel* thus sparked in him a mood of remorse and a resolve to change which were conscious enough to have been made explicit in his notebooks, and even in a conversation with Edmond de Goncourt, as recorded in Goncourt's *Journal.*[14]

Some time in 1888, after *L'Immortel* had come out and he was beginning to formulate a new novel (which was in fact to be *La Petite Paroisse,* conceived first at that time but not actually composed until after two plays, *La Lutte pour la vie* and *L'Obstacle,* as well as two novels, *Port-Tarascon* and *Rose et Ninette,* were produced) Daudet recorded for his own edification the following paragraphs:

Je voudrais que mon prochain livre ne fût pas trop cruel. J'ai eu la dernière fois [that is, in *L'Immortel*] le sentiment que j'étais allé trop loin. Pauvres humains! Il ne faut pas tout leur dire, leur donner mon expérience, ma fin de vie douloureuse et savante.

Traiter l'humanité en malade, dosages, ménagements; faisons aimer le médecin au lieu de jouer au brutal et dur charcuteur.

Et ce prochain livre qui serait tendre et bon, indulgent, j'aurais un grand mérite à l'écrire, car je souffre beaucoup. Fierté de ne pas imposer aux autres la mauvaise humeur et les injustices sombres de ma souffrance.

(I should like my next book not to be too harsh. The last time I had the feeling that I had gone too far. Poor human beings! I must not tell them everything, give them my experience, my painful and knowledge-filled last years. Treat humanity like a sick person, with careful dosages and consideration; let's cause the doctor to be loved instead of playing the role of brutal and tough butcher.

And this next book which should be tender and kind, indulgent— I'd have great merit for writing it, for I suffer a great deal. The pride of not imposing on others the ill humor and the somber injustices of my suffering.) [15]

Both the remorse and the new resolve are plain in these words. The "new" Tartarin of *Port-Tarascon* had his origins in this reflection that men must be treated like patients needing kindly and understanding attention rather than a cold and brutal revelation of disease. Daudet began to see his role as novelist not as the exposer of human evil, but as the consoler and healer. Daudet conceived that he could remain true to his ideal of rigorous devotion to the truth, however painful, and yet use his art to open the way to happiness rather than merely to assault man with his shame. After 1890 he was to proclaim himself a "*marchand de bonheur*" ("dealer in happiness,") in his art,[16] and casting aside the last vestiges of his objectivity, he set out purposefully to devote what he knew to be his very few remaining years, and his last creative energies, to the cause of human happiness.

VII

Disintegration

1 8 9 0 – 1 8 9 7

The novel *Port-Tarascon* marked a transition in Daudet's career not only to a new emphasis and viewpoint but also, unhappily, to a period of sharp decline in talent. *L'Immortel* had
been Daudet's last sustained burst of genuine emotional and
artistic energy, as it turned out. His powers of invention, and
his ability to breathe life into his creations, were plainly at low
ebb in *Port-Tarascon,* and events were to show that this was
no temporary fatigue. The root of the matter was, of course,
the wasting sickness that racked his body, sapped his strength,
and inhibited the play of his imagination. Matters grew steadily worse after 1890. Extensive walking was now out of the
question, and he could hardly manage even a short stroll without a helping hand. He thus went out less, and suffered from
the lack of immediate contact with the world he had once observed and described so avidly. Even more of a handicap was
the fact that it was growing difficult for him to sit for long at
a desk, and his fingers could hold a pen only with the shakiest
of grips. His handwriting deteriorated almost to illegibility and
he took more and more to composing his work aloud, dictating
to his secretary.

Under such conditions, one must acknowledge that it was an
act of tremendous courage for Alphonse Daudet to continue to
write at all after 1890. No doubt the work he did in those
years must be judged with the circumstances of composition in
mind. Daudet was now a man struggling by sheer will power

to keep himself feeling alive through the only activity he knew. Virtually cut off from his environment, he was writing, as it were, from habit and from memory. Most of the time it proved to be all he could do to keep a coherent plot running in his fiction, and to attain an acceptable level of prose clarity. Except for short bursts of inspiration, he found it largely beyond his powers to strive for fine style, subtlety of characterization, intricacy of structure, and artful narrative strategy. He was unable, that is, to apply in his work after 1890 the skills he had painstakingly developed for making literature of his observations and imaginings. The three novels, the handful of short stories, and the two plays (one in collaboration) that are the creative works of this final phase of his career testify chiefly to the dramatic deterioration in the author's capacities as an artist.

Yet this phase is not totally bleak. Two short stories, written almost at the very end of his life, miraculously revive the best qualities of Daudet's prime creative years, and there are pages of very distinguished writing in at least one of the novels. For those achievements alone the final phase of Alphonse Daudet's career would repay serious study. The decisive justification, however, for devoting attention even to these inferior works is simply that this phase of Daudet's career exists. What Daudet composed in these years is an integral part of what he was, in his lifetime, as a writer. His very triumph over his physical debility, though it takes a form that falls far short of being art, is a valuable and instructive clue to the creative process as it operated in the case of this writer. The quality of Daudet's mind, and the meaning of Daudet's career, are not to be grasped fully without taking account of what he produced in his struggle with his own failing powers.

In the light of Daudet's general artistic development, the new outlook sensed in *Port-Tarascon* could only signify a step backward. For the obligation he now seemed to feel to promote the happiness of his readers via fiction meant abandoning the tough-minded realism that had become one of his principal strengths. There was some measure of pride, dimly conscious, in Daudet's new outlook: because he was in constant pain himself, he proposed as a point of honor not to inflict his suffering on others, but to bend his energies rather to soothing the public's abrasive encounters with reality. This was a form of artistic *noblesse oblige*. But the new outlook was equally, and pathetically, a tacit admission that he no longer had the stamina to practice his art at its highest level. He seemed, indeed, to be willing to redefine his art so as to accommodate his weaknesses. And to accommodate those weaknesses, at this stage of his career, was a significant defeat, for the weaknesses were the very ones which had been associated with the uncertainty of his muse, and against which he had conducted a long, running battle in more vigorous days. It meant that he was yielding now, without a struggle, to his need to gain the affection of his readers rather than earn their admiration. It meant that he intended to play shamelessly and facilely on their emotions through the unrestrained recourse to pathos. It signaled his willingness to introduce and to justify preaching and moralizing in his fiction, and to substitute partisanship for the difficult virtue of objectivity. He was thus opening the door to all his potential artistic vices at once. His conception of himself as a *marchand de bonheur* amounted to the veritable abdication of his accumulated and hard-won qualities as an artist, and the substitution of a wholly artificial pose.

This final phase of Daudet's career opened with his last personal fling at the theater, the play *L'Obstacle*, first produced in December 1890. All through his career, from the very beginning, Daudet had been tantalized by his inability to score a solid success in the theater of the kind he had achieved in the novel and the short story. This failure had become a sore spot with him, and he never completely abandoned the ambition to produce one truly successful play. In L'Obstacle, which was a failure like the rest, he chose the facile path of sentimentality allied with a topical issue. The play concerns a marriage which is almost thwarted by the discovery of a possible hereditary taint in the man. There is, of course, a happy ending to preserve Daudet's new self-image as a purveyor of joy, but not before the audience is subjected to a long discussion of the laws of heredity, then much in the air because of recent scientific findings and because of the novels of Emile Zola. It is also worth noting that Ibsen's Ghosts had its first French production in May 1890; there is no concrete evidence that it influenced Daudet, but the production added to the topicality of Daudet's play six months later.[1] As for Daudet's choice of this theme, it could have been primarily inspired by personal anxieties. Daudet's older son was soon to be married, and the author was conceivably using his art to ventilate his own guilt and allay his fears over the possible taint he may have inflicted on his son because of his illness. Whatever the truth of his motivation, the play itself proved to be stilted, forced, and in places even silly. L'Obstacle did nothing whatever for Daudet's ambition to score a theatrical hit, and even less for his permanent reputation as a writer.

About this period Daudet was making notes for a new work, seeking to crystallize its outline into something more concrete than the vague generality which obsessed him. Although this project was never realized, it is a significant phase of his activity for what it reveals about his state of mind. For this project was really to be the consecration of his new self-image, a novel of both joy and wisdom, and a celebration of simple pleasures. He had named it La Caravane, and his conception was that of an episodic novel held within a framework: a family traveling the roads of France and stopping to hear the tales or discuss the problems of people along the way.[2] The work was to have philosophic pretensions, pointing in the aggregate of its epi-

sodes to true wisdom in the conduct of life. Daudet seems to
have dreamed of this project as his own equivalent of Montaigne's *Essais*, the classic work he most admired and which he
was constantly rereading. It was also intended to be an evocation of the joys to be found in nature, along the dusty roads
of the French countryside. Above all, it was to be an expression
of the author's warm feeling and respect for the poor and the
disinherited: peasants, migratory workers, and homeless wanderers whose lives are reduced to essentials because they have
no possessions or property.

It seems clear that the conception was not viable for fiction,
and would have turned out to be a compendium of Daudet's
worst faults had it ever been written: sentimental, preachy, and
fragmented beyond coherence. That he could have contemplated such a project seriously is comment enough on the low
state of his imaginative and creative energies. The conception
of the project is, however, the painfully faithful mirror of the
attitudes that dominated his thinking after 1890.

The nebulous preoccupations with *La Caravane* abruptly
gave way, in 1891, to a more pressingly immediate concern
which became, before the year was out, Daudet's shortest novel,
a work called *Rose et Ninette*. The subject of this brief novel
is the problem of divorce, and *Rose et Ninette* is sometimes
pointed out—the only distinction it has ever been accorded—as
the first French novel on this topic ever written. Just a few
years before, in 1884, the French legislature had passed a controversial law permitting divorce in France for the first time.
The law was still exciting lively controversy in 1891, and its
author, a deputy named Naquet, was a public storm center.
The fact that Naquet was a Jew only added to the violence of
the debate in those troubled times. Daudet entered the debate,
not in a spirit of religious dogmatism, of course, but rather as
a humane and perplexed observer. His point of view, which
recognizes the need for some way of solving the problem of

bad marriages, but which fears divorce as a threat to marriage, is summed up in the statement he recorded in the notes for his first draft of *Rose et Ninette:* "Non, le divorce n'est pas une solution. C'est la fin du mariage que le juif nous apporte là, mais il faut chercher autre chose." ("No, divorce is not a solution. It is the end of marriage as an institution which the Jew brings us with his law, but we must look for something else.")[3]

The editors of the Edition Ne Varietur suggest that the genesis of this novel was a divorce and its consequences to which Daudet had recently been witness in his circle of friends.[4] The more likely roots of his impulse to write *Rose et Ninette*, however, were, as in the case of *L'Obstacle*, deeply personal. The novel is dedicated to his son Léon, who had just married the granddaughter of Victor Hugo. The dedication reads, rather pointedly: "A mon cher fils/Léon Daudet/Au poète et au philosophe/Je dédie cette page de la vie contemporaine" ("To my dear son/Léon Daudet/To the poet and philosopher/I dedicate this page out of contemporary life"). It is well known that Daudet had had serious misgivings about the stability of this marriage. He had gone to the wedding with a heavy heart. The intent of *Rose et Ninette* would seem to have been, simply stated, to warn his son Léon of the dangers of divorce.[5]

The novel is painfully dull and unimaginative. Not for one moment do the characters come alive. The recently divorced Régis de Fagan, his two daughters Rose and Ninette, and the unhappily married Mme. Hulin are all cardboard puppets in a geometrical demonstration that accessible divorce undermines marriage, and that it is particularly the children who suffer when divorce does take place. The plot is barely serviceable, without dramatic conflict, and generates no interest on the part of the reader. The writing is perfunctory. It would be hard to imagine a purer example of the thesis novel. While the attitude to divorce which animates the book is neither simplistic nor dogmatic—it is, in fact, highly intelligent and generously humane—the novel is not art, but argumentation. Its very brevity, and its flat, expository style, are the clearest signs that Daudet himself did not get deeply involved in it as art, but viewed it as something he wanted to say, quickly. Indeed, the writing of this novel seems like a *coup de tête*, a sudden impulse carried out in the midst of other preoccupations. It was conceived and written with most uncharacteristic haste.

The fact that it was written at all speaks eloquently of Daudet's outlook regarding himself at this stage of his career. Most authors who have achieved some fame and are conscious of the nature of enduring literary glory are inclined to be circumspect about the work they will set their hand to, and sign. They manage their careers with an eye to posterity. *Rose et Ninette* seems to have been written in the conscious awareness that it was unworthy of an author ambitious for immortality. But Daudet was characteristically more interested at that moment in the welfare of his own family than he was in his reputation. *Rose et Ninette* bespeaks the specific anxiety about his son's marriage that was then uppermost in Daudet's mind, as well as his general concern for the declining ideal of the family, a theme that had first prominently entered his fiction in *L'Immortel*. The novel was thus a warmly human act, though it was not the act of a great artist. Under the circumstances it was bound to be didactic, sentimental, and contrived. The existence of *Rose et Ninette* is a measure of what Daudet valued most in 1891.

For some two years thereafter Daudet was occupied with various lesser tasks, journalism, translations, and collaboration on a play with Léon Hennique, while he continued to reshuffle various material for the still-cherished project of *La Caravane*. The play was Hennique's idea: he wished to dramatize an old short story of Daudet's called "La Menteuse," and Daudet's decision to help him with the task was an act of pure complaisance. Except that it added one more failure to Daudet's theatrical history, *La Menteuse* made no contribution to Daudet's career when it was produced in 1892. By late 1893 a new idea for an ambitious novel did finally crystallize out of some of the *Caravane* material combined with other matter having to do with a roadside chapel near Daudet's summer home at Champrosay. The novel which emerged out of this, *La Petite Paroisse*, was completed toward the end of 1894 and appeared as a book in 1895.

The roadside chapel that inspired the heart of *La Petite Paroisse* had been put up by a local citizen to the memory of his wife who, as everyone in the region knew, had left him for a younger man. Daudet was attracted, as one might expect, by a story with the built-in appeal of pathos, and, as his notebooks show, by a framework affording him the chance to make a probing and profound study of jealousy. The significant point is that Daudet was now choosing subjects which could be stated as abstractions rather than as human situations. The didactic temper now controlled his imagination completely. Further, Daudet's notes indicate that what interested him in this subject was the psychological trajectory by which the jealous man ends in forgiveness and renewed worship of the woman who had wronged him. Here was a further opportunity for the self-elected *marchand de bonheur* to point the way by fictional example to wisdom, triumph over passion, and the deep satisfactions to be found in pardoning the sinner. And that was, in fact, what the novel turned out to be: a sermon on forgiveness. It is obvious that in this theme Daudet was approaching via another route the subject that was becoming an obsession with him: the integrity of the family as an institution.

La Petite Paroisse is a full-length, ambitious novel, inevitably cast in the mold of the sentimental sermon which characterized Daudet's work of this period, but not without certain glimmers of the earlier talent that had brought him merited fame. Chiefly it is the character of Fénigan, the hero, who holds center stage. A typical Daudet figure, Fénigan is a man of gentle ways and sensitive responses who is wholly devoted to his young wife. What Daudet has rendered singularly well and movingly is the shifting range of emotions in Fénigan after his wife runs off with young Charlexis. We follow him as he suffers the first shock, and the welling-up of anger against the seducer, then anger against his wife, followed by a savage thirst for vengeance, directed against both wife and lover, which he is not prepared to discover in himself. The delineation of this inner struggle is masterful and leads convincingly to the slow subsiding of these unwonted violent emotions which his gentle temperament will not support. The return of calm perspective, eventually, induces a willingness to forgive which permits a happy ending.

Daudet's success in those parts of the novel which trace the emotions of Fénigan may be ascribed to the fact that he seemed to enter so fully and with such profound empathy into the travail of his protagonist that he was temporarily distracted from his didactic purpose. The result was a genuinely creative act in which a human being and his emotions come throbbingly alive under the author's skillful pen. The novel is in no sense autobiographical, but there would seem to be much of Daudet himself in Fénigan as there is in all of his protagonists who have this same passive, almost feminine disposition. This identification with self helps, no doubt, to explain his capacity to render the inner feelings of Fénigan so persuasively. However one explains it, this aspect of *La Petite Paroisse* does represent a sudden, limited re-emergence of Daudet's greatest gifts. Fortunately this aspect also constitutes the main focus of the whole novel as Daudet conceived the work. While the rest of the novel is dreary, lifeless, and unconvincing, the triumphant creation of the central character suffices to render this novel worthy of a serious reading.

Though jealousy is the focal center of the novel, and the

analysis of the hero's emotions its prime excellence, *La Petite Paroisse* is notable also for the presence of the extraordinary young villain, Charlexis. Presented as the corrupt scion of decaying nobility, a prince of noble blood and a jaded roué at the age of eighteen, Charlexis is scarcely a believable figure. His cold-blooded seduction of the simple Lydie, who is almost old enough to be his mother, does not ring true. But Daudet's invention of this curious figure is revealing. For he is another incarnation of the type of *jeune gredin*, young scoundrel, unprincipled, selfish, coldly unemotional, whom Daudet had earlier portrayed in the figure of Paul Astier, in both *L'Immortel* and the play *La Lutte pour la vie*. Charlexis is another representative of that disturbing young generation whom Daudet saw—not clearly, but distortedly, through the obsessive fears of a worried parent—coming of age all around him. The words of Charlexis himself so identify him, early in the book:

Pourquoi suis-je ainsi? d'où me vient cette expérience précoce, ce dégoût de tout et ces rides que je me sens jusqu'au bout des doigts? Serait-ce commun à ma génération, à ceux qu'on a nommés les "petits de la conquête," parce qu'ils sont nés comme moi vers l'année de la guerre et de l'invasion, ou seulement personnel à ma famille, au vieux sol épuisé par trop de moissons heureuses et qui réclame à présent une longue jachère?

(Why am I this way? where has this precocious experience come to me from, this disgust with everything and these wrinkles of old age which I feel on myself all the way to my fingertips? Could it be common to my generation, to those who have been called "the children of defeat" because they were born as I was about the time of the Franco-Prussian war and the invasion, or is it merely personal to my family, to the old soil exhausted by too many happy harvests, and now in need of lying fallow for a long period?) [6]

The hint of a generation corrupted by an attitude of anarchistic selfishness following the humiliation of the Franco-Prussian War, combined with the suggestion of decadent aristocracy, make of Charlexis a symbol of all the vices that were undermining family life, in Daudet's estimation. Charlexis is not merely the seducer who intrudes into Fénigan's marriage, he is also the product of a different generation, contemptuous of traditional virtues. The clash between generations and the collapse of the family unit are thus strong secondary themes in *La Petite Paroisse*, supporting the main theme of conjugal jealousy, and linking the work firmly to the other novels of the same period, in which Daudet showed similar preoccupations.

The invention of Charlexis is revealing for yet another reason. For in *La Petite Paroisse* he is the principal incarnation of evil, whereas in previous works of Daudet the most potent source of evil has generally been a woman. The figure of the cruel, perfidious, and domineering female, long a staple in Daudet's fictional world, is a striking absentee in *La Petite Paroisse*. Instead the principal traits of the type have, for the first time in Daudet's work, been transposed en bloc to the younger generation and to the opposite sex. This transposition suggests how far Daudet's creative imagination had shifted its standpoint from that of the dominant generation to that of the declining generation uneasily witnessing the rise of the young to dominance. With an old man's point of view, Daudet no longer tended to depict evil as a *femme fatale*, but rather as a cynical and unprincipled youth. In that sense the creation of Charlexis as the prime source of evil in *La Petite Paroisse* marks a distinct new stage in Daudet's evolution as a writer.

La Petite Paroisse stands out as the only full-length fiction of Daudet's, after *L'Immortel*, in which one can still find evidence of the greatness of his talent. If the dissection of jealousy is masterful, and the invention of Charlexis revealing, however, *La Petite Paroisse* is for the rest a simple and uninspired composition which belongs all too clearly to the author's declining years. The characters are wooden, the plot predictable, and the tone and manner of narration indulgently sentimental. It was in most respects a suitable product from a confirmed *marchand de bonheur* in full cry. But by the time it was completed late in 1894, Daudet's health and strength had dramatically ebbed, and one may properly wonder that it contained any quality at all worthy of critical attention. It was, indeed, to prove almost a last gasp of creativity, for little time now remained to him.

Fiercely determined to succumb neither in body nor in spirit to his painful illness, Daudet continued doggedly to work during the barely three years of his life from the time *La Petite Paroisse* was completed until his sudden death on December 16, 1897. His compositions of that period included several short stories, and a novel to which he devoted the main effort of his last resources of energy. The novel was *Soutien de famille*, one of the longest works of his career (only *Jack* and *Le Nabab* are longer), begun in January 1895 and completed two and a half years later. Since it was still appearing serially when he died, Daudet did not live to see *Soutien de famille* through the press in book form.

The last book which he did see through the press was, fittingly, the slim volume containing *Le Trésor d'Arlatan*, a work of rare power, one of the best creations of Daudet's career, and easily the finest piece of writing salvaged from the wreckage of his declining years. It was composed during a sudden burst of creative inspiration early in 1896, interrupting the work on *Soutien de famille*. The writing of the novel was also interrupted for a group of short stories which were published in 1896 in a collection named for the best story of the group, *La Fédor*, as well as for two stories composed for the foreign press, and published in French only after the author's death: "Premier voyage, premier mensonge," solicited and translated into English for a British publication by R. H. Sherard; and "La Fille de l'ogre," solicited and translated into German for Vienna's *Neue Freie Presse* by Theodor Herzl.[7]

The magnum opus of these final years, *Soutien de famille*, seems today to be primarily a monument to Daudet's iron will and personal pride. Judged apart from the physical suffering

and mental fatigue of its author, it is an embarrassing performance. The novel tells the story of the Eudeline family, concentrating on the period following the death of the father, hounded
into suicide by heartless creditors. The elder son, Raymond
Eudeline, a teenager thus catapulted into the role of family
provider (the *soutien de famille* of the title), is coddled and
protected by family and friends alike because of the burden
he bears, but he is unequal to the responsibilities. He grows up
selfish, lazy, and weak, using his "burden" as his constant excuse,
while his younger brother Antonin and his sister Dina actually
do the honest labor that supports the family. Only after years
of cynical and self-indulgent behavior does Raymond Eudeline
recognize the truth, admit his faults, and attempt restitution
to his brother by substituting for him in his compulsory mili-
tary service. The original cruelty which drove the father to
suicide was the work of a political figure, a member of the
Chamber of Deputies, who plays an important secondary role,
along with other political figures, throughout the novel. Indeed,
the world of the Palais Bourbon constitutes the principal back-
drop of the novel's action.

The novel is set in the 1880's, and bears the subtitle "moeurs
contemporaines." Its central happenings and characters derive
from real-life observations recorded in Daudet's notebooks
more than a decade before he began the novel. There are repeated references to the fatal gap between generations, the cool
and calculating cynicism of the new youth, and the collapse
of family feeling and discipline: all themes amply developed in
L'Immortel, La Lutte pour la vie, and other works. And his
conception of his own role as *marchand de bonheur*, incessantly
talked about with friends and recorded in his private notebooks
for years, now intrudes directly into *Soutien de famille*, as the
author describes a small shop opened by Mme. Eudeline and
her daughter Dina, and in a personal aside indicates that he
knows the shop well:

Que de fois je me suis arrêté sur le trottoir à contempler avec
envie ce brillant et paisible intérieur, alors que je rêvais de m'in-
staller marchand de bonheur en plein Paris. Vous lisez bien, marchand de bonheur. Ce fut un temps ma fantaisie d'adopter cette profession bizarre, de mettre mon expérience de la vie et de la souffrance au service d'une foule de malheureux qui ne savent pas dis-
cerner ce qu'il y a de bon, ce qu'on peut extraire encore d'agréable
de l'existence la moins favorisée. Pour le débit de cette denrée
précieuse et rare qu'on appelle le bonheur, le magasin de Mmes
Eudeline me semblait le cadre idéal, comme douceur, silence,
netteté, sérénité.

J'aurais probablement changé d'avis, si, caché dans quelque coin,
j'avais assisté, un soir d'avril 1887, à la rentrée de Mlle Dina . . .

(How many times have I stopped on the sidewalk to contemplate
enviously that bright and peaceful interior, in the days when I
dreamed of setting myself up as a dealer in happiness right in the
heart of Paris. You read that correctly, a dealer in happiness. It
was for a time a fantasy of mine that I would adopt that bizarre
profession, that I would place my experience of life and of suffering
at the service of a whole mass of unfortunates who don't know
how to discern the good that there is to be got, the pleasantness
that one can still extract, even from the least favored existence. For
the retailing of that rare and precious commodity called happiness,
the shop of Mesdames Eudeline seemed to me the ideal setting for
its comfort, silence, cleanness and serenity.

I should probably have changed my mind if, hidden in some
corner, I had been present one evening in April 1887, when Miss
Dina returned to the shop . . .) [8]

There is no need to complete the quoted passage; it has been
given at sufficient length to suggest as fully as need be the
quality of imagination and of prose that Daudet was able to
muster for this final novel.

Restricted in movement and social contact, broken up with
pain and fatigue, Daudet was clearly "writing from memory,"
exploiting well-worn themes and ideas, dredging up old memories for a plot, even reusing old characters and milieux. He was
not at all recording *moeurs contemporaines*, but a world remembered, ten years behind him. Above all, he was self-

indulgently going back to old habits of personalizing his narrative with familiar asides and sentimental reflections. The reader's embarrassment with *Soutien de famille* comes from this accumulation of evidence that all power of new invention had been exhausted in Daudet, and all discipline of style, thought, and structure eroded. The very length of the book, for so slight a tale, is enough to reveal how verbose and slack the writing is, how ill-managed the plot, and how dimly conceived the characters. The attempt to blend the political world, the commercial world, and the world of the white collar functionary is perhaps the clumsiest of its kind in Daudet's long career.

All the indications suggest the pathetic truth about *Soutien de famille*: that in a heroic effort to keep his mind intact from his illness, Daudet, to occupy himself, conceived a plan for a work in the mold of his best novels of realism which he simply had not the creative energy left to execute worthily. What remains, where once there had been acute observation, a gift for satire, and the rigor of objectivity, is pathos and sentimentality, pity for the weak, scorn for the cruel, and a tender and sermonizing concern for the integrity of the family circle as the true source of individual happiness. This obsessive theme, evident in all his work since *L'Immortel*, became at last the dominant central focus and controlling idea in this irretrievably mediocre swan song to the novel, *Soutien de famille*. To such a low estate had the creative powers of Daudet been brought, at the end, by time and illness.

Happily, however, Daudet's long and occasionally glorious career did not fade out quite so ignominiously. *Soutien de famille* is a conception that went back to early 1895. During 1896 a few shorter works, and most notably "La Fédor" and *Le Trésor d'Arlatan*, materialized in time to prove that the old spark of brilliance was not yet dead, and to close his career with genuine distinction. What all of these shorter works have in common is that they are intensely personal, drawn from the author's own life, and generally from distant memory, as though in the twilight of his years Daudet felt impelled to recapture the emotions and events of his youth. Throughout his career, of course, his very best work had always been drawn, in some degree, from his most intimate self. Now at the end of his career he seemed to be guided by some instinct, in short and fitful bursts of inspiration, back to the short story form and the personal confession in which he had triumphed as a young beginner. Like the hero of his own early story "L'Homme à la cervelle d'or," he drew on the last remaining riches in the stored treasure of his own brain. His creative instincts had brought him finally, after many a twist and turn, back full circle to his beginnings and his true self.

Before discussing "La Fédor" and Le Trésor d'Arlatan, the two gems of this period, something must be said of the only other story of exceptional interest in the group, "Premier voyage, premier mensonge," a reminiscence, without fictional trappings, of a real event in Daudet's boyhood in Lyons, involving truancy from school and a boat ride on the Rhone river. In an extraordinary feat, Daudet dictated this story aloud, guided only by a few written notes, to the journalist R. H. Sherard who had asked him for something yet unpublished which could be translated for first publication in England. The text is so smoothly composed, the details so vividly recalled, the tone so warm and winning, that it seems hard to believe the story is the product of a spontaneous narration. To be sure, Daudet had long meditated the material, to the point where it had taken literary shape in his mind. Nevertheless, the composition of "Premier voyage, premier mensonge" was essentially a feat of impromptu storytelling. The testimony of Edmond de Goncourt, Jules Renard, and many others assures us that Daudet possessed to an extraordinary degree the natural ability to tell a story aloud, and that he was most effective when narrating his own experiences.[9] All attest to the spellbinding vividness, the skill, and the charm with which he could hold forth. In "Premier voyage, premier mensonge" we have a precious written transcript of such an oral performance.

The source of "La Fédor" in Alphonse Daudet's personal life is well known and but thinly veiled. For in it he fictionalized the death of Marie Rieu, who had been his mistress for so much of the period of his apprenticeship. Daudet's relationship with Marie Rieu had been frequently stormy, but out of weakness—and perhaps pity—he had been unable to break it off, cleanly, until his marriage in 1867. The announcement of the marriage of course aroused deep resentment in Marie Rieu, who threatened revenge on both Daudet and his bride. Much to Daudet's relief, no doubt, Marie Rieu died shortly thereafter. Nearly thirty years later Daudet was moved to recall his feelings on learning of her death, casting his recollection in the form of a short story which can also be considered a sort of final chapter or epilogue to his novel *Sapho*, in which the same relationship had been explored.

The short story Daudet imagined to incorporate this memory out of his past was constructed around the funeral of the former mistress, transformed into an actress named Louise Fédor, known to the public as "La Fédor." The principle of construction was apparent in the first title Daudet gave the story, for journal publication: "L'Enterrement d'une étoile." To portray himself, Daudet created the character of François du Bréau, a marquis married but two years and delighted with his gentle young wife and baby. An old friend informs him of the death of his former mistress, La Fédor, and prevails upon him to attend the funeral as an act of charity. The story then focuses centrally on the reactions of François du Bréau at the funeral: he encounters other former lovers of hers, and in conversation hears of still others; he learns of caprices and treacheries on her part unsuspected at the time; he watches, fascinated, the comportment at the funeral—comic or callous—of those who had been associated with her career or private life; and he re-experiences with unexpected vividness both the pain and the pleasure of his relationship with her. By the end of the afternoon François du Bréau is eager and grateful to return to his family and the warm comfort of domestic respectability.

The ending of the story, with its implicit rejection of the bohemianism of artists and its stress on the joys of family life, belongs of course to the sermonizing *marchand de bonheur* Daudet had become by 1896. But the story's essence carries us back to Daudet's finest period when his combination of observant eyes and acute sensitivity could produce memorable results. In "La Fédor" the analysis of the conflict in François du Bréau, entranced by the behavior of the others present at the funeral even as he is pained by what they tell him, is accomplished with masterful subtlety. His urge to flee the scene, counteracted by a rather helpless fascination with it, echoes in miniature for the reader the whole character of his bittersweet relationship with La Fédor, and reveals the vacillating temper which has been the root of all his suffering. The most impressive aspect of "La Fédor," one must grant, is Daudet's rather coolly objective analysis of himself. In addition, the story describes the details, the atmosphere, and the participants at the funeral with all of the perceptive irony which Daudet at his best had always commanded. The central segments of the story, devoted to the funeral itself and to the reactions of François du Bréau, constitute a magnificent achievement. Though little known, "La Fédor" deserves to be added to that select group of short stories from *Les Lettres de mon moulin* and from *Contes du lundi* which have gone round the world as the best-known part of Daudet's literary legacy, and the basis of his enduring fame.

Even more deserving of rescue from neglect than "La Fédor" is the last story Daudet wrote, *Le Trésor d'Arlatan*. Much longer than any of Daudet's short stories, but not long enough to be called a novel, this work was composed in early spring 1896 and was published in a handsome illustrated volume by itself in January 1897. That this remarkable composition had special significance for the author is evident from his decision to accord it this separate book publication. In part, that special significance is indicated by its dedication to the memory of his cousin Timoléon Ambroy, who for nearly forty years had been his faithful correspondent, confidant, and warm personal friend, and whose death early in 1896 had been the immediate occasion of his writing it. Hearing of the death of "le vieux Tim," as he called him, Daudet put aside *Soutien de famille* briefly in order to set down a tale, as a memorial to his friend, which he based on an incident from his own life in which Timoléon Ambroy had played a part. That incident had occurred just exactly thirty years before, in early 1866, when Daudet had accepted Timoléon Ambroy's suggestion that he leave Paris and return in solitude to the healing atmosphere of his native Provence, to a small house which Tim was able to put at his disposal. The therapeutic sojourn was made necessary, as Tim knew from his young cousin's letters, by the misery of Daudet's relationship with Marie Rieu. Daudet hoped to forget her, and to get some writing accomplished, in this Provençal hideaway. It was during that sojourn that the first draft of *Le Petit Chose* was written.

Thirty years later Daudet transposed this event fictionally with certain modifications. Daudet himself became a writer named Henri Danjou, a "Franciot" or northerner and therefore an alien in Provence. His cousin was dubbed Tim de Logeret, and the house near Arles became a hunting cabin in the Camargue. Marie Rieu became Madeleine Ogé, an actress and singer of renown both in Paris and in the provinces. Using the sultry, and vaguely ominous, atmosphere of the Camargue to powerful effect as the background, Daudet interwove the story of the brooding author, Henri Danjou, with that of the deeply disturbed adolescent, Zia, whose task it was to prepare Danjou's meals for him. Zia is fifteen years old, and so obsessed by evil visions that she has repeatedly been deemed unworthy of experiencing her "bon jour"—the ceremony of the first communion. Her inability to rid herself of these demonic visions parallels the torment of Danjou, haunted by episodes of cruelty and infidelity in Madeleine Ogé yet unable to rid himself of his fleshly enslavement to her.

Zia and Danjou suffer their private torments separately until both become tantalized—each for a different reason—by the mysterious treasure of the shepherd Arlatan. At that point their two stories intersect and echo each other ironically. For Arlatan's treasure is nothing more than a collection of lewd photographs, for which he has made extravagant claims of magic curative powers. The sophisticated Danjou is driven to pay for a look at the treasure, not because he believes in the curative powers, but because a chance remark of Arlatan's has led him to believe that the treasure contains a photograph of Madeleine Ogé, and he is too weak to resist the temptation to look at it. Nevertheless, when Arlatan crudely narrates the obscene circumstances in which he came by the photograph, Danjou finds to his surprise that he is so disgusted he leaves Arlatan's hut feeling cured forever of his obsession with Madeleine Ogé. The simple Zia, on the other hand, pays to see Arlatan's treasure because of her insatiable craving for immersion in evil and for the voluptuousness of guilt. Her naïve hope for a cure rests on the notion of thus purging her wickedness once and for all. Instead of a cure, however, Zia carries away from Arlatan's hut the seeds of her destruction. For Danjou accidentally sees her come out, which so overwhelms her with intensified shame and guilt that she flees and drowns herself.

In the sober and restrained style which characterized that very early tale of dark Provençal passions, "L'Arlésienne," Daudet recounts the grim events of *Le Trésor d'Arlatan* simply and without ornament or literary flourish. The individual characters with their brooding tensions and strange ways, and the eerie atmosphere of the Camargue, are evoked with brief, sure-handed skill. The story itself is allowed to unfold with its natural order and pace, and without artificial heightening of suspense. The simplicity of presentation powerfully enhances the impact of this strongly moving tale. Even at the end, where one might have expected Daudet to yield to the temptation to moralize, as had been his wont in all his other works of this period, he finds the discipline to state the symbolic import of Arlatan's treasure and its effects with the classical pithiness of a maxim, and without any pretensions to prescriptive wisdom: "Ce trésor d'Arlatan ne ressemble-t-il pas à notre imagination, composite et diverse, si dangereuse à explorer jusqu'au fond? On peut en mourir ou en vivre." ("This treasure of Arlatan's—does it not resemble our human imagination, composed of many and varied elements, so dangerous to explore all the way to the bottom? One can die from it, or live from it.")[10] The reader is allowed to quit the story without false comfort and with a foreboding sense of the potential violence in the unplumbed depths of the human psyche.

Le Trésor d'Arlatan is an inexplicable, almost miraculous, literary fact. There is nothing comparable, in quality of writing or quality of imagination, in any other work of this period of Daudet's decline. It is as though, in the midst of more pedestrian preoccupations, for no clear reason, a fragment of Daudet's youth—not only subject matter, but style, structure, and outlook as well—floated to the surface of his consciousness and found expression suddenly. Le Trésor d'Arlatan is not only as impressive as any of the Lettres de mon moulin, it belongs among them in spirit. For it contains all their excellences: keen insight into human nature, sensitive appreciation of the Provençal atmosphere, a flair for the dramatic, even touches of gaiety and wit, and a gift of vivid expression; and it mysteriously avoids all the accumulated faults and self-consciousness of his work after 1890. It is part of the enigma of the creative process that *Le Trésor d'Arlatan* could have come from the pen of a writer whose powers were then in a state of patent deterioration. However one explains this particular enigma—a sick man's obsession with his own youth, the death of a close friend, a Proustian moment of privileged memory—we must be grateful for the existence of *Le Trésor d'Arlatan* as a fitting capstone to the career of Alphonse Daudet, and a farewell testament to what was best in his art after the more dubious elements have been stripped away.

VIII

Conclusions

"J'écris uniquement pour le plaisir, pour le besoin de m'exprimer, parce que je suis un sensitif et un bavard" ("I write solely for pleasure, out of the need to express myself, because I am sensitive and garrulous"). When Alphonse Daudet offered that definition of himself, in the summer of 1896, during a discussion with Edmond de Goncourt about writers' motivations, he came as close to the truth about his work as he had ever come, as though he had been suddenly, near death, vouchsafed a last insight.[1] As a writer Alphonse Daudet was, after all, very largely a creation of his own will power and his intellect—he made himself into a serious man of letters by sheer hard work. But when his created self disintegrated under the impact of a wasting illness, in the 1890's, there stood revealed in the final, almost instinctive compositions, that foundation of pure natural resources on which Daudet had built. Those natural resources were the "sensitif" and the "bavard" in him. They were the innate talents which were the true basis of Daudet's career. They define the extent to which Daudet can be called a "natural" writer. He was assuredly right in claiming that it was not for posterity—which Goncourt gave as his own motivation—nor yet for money, fame, or social prominence that he engaged in writing, but, at bottom, because writing offered the obvious outlet for his dominant personal traits: the compulsive talker and the man of extraordinary sensitivity.

Bavard is a deliberately irreverent word designating Daudet's gifts as a storyteller, but it contains its own truth. In origin, Daudet's ability to manage a narrative effectively was oral—like so many Frenchmen from the Midi he came by a delight in vivid speech naturally, and learned as a matter of regional custom how to hold the interest of others when he had a tale to recount. The quality of Daudet's oral skill was widely and publicly attested throughout his life. What his literary career demonstrates is that he was able to transmute this oral skill into a major asset on the written page—indeed into one of his greatest distinctions as an artist. For he developed to a high degree the art of spinning a narrative so as to entice and enchant, preserving suspense and distributing surprises, without blurring the story line. To go from short stories to novels, Daudet learned to refine the technique in subtlety and complexity so as to be able to interweave, without confusion, several concurrent plots. This art ultimately evolved into one of the most sophisticated tools in his craft, and because it had its roots in his very nature, it survived even the years of disintegration. No more superbly managed narrative exists in all Daudet than his final composition, *Le Trésor d'Arlatan*.

His natural talent as a *bavard* was not only for the strategy of narration, but for the manner as well. Daudet was able to adapt to written forms many of the verbal tricks by which a speaker establishes rapport with an audience. The frequent interpolations in his fiction of asides from author to reader have exactly that intention. The reader is made pleasantly aware of the persona of the narrator when the device is skillfully used, as, for example, in *Les Lettres de mon moulin*. Daudet showed consistent fondness, too, for the informality of tone which first-person narrative can impart. This preference also was related to his gifts as a talker. Such writing can take on the loose syntax and personal idiosyncracies of conversation. Thus it is a rare novel of Daudet's in which a part of the action is not handled in the form of letters, or a diary, or extensive segments of dialogue, so that the style of a personality is imprinted in the words. Daudet called such writing *littérature debout,* "stand-up writing," to suggest its kinship with spoken or declaimed material.[2] First-person narrative became his favorite means of dissipating literary solemnity and "speaking" to his readers. Much of what is usually meant by Daudet's "charm" reduces itself to this warmth and intimacy of narrative manner, the outgrowth of Daudet's fundamental talent as a *bavard.*

Daudet's greatest natural endowment as a writer, however, was surely not his oral facility but his sensitivity. His own term, *sensitif,* is again inadequate, for what he had was a phenomenally high threshold of awareness of the world he inhabited. "Quelle merveilleuse machine à sentir j'ai été, surtout dans mon enfance," he remarks of himself in his *Notes sur la vie.* "Fallait-il que je fusse poreux et pénétrable; des impressions, des sensations à remplir des tas de livres et toutes d'une intensité de rêve." ("What a marvelous piece of machinery for feeling things I was, especially in childhood . . . How porous and penetrable I would have to have been; impressions, sensations enough to fill piles of books, and all with the intensity of a dream.")[3] This was indeed the wealth which fed his art, the stuff of all his books. With that insight into himself which was but another aspect of his great sensitivity, Daudet used to concede—not without some pride—that he lacked imagination, the power of invention. All he wrote was drawn from life, he maintained.[4] No student of his career can doubt that the hypersensitive antennae with which he perceived life were his highly effective substitute for imagination. His keen awareness of the world around him, his perspicacity in noting the telling detail of appearance or conduct, his ability to empathize with those he was observing, all are part of his sensitivity, the marvelous equipment which provided all the raw material for his fiction. It was an impressive talent of Daudet's displayed from the beginning to the end of his career, to be able to render with immediate vividness the feel, the texture, the surface appearance of people, places, and things. *Le Trésor d'Arlatan* is again proof, with its intensely felt atmosphere of sensuality and mystery in the Camargue, that this ability survived in Daudet to the very end of his life.

It seems an inescapable first conclusion, therefore, from this close examination of Alphonse Daudet's career, that the gifts which made a writer of him, the best of himself out of which his enduring achievements came, were his acute sensitivity and his natural storytelling faculty. Whatever there was of greatness in Daudet was born of these twin endowments.

However, Daudet's career amply demonstrates also that these twin endowments were complicated by several factors of personality and circumstance which seriously affected their growth and their yield. Daudet's entire life was, for example, conditioned by a basic conflict in his personality which pitted a craving for affection against an imperious need to feel independent. A fundamental insecurity in his nature also took its toll, in painful indecisiveness and an inability to make strong and deep commitments. His southern heritage proved a mixed blessing, enchanting and shaming him by turns as he observed its impact on himself and others. The family's financial troubles in his youth, his place in the family as the youngest boy, his myopia and his small stature, all influenced the ways in which he developed and utilized the twin endowments with which he was born. If the urge to tell stories and to communicate the perceptions which his extraordinary sensitivity opened to him were compelling within him, and demanded some outlet, his anxieties and his pride, his fears, his insecurities, and his emotional needs, all made it difficult for him to achieve single-minded devotion to literature as a career, or even to maintain that necessary faith in his own genius which the practice of art demands. Though born with the endowments a writer must have, Daudet grew up with personality pressures which kept those endowments from forming the central driving motivation of his life. As a writer Daudet suffered from an uncertain muse. His was a career that was constantly shifting, eternally in search of itself, condemned to restless change. Nothing fully satisfying to either author or reader can be achieved under the sway of so unsteady an artistic vision. And that is the second conclusion to which the pattern of Daudet's career inescapably leads.

From these two conclusions it appears that Daudet's career is a product of the struggle between his innate abilities and his emotional disabilities. For the most part this struggle proceeded at a conscious level. In the beginning the specific issue was whether or not he would or could be a writer at all. His need for the moral support of some kind of collaborator or companion in his work resulted from that initial struggle. His early efforts convinced him that he could produce nothing without some encouraging presence, a human sounding board to test his ideas, who would not, however, pose a threat to his sense of independence.

During his apprentice years Daudet struggled to find his bent, concluding at an early point that he was not a poet, later risking the plunge into the sustained creation of a novel when he feared that his attention to shorter compositions might mean that he lacked staying power. His first successes assured him that he did not lack *souffle*, but disturbed him by their heavy dependence on his Provençal origins and his own personality. The struggle thus renewed itself over the question of variety and versatility. Impelled by the effects of maturity, aided by intelligence and determined discipline, Daudet overcame his disabilities and deepened his talents enough to become an impressive novelist of manners, exercising extraordinary will power against much of his inner nature in order to make of himself an objective realist. Objectivity, in turn, provided only a temporary equilibrium in the author, and the struggle was soon joined again as Daudet began to allow more play to his subjective opinions, and to show a long-suppressed urge to espouse or attack causes. This tendency culminated in a novel of such unredeemed vehemence (*L'Immortel*) that it was as much remorse as physical decline which produced his final shift in the long struggle, the strange phase of the *marchand de bonheur* during which Daudet wished to impart healing powers to his work. Daudet's fascinating last creations, "La Fédor" and *Le Trésor d'Arlatan,* may be understood as the products of a moment in the author's consciousness when, the long struggle stilled at last by his physical collapse, he had a momentary reinfusion of his twin endowments, in full force and without encumbrances.

Such an understanding of the evolution of Daudet's career can provide the basis for assessing the value of his achievement and defining the place that ought to be his in the literary history of his times. Certainly his achievements must be stated in terms of his most eminent gifts. Among his short stories and his novels, the best works will be remembered first of all because they are excellent yarns, artfully unfolded. Secondly, they will be remembered because, in characters and settings, they vibrate with the authentic texture of life, they are alive and breathing, they are the product of a truly responsive sensibility.

Unfortunately, there is no single work which is not marred in some degree by an excess of sentimentality, an exaggerated character, an instance of bad taste, or an obtrusive archness of manner. Daudet regularly succumbed to the temptation of the facile effect, trying to reach too wide and varied an audience. That is the price Daudet paid for his uncertain muse. It prevented him from ever taking a place in the very front rank among the artists of his time. It is not, of course, the fact that Daudet's works were all imperfect which keeps him from the front rank. "Even the greatest works of art fall short of perfection," Alfred North Whitehead had occasion to remind us.[5] Rather it is a question of the proportion of excellences to faults in each work, and of the obtrusiveness with which those faults strike the reader. Reading Daudet is a frustrating and less than satisfying experience because one is always naggingly conscious of the flaws which diminish even the very greatest of his works. The flaws in Daudet's work are always an integral part of his total conception, for the flaw is in Daudet himself. The fully satisfying masterpiece seems instead to be a conception of irresistible power, whose imperfections are merely in the details of execution.

Though not among the rare geniuses of the very front rank, Daudet deserves a prominent place among those immediately next in rank as a creative artist. His literary achievement, in both quality and quantity, towers above that of the vast majority of his competing contemporaries, who are mostly now forgotten. Daudet is not quite the equal of Flaubert or Zola, but he remains a major figure in French literature. For he is among the comparative handful of his generation who survive. Moreover, even the amount of his creative work which promises to live on is impressive: the novels *Le Petit Chose, Tartarin de Tarascon, Fromont jeune et Risler aîné, Le Nabab,* and *Sapho;* the play *L'Arlésienne;* at least a dozen stories from the *Lettres de mon moulin* and *Contes du lundi* collections; and in all probability the novella *Le Trésor d'Arlatan.* Their appeal is varied: *Tartarin* and a few of the short stories have the purest merriment for its own sake to be found in France in the nineteenth century; *Sapho* and *L'Arlésienne* each embodies a powerfully penetrating analysis of the dark roots of physical passion; *Fromont jeune et Risler aîné* and *Le Nabab* are entrancing tales spiced with a vivid evocation of the atmosphere of Paris under Napoleon III. Whatever the evident imperfections of these works, they will not soon lose their audience, for they have so high a level of intrinsic worth as to outweigh the imperfections handily.

Still, predicting the future reputation of works of art is a notoriously risky business, and one must be given pause by the fact that time has already dealt rather harshly with Daudet's work. Perhaps only one quarter of his total production is now still regularly sold and kept in print, and even that fraction promises to decrease. This study of Alphonse Daudet's career may, nevertheless, conclude with a prediction which rests on firmer ground: namely, that Daudet's career itself is his most durable achievement, and that as long as men are curious about France in the second half of the nineteenth century, Daudet and his writings are not going to be forgotten, even if the audience for his individual works were to dwindle to insignificance. For the more one studies his career, the more one is impressed with the fact that he is perhaps the most representative man of letters of his age. And it is, once again, to his extraordinary sensitivity that this may be attributed.

Throughout his career Daudet was so constantly aware of the ideas and the public concerns which were in the air, and he responded to them so directly—one is tempted to say, so helplessly—that his career ended by being a sort of mirror of his times. His beginnings reflected the wide popularity in those years of the poetry of Victor Hugo and Alfred de Musset, and of the journalistic style of the *chroniqueurs* and fantasists. As his career developed, he responded directly to the aesthetic preoccupations of his time in literature: realism, Naturalism, impressionism and the "écriture artiste" of the Goncourt brothers, even Symbolism and the psychological novel. Politically and philosophically, too, his work underwent the influence of the changes and controversies of the day: the problems of industrialization and urbanization; the decline of monarchy and the rise of republicanism; Schopenhauerian pessimism and social Darwinism as life philosophies; the disintegration of family and the debate over divorce. All these issues and many others found their way into the fictional world Daudet created. Suffering the inherent defect of his greatest quality, Daudet seemed responsive to everything, without distinction or discrimination. He was thus led, too often, to write about trivial and transitory matters. But the very fabric of the life of his day is therefore faithfully reflected in his work, both the kind of life writers and artists then led, and the nature of daily existence for the average man as well.

The permanent value of the corpus of Daudet's work, then, and of the evolution of his career, is documentary. He felt personally, and gave expression to, every significant change in mood, every new concern, which preoccupied his contemporaries. As *témoignage*, as witness to an age, Daudet's works are historians' gold, for there is nothing else quite like them. The *Journals* of the Goncourt brothers are no doubt a better source of information concerning literary gossip and personality quarrels in that period. The novels of Zola are more powerful, but limited as reflections of their times by Zola's bias. Numerous historians have chronicled the publicly-known political events of the era ably. But if one wishes to acquire some intimate idea of what it felt like in a daily way for the ordinary individual to be alive in France between 1860 and 1890, there is no better path to that knowledge than the study of the works and the career of Alphonse Daudet. The quality of life in that era breathes from his every page. And there is a very handsome dividend of aesthetic pleasure to be culled along the way.

BIBLIOGRAPHY · NOTES · INDEX

Bibliography

WORKS BY ALPHONSE DAUDET

Oeuvres Complètes Illustrées, Edition Ne Varietur, 20 vols. Paris: Librairie de France, 1929–31. This is the indispensable edition for scholars, containing numerous texts not otherwise published in book form, all prefaces written by Daudet for other people's books, material from Daudet's personal notebooks, details concerning each first edition, and extracts from book reviews of the time, in addition to carefully printed texts of the main works. However, most of the correspondence, and some of the short works published in newspapers, do not appear in this edition; and the personal notebooks have been excerpted only, often with proper names deleted and other editorial alterations. The ideal complete works does not yet exist.

La Doulou: La Vie: Extraits des carnets inédits de l'auteur, preface by André Ebner, Daudet's last secretary. Paris: Fasquelle, 1931. This separate edition includes more material than is given in the text of *La Doulou* included in the *O.C.*, above (vol. XVII).

Contes du Lundi, ed. J.-H. Bornecque, 2 vols. Paris: Arthème Fayard, 1947.

Lettres de mon moulin, ed. J.-H. Bornecque, 2 vols. Paris: Arthème Fayard, 1948. Now rare, these inexpensive paperbacks contain valuable documentation in the introduction and notes.

Marchand de Bonheur. Paris: Thomas Nelson and Sons, 1932. An anthology of sentimentality, selected from all periods of his career, and proving that it was a running theme in his work, in case anyone ever doubted it. A sort of autobiography made up of extracts from Daudet's memoirs is included.

Les Mères. Paris: Alphonse Lemerre, 1897. An anthology of excerpts reflecting Daudet's concern with family values as expressed in the creation of "mother" types in his fiction. Revealing chiefly because it proved possible to concoct such an anthology.

Le Petit Chose, ed. J.-H. Bornecque. Paris: Fasquelle, 1947. Long, detailed introduction and notes make this the indispensable edition of this novel.

OTHER WORKS CITED AND CONSULTED

Albalat, Antoine. *L'Amour chez Alphonse Daudet: Essai.* Paris: Ollendorff, 1884. Daudet's pessimism about love: a superficial study.

——— *Gustave Flaubert et ses amis, avec des lettres inédites.* Paris: Librairie Plon, 1927.

——— *Le Mal d'écrire et le roman contemporain.* Paris: Flammarion, 1895.

——— *Souvenirs de la vie littéraire.* Paris: Arthème Fayard, [1921].

Aldington, Richard. *Introduction to Mistral.* Carbondale: Southern Illinois University Press, 1960.

d'Alméras, Henri. *Avant la gloire: Leurs débuts,* first series. Paris: Lecène-Oudin, 1902.

L'Apothéose d'Alphonse Daudet à Fontvieille. Avignon: Rullière frères, 1936. Proceedings of celebration inaugurating Daudet museum in windmill at Fontvieille.

Arène, Paul. "Juvénilia," *Gil Blas,* May 10, 1885. An interesting tribute to Daudet's originality as a writer.

——— "Lettre à Edouard Drumont," *Le Livre,* March 10, 1884. Arène's reply to an article in the same journal by Drumont, on the authorship controversy surrounding *Les Lettres de mon moulin.*

——— "Pour un fait personnel," *Gil Blas,* December 16, 1883.

Arène's version of how *Les Lettres de mon moulin* were written.

———— *La Veine d'argile: Contes inédits*, preface by Hubert Dhumez. Paris: Librairie Plon, 1928. The preface by Hubert Dhumez is a partisan statement on the Arène side of the authorship controversy surrounding *Les Lettres de mon moulin*.

Artinian, Artine. "Daudet's 'petit homme bleu,' " *Modern Language Notes*, February 1954, pp. 111–114.

Ashleman, Lorley Ada. *La Société française d'après l'oeuvre d'Alphonse Daudet*. Paris: Editions de la "Mutuelle des Auteurs," 1910.

Auchincloss, Louis. *Reflections of a Jacobite*. Boston: Houghton Mifflin Co., 1961. Interesting evaluation of Daudet by practicing novelist, "Early Reading and Alphonse Daudet," pp. 1–9.

Auriant. "Le Double visage d'Alphonse Daudet," *Maintenant*, no. 8, 1948, pp. 73–106. A vehement attack, summarizing all charges ever brought against Daudet. A prime specimen of the revisionist literature about Daudet.

———— *Quatre héros d'Alphonse Daudet*. Paris: Mercure de France, 1948. Details the real-life background of Tartarin and of three characters in *Sapho*.

———— "Sept lettres inédites d'Alphonse Daudet et une de Paul Arène," *Mercure de France*, December 1947, pp. 767–770.

———— "La Véritable histoire du Nabab," *Le Manuscrit Autographe*, nos. 27, 28, and 30, 1930.

Badesco, Luc. "Les Débuts parisiens d'Alphonse Daudet: Légende et vérité," *Revue d'histoire littéraire de la France*, October–December 1963, pp. 581–618. Painstaking research corrects some earlier errors, but is tendentiously argued.

Bale, Katherine. *La Provence à travers l'oeuvre d'Alphonse Daudet*. Aix-en-Provence, 1927.

Barbey d'Aurevilly, Jules. *Le Roman contemporain*. Paris: A. Lemerre, 1902.

Baumont, Georges. "A propos de 'L' Agonie de la *Sémillante*, ' "

Revue d'histoire littéraire de la France, January–March 1935, pp. 90–95.

Beaume, Georges. *Les Lettres de mon moulin d'Alphonse Daudet*, "Les Grands événements littéraires." Paris: E. Malfère, 1929.

Benoit-Guyod, Georges. *Alphonse Daudet, son temps—son oeuvre*. Paris: Éditions Jules Tallandier, 1947. A rather standard and traditional life and works.

Bérenger, Henry. *La France intellectuelle*. Paris: Armand Colin, 1899.

Bergman, J. *Die Provence und die Provenzalen in der Schilderung Daudets*. Münster, 1933.

Beuchat, Charles. *Histoire du naturalisme français*, 2 vols. Paris: Éditions Corrêa, 1949.

Billy, André. "Les Origines d'Alphonse Daudet," *Le Figaro littéraire*, October 27, 1951. Suggestive review of Bornecque's study.

Blavet, Emile. *La Vie parisienne*, vol. 2. Paris: Ollendorff, 1886. Interview with Daudet in 1885, bearing especially on candidacy for the French Academy.

Blechmann, Wilhelm. "Die Kunstform einer Daudetschen Novelle ("La Chèvre de M. Seguin"), " *Germanisch-Romanische Monatsschrift*, April 1962, pp. 193–202. Rather muddled attempt to locate Daudet's charm in the writing style and structure of one short story.

Bloy, Léon. *Belluaires et porchers*. Paris: P.-V. Stock, 1905. Essay on Daudet, called "Le Voleur de gloire," is one of the most bitter in print, stressing plagiarism—pp. 37–50, dated December 1888.

Bonfils, Juliette. *Paul Arène: Poète, félibre et conteur*. Aix-en-Provence: Aux éditions du feu, 1933. Adds some minor details (pp. 183–198) to the Daudet-Arène controversy.

Bonnet, Batisto. *Un Paysan du midi: Le "baïle" Alphonse Daudet*. Paris: Flammarion, 1912.

Bonnetain, Paul. "Autour d'un livre," *Le Figaro*, December 14, 1890. Interview concerning *Port-Tarascon*.

Bonnières, Robert de. *Mémoires d'aujourd'hui*, second series.

Paris: Ollendorff, 1885. Subtle insinuations against Daudet's character.

Bordeaux, Henry. *Les Ecrivains et les moeurs.* Paris: Albert Fontemoing, 1900.

Bornecque, J.-H. "Alphonse Daudet et l'amour fatal," *Le Monde,* February 6, 1951. Interesting analysis of the play *L'Arlésienne.*

————*Les Années d'apprentissage d'Alphonse Daudet.* Paris: Librairie Nizet, 1951. The most thorough study in print on Daudet, and a serious effort to penetrate the "legend." Confined to period before Daudet's fame, turgid and digressive at times, but permanently valuable.

————and Luc Badesco. "Controverse autour d'Alphonse Daudet," *Revue d'histoire littéraire de la France,* July–September 1964, pp. 473–478. Sharp-toned exchange of letters provoked by M. Badesco's article (q.v.).

Brisson, Adolphe. *La Comédie littéraire: Notes et impressions de littérature.* Paris: Armand Colin, 1895.

————*Portraits intimes, second series.* Paris: Armand Colin, 1904. Revealing personal interview with Daudet, pp. 245–253.

Brivois, Jules. *Essai de bibliographie des oeuvres de M. Alphonse Daudet.* Paris: Librairie L. Conquet, 1895.

Bruyère, Marcel. *La Jeunesse d'Alphonse Daudet.* Paris: Nouvelles Editions Latines, 1955. Carefully researched. Stops at 1857.

Buet, Charles. *Grands Hommes en robe de chambre.* Paris: Société Libre d'Edition des Gens de Lettres, 1897. Article on Daudet is full of unfavorable innuendoes.

Burns, Mary. *La Langue d'Alphonse Daudet.* Paris: Jouve et Cie., 1916. Concentrates on Daudet's vocabulary, with rather inconclusive results.

Caillat, J. *Le Voyage d'Alphonse Daudet en Algérie (1861–62).* Algiers: Jules Carbonnel, 1924.

Carter, Boyd G. "Alphonse Daudet and Darwinism," *Modern Language Quarterly,* March 1945, pp. 93–98.

———— "Alphonse Daudet: In Memoriam," *French Review*, October 1940, pp. 21–25.

Céard, Henry. *Lettres inédites à Emile Zola*, annotated by C. A. Burns. Paris: Nizet, 1958.

Chassé, Charles. *Styles et physiologie: Petite histoire naturelle des écrivains*. Paris: Albin Michel, 1928. Daudet's skill is more auditory than visual.

Chaumeix, André. "Alphonse Daudet critique," *Le Gaulois*, April 19, 1924.

Chauvelot, Robert. *Gustave Flaubert et Alphonse Daudet*. Monaco: Imprimerie de Monaco, 1927.

Chevalier, Adrien. *Humbles Essais*. Paris: Bibliothèque de l'Association, 1903.

"Chez Alphonse Daudet" (unsigned interview), *Le Temps*, January 27, 1893. Daudet on raising children—an example of myth-making.

Claretie, Léo. "Maîtres et jeunes," *La Vie contemporaine*, April 15, 1896, pp. 124–135.

Clauzel, Paul. *Gloires Nîmoises*. Nîmes: Chastanier, 1901.

Clemenceau, Georges. *Le Grand Pan*. Paris: Charpentier, 1896.

———— "La Mort d'Alphonse Daudet," *L'Aurore*, December 18, 1897.

Clogenson, Y. E. *Alphonse Daudet peintre de la vie de son temps*. Paris: J. B. Janin, 1946. Well-intentioned, standard view of the life and works.

Conrad, Joseph. "Alphonse Daudet," *The Outlook*, April 9, 1898. Judicious and perceptive post-mortem evaluation of Daudet.

Crawford, Virginia M. *Studies in Foreign Literature*. Boston: L. C. Page and Co., 1899.

Dambska-Prokop, Urszula. *Le Style indirect libre dans la prose narrative d'Alphonse Daudet*. Cracow: Jagellonne University Press, 1960.

Daudet, Mme. Alphonse. "Le Cinquantenaire de l'*Arlésienne*," *Les Annales politiques et littéraires*, October 1, 1922.

———— *Fragments d'un livre inédit*. Paris: Charavay Frères, [1885].

——— *Souvenirs autour d'un groupe littéraire.* Paris: Charpentier, 1910.

Daudet, Ernest. "La Jeunesse d'Alphonse Daudet," *La Revue hebdomadaire*, February 24, 1912, pp. 447-474.

——— *Mon frère et moi.* Paris: Librairie Plon, 1882.

Daudet, Léon. *Alphonse Daudet.* Paris: Fasquelle, 1898.

——— *Quand vivait mon père.* Paris: Grasset, 1940.

——— *Sauveteurs et incendiaires.* Paris: Flammarion, 1941.

Daudet, Lucien. *Lettres familiales d'Alphonse Daudet.* Paris: Librairie Plon, 1944.

——— *Vie d'Alphonse Daudet.* Paris: Gallimard, 1941. Well-written but necessarily conditioned by filial piety.

——— *Les Yeux neufs. L'Age de raison.* Paris: Flammarion, 1921 and 1923. Autobiography of Daudet's second son, in two volumes.

Deffoux, Léon. "Alphonse Daudet et le naturalisme," *Les Nouvelles littéraires*, July 13, 1929.

Degoumois, Léon. *L'Algérie d'Alphonse Daudet.* Genève: Editions Sonor, 1922.

Delaporte, P. V., S.J. *Etudes et causeries littéraires*, first series. Paris: Desclée, de Brouwer et Cie., 1900. A Jesuit priest finds Daudet's work morally harmful.

Delattre, Floris. *Dickens et la France.* Paris: Librairie Universitaire, 1927. Argues for direct but minor influence of Dickens on Daudet.

Delvau, Alfred. *Du Pont des Arts au Pont de Kehl: Reisebilder d'un Parisien.* Paris: Achille Faure, 1866.

——— *Le Grand et le petit trottoir.* Paris: Achille Faure, 1866. A novel in which Daudet appears as Henry de la Barthelasse.

Demont-Breton, Virginie. *Les Maisons que j'ai connues*, vol. II: *Nos amis artistes.* Paris: Librairie Plon, 1927.

Descaves, Lucien. *Souvenirs d'un ours.* Paris: Les Editions de Paris, 1946.

Desprez, Louis. *L'Evolution naturaliste.* Paris: Tresse, 1884.

Diederich, Benno. *Alphonse Daudet, sein Leben und seine Werke.* Berlin: Schwetzke, 1900.

Dobie, G. V. *Alphonse Daudet*. London: Thomas Nelson, 1949. Primarily biographical, thorough and careful on facts, but excessively traditional in interpretations. Valuable compendium of information, but not very illuminating about Daudet as artist.

"The Domesticated Daudet" (unsigned article), *Times Literary Supplement*, London, October 26, 1951. Interesting British estimate of Daudet apropos of new translation of *Sapho*.

Doumic, René. *Portraits d'écrivains*. Paris: Paul Delaplane, 1892.

Draugelattes, Wilhelm. "Bemerkungen über den Stil in Alphonse Daudets *Lettres de mon moulin*," Fifth Annual Report, Städtische Realschule, Eberswalde, 1909. Mechanical enumeration of Daudet's repetitive devices.

Drumont, Edouard. *Figures de bronze et statues de neige*. Paris: Flammarion, 1900. Personal reminiscences about Daudet, pp. 147–162.

——— "*La France Juive*" *devant l'opinion*. Paris: Marpon et Flammarion, 1886.

——— "Le Mouvement littéraire," *Le Livre*, February 10, 1884. Partisan comments on the controversy over authorship of *Les Lettres de mon moulin*.

Dubois, Jacques. *Romanciers français de l'instantané au XIX*ᵉ *siècle*. Brussels: Palais des Académies, 1963. Analysis of impressionistic techniques in the prose style of Daudet and of several contemporaries.

Edwards, Tudor. *The Lion of Arles: A Portrait of Mistral and His Circle*. New York: Fordham University Press, 1964.

Faguet, Emile. *Propos littéraires*, fourth series. Paris: Société française d'imprimerie et de librairie, 1907. Perceptive review article on *Notes sur la vie*.

Favreau, A. R. "Alphonse Daudet and Anselme Mathieu: Some Unedited Letters," *Romanic Review*, February 1945, pp. 38–42.

——— "British Criticism of Daudet, 1872–1897," *PMLA*, June 1937, pp. 528–539.

Floret, Jean-Marie. *La Vérité sur Tartarin de Tarascon*. Tarascon: Librairie Gardiol, 1947.

Formentin, Charles. "La Rupture Daudet-Goncourt," *Le Jour*, May 30 and 31, 1896. Gossipy details concerning Daudet's misunderstanding with Goncourt over the French Academy election.

France, Anatole. "L'Incident Daudet-Tourguénef," *Le Temps*, February 12, 1888.

Fricker, Elsa. *Alphonse Daudet et la société du Second Empire*. Paris: E. de Boccard, 1937. Daudet as mirror of the age of Louis Napoleon, more than of the Third Republic. Good documentation of Daudet's remarkable sensitivity to environment.

Geffroy, Gustave. "Alphonse Daudet, A propos des trois Tartarin," *La Lecture*, January 10, 1891, pp. 17–24.

George, W. L. "Tartarin: The French Comic Giant," *Oxford and Cambridge Review*, London, July 1912, pp. 67–75.

Germain, André. *La Bourgeoisie qui brûle: Propos d'un témoin (1890–1940)*. Paris: Editions Sun, 1951. Memoirs of the first husband of Daudet's daughter Edmée.

Gerstmann, Adolf. *Alphonse Daudet: Sein Leben und seine Werke bis zum Jahre 1883*. 2 vols. Berlin: A. B. Auerbach, 1883.

Gille, Philippe. *La Bataille littéraire*, third series: 1883–1886. Paris: Victor-Havard, 1890. Very revealing interview in 1885, especially concerning Daudet and the French Academy.

Goncourt, Edmond et Jules de. *Journal: Mémoires de la vie littéraire*, ed. Robert Ricatte, 4 vols. Paris: Fasquelle et Flammarion, 1956. Indispensable! But still requires exercise of caution because so much of it is gossip and hearsay rather than fact.

Gosse, Edmund. *French Profiles*. London: William Heinemann, 1905.

Gottschalk, Walter. *Die Humoristische Gestalt in der Französischen Literatur*. Heidelberg: Carl Winter Verlag, 1928.

An attempt to separate humor from comedy, satire, and irony in French literature.

Gourmont, Rémy de. "M. Alphonse Daudet," *Mercure de France*, January 1898, pp. 216–219. An obituary article, unfriendly, even harsh in places.

Guiches, Gustave. *Au banquet de la vie*. Paris: Editions Spes, 1925.

——— *Le Banquet*. Paris: Editions Spes, 1926.

Guillemot, Maurice. "Alphonse Daudet et l'Académie," *Le Figaro*, April 7, 1896. One of the interviews which angered Goncourt because Daudet would not say no categorically to the French Academy.

Gullette, Cameron C. "The Critic's Candidate," *Modern Language Journal*, March 1933, pp. 401–409.

Guth, Paul. "Pour un centenaire d'Alphonse Daudet, ou La Sensibilité française," *Revue hebdomadaire*, August 1939, pp. 35–48.

Halpérine-Kaminsky, E. *Ivan Tourguéneff d'après sa correspondance avec ses amis français*. Paris: Charpentier, 1901. Contains the most responsible account (together with additional new information) of the so-called "Incident Daudet-Tourguéneff" in 1888.

Henry, Martin A. "The Problem of Artistic Creation in Alphonse Daudet's Works," unpublished dissertation, Princeton University, 1944. Daudet's aesthetic theories, and practice, until 1874. Relies too heavily on limited and not always trustworthy sources.

Hermant, Abel. *Discours*. Paris: Société d'éditions littéraires et artistiques, 1903.

Hoche, Jules. *Les Parisiens chez eux*. Paris: E. Dentu, 1883.

"Hommage à Alphonse Daudet," *Les Cahiers d'Occident*, second series, no. 8, Paris, Librairie de France, 1930.

Huret, Jules. *Tout yeux, tout oreilles*. Paris: Charpentier, 1901.

——— "Yvan Tourguénieff," *Le Figaro*, November 5, 1893.

Jakob, Gustave. *L'Illusion et la désillusion dans le roman réaliste français (1851–1890)*. Paris: Jouve et Cie., 1912.

——— *Die Pseudogenies bei Alphonse Daudet*. Borna-Leipzig:

R. Noske, 1906. Superficial analysis of Daudet's use of the *raté* type.

James, Henry. *Partial Portraits.* London: Macmillan and Co., 1888.

Jenkins, T. A. "Three Notes to Alphonse Daudet's Stories," *Modern Language Notes,* May 1907, p. 152.

Jolly, Maria. *Die Stilmittel Alphonse Daudets in der Schilderung der Provence.* Würzburg, 1931.

Jourdain, Frantz. *Au pays du souvenir.* Paris: Les Editions G. Crès, 1922.

Kruglikoff, Alexander. *Alphonse Daudet et la Provence.* Paris: Jouve et Cie., 1936. Thorough but unimaginative and narrow-gauge study.

Kurz, Harry. "Daudet's Atmospheric Sensibility," *PMLA,* December 1929, pp. 1179–1200.

La Jeunesse, Ernest. *Les Nuits, les ennuis, et les âmes de nos plus notoires contemporains.* Paris: Perrin, 1896. Sentimental essay on Daudet, pp. 81–98.

Lancier, Elisabeth. *Kind und junger Mensch in den Werken Alphonse Daudets.* Münster, 1935.

Larroumet, Gustave. *Etudes de littérature et d'art,* fourth series. Paris: Hachette, 1896.

Latzarus, Bernard. "Alphonse Daudet et les Académies," *Mémoires de l'Académie de Nîmes,* seventh series, vol. XLIX (1931–32).

Launay, Robert. "La Caricature dans l'art d'Alphonse Daudet," *Mercure de France,* June 1, 1940.

Lavondès, Arthur. *Alphonse Daudet.* Nîmes: Clavel-Ballivet, 1883.

Lazare, Bernard. *Figures contemporaines: Ceux d'aujourd'hui: Ceux de demain.* Paris: Perrin, 1895. Rather scornful and sarcastic attack on Daudet.

Le Roux, Hugues. *Portraits de cire.* Paris: Lecène, Oudin et Cie., 1891. Contains long essay, "Notre Patron, Alphonse Daudet," which was printed separately in 1888 in a tiny volume now rare.

Lindemann, Hermann. *Alphonse Daudet als Humorist.* Meiningen, 1896.

Lorrain, Jean. *Du temps que les bêtes parlaient: Portraits littéraires et mondains.* Paris: Editions du Courrier Français, no date.

Loti, Pierre. *Reflets sur la sombre route.* Paris: Calmann-Lévy, 1899.

Mantoux, Charles. *Alphonse Daudet et la souffrance humaine.* Marseille: Imprimerie Ricord, 1941. Rather sentimental admiration for Daudet's devotion to the theme of suffering.

Margueritte, Paul and Victor, Gustave Geffroy, Auguste Marin, Gauthier-Ferrières. *Alphonse Daudet, 1840–1897.* Paris: Bibliothèque Larousse, no date.

Martinet, Yvonne. *Alphonse Daudet (1840–1897). Sa vie et son oeuvre. Mémoires et récits.* Gap: Imprimerie Louis-Jean, 1940. Contains much hard-to-find information, but is too random and fragmentary in method to be a satisfying life and works.

Matthews, Brander. *The Historical Novel and Other Essays.* New York: Scribner's, 1901. High praise for Daudet, in essay intended to introduce complete works in English translation.

Maurice, Arthur Bartlett. *The Paris of the Novelists.* New York: Doubleday, Page and Co., 1919.

Mertens, Eberhard. *Autobiographisches in Alphonse Daudets Werken.* Münster, 1937.

Michel, Louis. *Le Langage méridional dans l'oeuvre d'Alphonse Daudet.* Paris: Editions d'Artrey, 1961. A study of regional vocabulary, noting Daudet's errors of usage and grammar.

Mirbeau, Octave. *Les Grimaces,* no. 21, December 8, 1883. An extreme denunciation of Daudet as a plagiarist, wildly inaccurate, but historically significant as the piece that started the still-smouldering Daudet-Arène controversy.

Monval, Jean. "A propos d'un centenaire: Alphonse Daudet et François Coppée: Lettres inédites," *Revue des Deux Mondes,* May 1, 1940, pp. 166–176.

Moore, Olin H. "The Naturalism of Alphonse Daudet," *Modern Philology*, July 1916, pp. 157–172.

Mouquin (Le Professeur). "La Maladie d'Alphonse Daudet," *Histoire de la médecine*, February 1955, pp. 41–55.

Mülbrecht, Kurt. *Die Dramatisierungen der Daudetschen Romane*. Königsberg, 1916.

Munro, William Angus. *Charles Dickens et Alphonse Daudet, romanciers de l'enfant et des humbles*. Toulouse: Edouard Privat, 1908. Points to some superficial similarities, and some differences, and argues for direct influence of Dickens on Daudet.

O'Faolain, Sean. *The Short Story*. New York: Devin-Adair, 1951. An essay, called "Alphonse Daudet or the interrupted Romantic" (pp. 35–75), argues that Daudet's stories are his best work because they reflect a genuine childlike view of the world. Sensitive insights but often inaccurate.

Pellissier, Georges. "Alphonse Daudet romancier," *Revue encyclopédique*, January 15, 1898, pp. 65–68.

Perret, Louis. "L'Idée royaliste chez nos principaux royalistes: Alphonse Daudet," *Revue Catholique et Royaliste*, July 20, 1902, pp. 243–247.

Pottecher, Maurice. "Portraits et souvenirs: Alphonse Daudet," *Le Monde Français*, August 15, 1947, pp. 287–289. Gossipy reminiscences, offering more personal testimony to the warmth and kindness Daudet showed to young writers.

Poujol, Jacques. "*L'Evangéliste* d'Alphonse Daudet," *PMLA*, June 1951, pp. 332–350.

Pritchett, V. S. "Daudet's *Sapho*," *The New Statesman and Nation*, London, September 22, 1951.

Proal, Jean. "Le Moulin de Paul Arène ou l'état actuel d'un vieux procès," *Synthèses: Revue européenne*, Brussels, no. 103, December 1954, pp. 199–204. A partisan summary of *Aréniste* arguments.

Proust, Marcel. "Portrait d'Alphonse Daudet," *La Presse*, August 11, 1897. This essay is conveniently accessible in the Édition Ne Varietur of Daudet's complete works, vol.

XVII, pp. 62–64. Interesting portrait of the man, rather than his work.

Ransome, Arthur. *Portraits and Speculations.* London: Macmillan and Co., 1913.

Ratti, Gino A. *Les Idées morales et littéraires d'Alphonse Daudet d'après ses oeuvres.* Grenoble: J.-L. Aubert, 1911. First systematic study—rather superficial, dealing with too many ideas too briefly.

Régnier, Henri de. "Alphonse Daudet," *Les Nouvelles littéraires,* January 27, 1934.

Renard, Jules. *Journal.* Paris: Gallimard, 1935.

Robert, Guy. *La Terre d'Emile Zola: Etude historique et critique.* Paris: Les Belles Lettres, 1952.

Robert, Louis de. *De Loti à Proust: Souvenirs et confidences.* Paris: Flammarion, 1928. An account of strained relations between Daudet and Zola.

Roche, Alphonse. "La Part du provençal dans 'Le Curé de Cucugnan,' " *French Review,* March 1941, pp. 387–402. Shows how Daudet's French version of this story reflects linguistically the Provençal original of Roumanille.

Rogers, Franklin R. "Mark Twain and Daudet: *A Tramp Abroad* and *Tartarin sur les Alpes,*" *Comparative Literature,* Summer 1964, pp. 254–263. An attempt to show that Daudet borrowed episodes from Mark Twain.

Rosny, J.-H. *Portraits et souvenirs.* Paris: Compagnie Française des Arts Graphiques, 1945. Daudet as a conversationalist.

―――― *Le Termite.* Paris: Albert Savine, 1890. A novel in which Daudet is portrayed as Guadet.

―――― *Torches et lumignons: Souvenirs de la vie littéraire.* Paris: Editions "La Force française," 1921.

Rossat-Mignod, Suzanne. "Le 'Réalisme' d'Alphonse Daudet," *La Pensée,* nos. 42 and 43 (double issue), 1952. A Marxist attack on the failure of social conscience in Daudet.

Sachs, M. "Alphonse Daudet and Paul Arène: Some Unpublished Letters," *Romanic Review,* February 1964, pp. 30–37.

———— "Alphonse Daudet's Tartarin Trilogy," *Modern Language Review*, April 1966.
———— "Manuscript Evidence Concerning *Les Lettres de mon moulin*," *PMLA*, December 1959, p. 638.
———— "The Role of Collaborators in the Career of Alphonse Daudet," *PMLA*, March 1958, pp. 116–122.
Saylor, Guy Rufus. *Alphonse Daudet as a Dramatist*. Philadelphia: University of Pennsylvania Press, 1940. An inconclusive analysis of Daudet's lack of success in the theater.
Sherard, Robert H. *Alphonse Daudet: A Biographical and Critical Study*. London: Edward Arnold, 1894. Apart from a few personal details to be found nowhere else, this is inconsequential journalism.
Symons, Arthur. *Studies in Prose and Verse*. London: J. M. Dent, 1904. Interesting post-mortem evaluation of Daudet (dated 1898) on pp. 108–116.
Trivas, Mary. *Auto-observation d'un tabétique de qualité*. Paris: Les Editions Véga, 1932. *La Doulou* studied as a medical record.
Vanel, G. *Une Restitution littéraire: "Le Curé de Cucugnan" et son véritable auteur*. Caen: L. Jouan, 1910. Attributes the original story to Blanchot de Brenas, not to Roumanille, as Daudet had.
Véran, Jules. "Correspondance inédite d'Alphonse Daudet et de Frédéric Mistral," *Hommes et Mondes*, April 1948, pp. 605–614. No revelations here, but good specimens of Daudet's natural warmth of expression in his letters.
Vialar, Paul. "Alphonse Daudet et les personnages du roman," *Les Lettres françaises*, February 12, 1948. Favorable commemorative article, good insights.
Vier, Jacques. "Sur la jeunesse d'Alphonse Daudet," *Revue d'histoire littéraire de la France*, April-June 1956, pp. 243–251. Review article on Bornecque's thesis, severely critical of Daudet.
Vincent, Jose. "Tartarin et Don Quichotte," *La Croix*, September 22–23, 1929.

Bibliography

Wandschneider, Wilhelm. *Sprachgebrauch bei Alphonse Daudet: Wortstellung und Verb.* Wismar, 1898.
Wenzel, Daniel. *Der literarische Impressionismus dargestellt an der Prosa Alphonse Daudets.* Munich, 1928.
Whitehead, Alfred North. *Modes of Thought.* New York: Macmillan, 1938.
Wolff, Albert. *La Gloire à Paris: Mémoires d'un Parisien.* Paris: Victor-Havard, 1886.

Notes

Note: References to the writings of Alphonse Daudet are to the *Oeuvres Complètes Illustrées* in twenty volumes, Paris, Librairie de France, 1929–1931 (Edition Ne Varietur). In these notes O.C. designates that collection, and Roman numerals designate its individual volumes.

I. MYTH AND REALITY

1. As a representative specimen of such standard reference sources, I cite the *Columbia-Viking Desk Encyclopedia* (1953): "He wrote with charm and gentle satire of his native Provence in *Lettres de mon moulin* and *Tartarin de Tarascon*, his most enduring works." The standard reference sources in France follow the same general lines, the *Petit Larousse* (1960) offering: "Bien qu'il se soit rattaché à l'école naturaliste, son oeuvre possède assez de variété pour qu'on y trouve souvent l'émotion humaine et la poésie." (Although he attached himself to the Naturalist school, his work as a whole possesses enough variety so that one can often find in it warmth of human feeling, and poetry.)

2. Auriant, "Le Double visage d'Alphonse Daudet" in *Maintenant*, no. 8, 1948, pp. 73–74. This is perhaps the most detailed of the recent revisionist studies attacking Daudet. Auriant's own vigorous French for the passage quoted in translation runs thus: "Nulle 'gloire' ne fut plus sophistiquée, plus fabriquée, plus artificiellement agencée et soufflée que la sienne . . . Une légende l'auréole, créée par lui-même, soigneusement entretenue par ses ayants droit qui veillèrent jalousement à ce qu'elle se perpétuât intacte . . . Tous les jugements . . . sont à reviser. Le moment est venu pour Alphonse Daudet de sortir de la légende et d'entrer, dépouillé de son faux prestige, dans l'histoire littéraire où sa place n'est pas parmi les maîtres, comme on a cherché à faire accroire de son vivant, ni même parmi les petits maîtres du XIXᵉ siècle, mais à la suite des romanciers discrédités ou disqualifiés."

3. Jacques Vier, "Sur la jeunesse d'Alphonse Daudet" in *Revue*

d'histoire littéraire de la France, April–June 1956, p. 243. The original French: "un des plus ingénieux parasites de notre littérature."

4. Luc Badesco, "Autour d'Alphonse Daudet: Controverse" in *Revue d'histoire littéraire de la France*, July–Sept. 1964, p. 478. Badesco's own words: "ce besoin, soigneusement calculé, de refaire son devenir et d'opérer, à tout prix, une conversion rétrospective de l'illusion à l'existence." Badesco's detailed study of what he considers to be Daudet's penchant for myth-making is to be found in his article "Les Débuts parisiens d'Alphonse Daudet: légende et vérité" in *Revue d'histoire littéraire de la France*, Oct.–Dec. 1963, pp. 581–616.

5. Henry James made his remark in August 1883 in an article in *The Century* but it is quoted here as subsequently reprinted in *Partial Portraits* (London, 1888), p. 195. Octave Mirbeau made his attack in a publication he edited himself, *Les Grimaces*, no. 21, Dec. 8, 1883.

6. This episode occurred in 1896. For years Edmond de Goncourt had planned to establish a rival literary academy, out of contempt for the official one. His plan was embodied in a will, directing that the proceeds of his estate be used to create an academy of ten members. In that will Alphonse Daudet was named an executor and first president of the new academy. Daudet was fully aware of the contents of the will and had shown his own contempt for the official French Academy in his novel *L'Immortel* (1888). It came as a shock to Goncourt, therefore, when it was widely rumored that Daudet was a candidate for the French Academy in 1896. It seemed a betrayal by his friend. Goncourt confronted Daudet directly with this question, and recorded the result, under the date of "Dimanche 22 mars" in his *Journal* (IV, 953): "On cause au *Grenier* de ce désir de l'Académie . . . Et comme on ne trouve pas très catégorique le refus de Daudet, je jui demande, ce soir, très nettement ce qu'il ferait si on le nommait à l'Académie sans les formalités qui sont d'ordinaire demandées. A quoi Mme Daudet me répond presque avec violence: 'Eh bien, il acceptera!—Il reste toujours la question de la lettre,' ajoute au bout de quelques instants Daudet, sans dire s'il l'écrira ou s'il ne l'écrira pas. Décidément, je crois qu'il n'y a que moi qui n'ai pas faim et soif d'un fauteuil, et j'ai peur, diable m'emporte! que Daudet en ait, tout en le cachant, aussi envie que Zola." ("The talk at the *Grenier* [the attic room in Edmond de Goncourt's house in which his literary salon assembled] is of the desire to be a member of the French Academy . . . And since Daudet's refusal

is not found to be very categorical, I ask him, this evening, point blank, what he would do if they named him to the Academy without the formalities which are ordinarily required. [The formalities include a formal letter declaring one's candidacy, and a vote-soliciting call paid to the home of each academician.] To which Mme. Daudet answers almost violently: 'Why, he will accept!— There still remains the question of the letter,' adds Daudet, at the end of a few moments, without saying whether or not he will write it. I believe I am decidedly the only one who does not hunger and thirst after a seat in the Academy, and I fear, the devil take me, that even while he hides his feeling, Daudet longs for one as much as Zola.")

7. Although the best-known instance, *Le Petit Chose*, was put forth as fiction, it quite typifies Daudet's casual approach to the facts of his own life. In his series of articles, *Histoire de mes livres*, and in his reminiscences, he regularly shows a conveniently selective memory, and sometimes is guilty of deliberate distortion. Something of the scope of this personal myth-making by Daudet can be gauged by the amount of Jacques-Henry Bornecque's study *Les Années d'apprentissage d'Alphonse Daudet* (Paris, 1951) which had to be devoted merely to setting the record straight. It should, however, be emphasized that Daudet's activities in this area were all rather innocuous, and the result of petty vanity for the most part: making himself younger, or poorer, or more altruistic, or more innocent than was the case. It is all too trivial to support any dark conspiracy theory.

8. The most complete edition of Daudet's works, the Edition Ne Varietur, for example, was prepared under familial supervision, and quotations from Daudet's personal notebooks and other such peripheral material show signs of rather careful editing, including suppression of entire passages, of proper names, and so forth. Lucien Daudet recounts openly (in his *Vie d'Alphonse Daudet*, p. 41) the fact that, rather than allow publication, he arranged to have a friend burn a group of potentially informative letters addressed to Daudet by his mistress Marie Rieu. Various scholars, including the present writer, have had the experience of being denied permission to publish, or sometimes even to see, existing documents. Protection against lawsuits, or protection of the market value of autograph material, has doubtless motivated some of this behavior. There is also an acute sensitivity in the family about anything touching on Daudet's sexual history, whether it be his long and significant liaison

with Marie Rieu before marriage, or occasional infidelities after marriage, or discussions of his syphilis whose third-stage manifestations were the basis of Daudet's terrible physical suffering in the last years of his life. Whether understandable or not, the pattern of obstruction, concealment, and distortion has unquestionably added up to deliberate myth-making.

9. Charles Beuchat, *Histoire du naturalisme français*, vol. I, *Le Naturalisme en marche* (Paris, 1949), pp. 355–356. The original French is as follows: "Faut-il classer Alphonse Daudet parmi les naturalistes . . . ? Par sa méthode de travail et par son oeuvre, Alphonse Daudet est bien de la famille de Flaubert, des Goncourt et de Zola . . . Mais par delà ce Daudet réaliste—et c'est le motif de notre hésitation à le classer—il faut chercher le novateur qui apporta à la doctrine naturaliste une sensibilité frémissante et qui rejeta le dogme de l'impassibilité si cher à Flaubert."

10. Declarations of independence were so frequent with Daudet as to constitute almost a tic, which one is tempted to interpret psychologically. Perhaps the most explicit statement of his in print on the subject is in the preface he wrote for Edmond Lepelletier's collection of short stories, *Les Morts heureuses* (Paris, 1886, pp. vi–vii): "Vous êtes ce que j'ai essayé d'être depuis près de trente ans que j'écris, un Indépendant. Oh! oui, pas de systèmes, pas d'écoles, ni surtout de critérium trop inflexible. Songeons à l'ingénieux outillage des marins qui font tout flotter sur les navires, les feux dans les suspensions, les cristaux dans les encoches des tablettes, et même la boussole, au milieu du pont, sous les étoiles. Ainsi doivent aller nos jugements sur les hommes, l'art, la vie. Toute stabilité est impossible, toute inflexibilité absurde et dangereuse à bord de notre grand bateau qui roule et qui tangue éternellement, en route vers l'inconnu." ("You are what I have tried to be for the nearly thirty years that I've been writing, an Independent. Yes, indeed, no systems, no schools, and especially no overly inflexible criterion. Think of the ingenious instrumentation of sailors, who keep everything free-floating on boats, the lights in their hanging brackets, the stemware in their slots in the tables, and even the compass, in the middle of the bridge, out under the stars. So must we proceed in our judgments on men, art, life. All stability is impossible, all inflexibility absurd and dangerous aboard our great vessel which rolls and pitches eternally, headed for the unknown.")

11. A novel called *Léo et Chrétienne Fleury* was accepted for publication in the *Gazette de Lyon* in 1856, according to Ernest

Daudet (*Mon frère et moi*, pp. 143–144), but the journal collapsed
before publication could begin and the only existing manuscript
was lost somehow by the editor.

12. Daudet was perfectly serious about abandoning literature in
1872, after his play *L'Arlésienne* proved a flop; and his decision to
become drama critic for *Le Journal officiel* was, at his wife's insistence, a sort of compromise decision between never writing again
and continuing his career. (See L. Daudet, *Vie d'Alphonse Daudet*,
p. 96.) Adolphe Brisson recounts that Daudet insisted he had missed
his calling, that he should have been an editor of a journal, and that
in the 1880's he had, only because of his wife's insistence, turned
down a very serious offer to become the editor of an international
magazine, backed by a wealthy American woman. (A. Brisson,
Portraits intimes, second series, pp. 249–250.) Edmond de Goncourt's *Journal* (III, 1121, and IV, 8) records Daudet's wistful
longings in the early 1890's to start a journal with his own money,
to be called *Journal de Champrosay*. He apparently considered editing other people's work as a solution to the increasingly difficult
time he was having with his own creative work because of his
illness.

II. ORIGINS

1. According to the family tradition, as reported in Lucien
Daudet's biography of his father (p. 16), Alphonse was supposed
to have been the *sixteenth* child born to the couple, thirteen of them
being dead. That tradition seems improbable, and Marcel Bruyère's
careful research (in *La Jeunesse d'Alphonse Daudet*, Paris, 1955)
seems to have established a more plausible truth in this matter, for
he points out (pp. 35–36) that the public records reveal only four
births officially noted in the family before Alphonse, of whom two
failed to survive. Still, one cannot help but be intrigued by the
existence of this family tradition, which suggests that the propensity
for myth-making was not confined to the special personality of
Alphonse.

2. The growth of this particular reputation for unreliability
clearly got under Daudet's skin in the end, suggesting that he was
genuinely unconscious of its origins in himself, and had no idea
how to stop it. When he challenged a minor journalist, Albert
Delpit, to a duel in 1883 over an article that was less than compli-
mentary, Daudet made it clear to Edmond de Goncourt that it was
the charge of unreliability—that he was a "Carthaginian"—which got

to him: "Vous savez, c'est toujours la même chose . . . la continu-
ation de la légende qui s'est faite sur moi: j'ai trahi tous mes amis
et personne n'est plus habile que moi pour envelopper une perfidie
dans de belles phrases . . . Enfin, ce mot *Carthaginois* commence
à m'agacer." ("You know, it's always the same thing . . . the con-
tinuation of that legend which has grown up about me: that I have
betrayed all my friends and that no one is cleverer than I at wrapping a perfidious action in fine phrases . . . In the end this word
Carthaginian is beginning to irritate me.") *Journal*, III, 258.

3. *O.C.*, XVI, *Notes sur la vie*, 1.
4. See especially *O.C.*, II, 9.
5. *O.C.*, II, 17.
6. Drumont's French, "Tu n'aimes pas les magistrats, tu n'aimes
pas les huissiers, tu n'aimes pas les sergents de ville, tu n'aimes pas
les académiciens, tu n'aimes aucun corps constitué," occurs on page
259 of the work cited. Daudet told the same anecdote about his
father, in almost the same words, to Edmond de Goncourt (see
Journal, III, 296). And in Daudet's novel *L'Immortel* a venerable
member of the French Academy is made to say: "Tous les corps
constitués sont lâches" ("All organized groups are cowardly"). *O.C.*,
XI, 165.
7. E. Daudet, *Mon frère et moi*, pp. 143–146. See also Ernest's
article "La Jeunesse d'Alphonse Daudet," published in 1912 and
reproduced in *O.C.*, I, 103.
8. See the reconstruction of Daudet's sojourn in Alès in chapter
VI of Bornecque's *Années d'apprentissage*.
9. *O.C.*, XVI, *Notes sur la vie*, 33.

III. THE APPRENTICE YEARS: 1857–1868

1. *O.C.*, XII, 2: "serré contre mon frère, le coeur angoissé,
j'éprouvais une terreur involontaire."
2. See Bornecque, *Années d'apprentissage*, p. 140.
3. *O.C.*, I. 1. The stanza can be rendered in plain English prose
as follows: "Day-old infants, oh newly-born, tiny mouths, tiny
noses, tiny half-closed lips, trembling limbs so fresh, so white, so
pink."
4. *O.C.*, I, 11–12. A plain English rendering of this stanza would
read as follows: "I do not love you; there, I've said it; I detest you.
I fear you as one fears the fires of hell, as one fears typhus, cholera,
the plague; I hate you unto death, Madame; but, my God! tell me

why I weep when I have gone two days without speaking to you and without seeing you at all."

5. It is the general estimate that Alphonse Daudet can be considered to have been a confirmed anti-Semite, yet the matter is unusually complex, and by no means so clear. If it is true, as some have reported, that in his last years Daudet was wont to identify himself as an anti-Semite, that was clearly a matter of abstract theory with him. In practice there is nothing in his writings or public utterances or choice of associations that can be properly called anti-Semitic. Indeed, it would be quite contrary to his character for him to feel and act committed to any opinion so strong as a form of race hatred. That was far more in the style of his son Léon who was in many respects the exact opposite of his father. One may suspect that some of the attacks on Alphonse Daudet over the years have represented a sort of backlash from the feelings his militant son generated. If so, it would constitute the curious and doubtless unprecedented cultural phenomenon of the sins of the son being visited on the father. In any event, the no doubt fascinating question of Alphonse Daudet's degree of anti-Semitic feeling has no valid place in a discussion of his artistic career. For as far as close study of his life and work can reveal, there is nothing in his creative writing which was in any way influenced by any personal opinions he may have entertained on the Jewish question.

6. O.C., I, 95–96. The following is a plain English version of the lines cited, which conclude the poem "La Double conversion": "Let love have its way, my sweet, and let's follow the impulse it is inspiring in us . . . And we shall flee, as we would the plague, theology and all that . . . The whole earth is in love, so come away and let us love each other somewhere." "—Yes, but let's not get home too late!"

7. For an account of the brief history of this publication, see Bornecque, *Années d'apprentissage*, pp. 307–310.

8. O.C., I, *Le Roman du Chaperon-Rouge. Scènes et fantaisies*, 78.

9. O.C., II, 161–175.

10. O.C., I, *Le Roman du Chaperon-Rouge, Scènes et fantaisies*, 23–24.

11. O.C., XIX, 101.

IV. FIRST SUCCESSES: 1868–1874

1. A very carefully researched and persuasive reconstruction of

the circumstances of composition of this novel, and an interpretation of its significance, can be found in J.-H. Bornecque's introduction to his critical edition of *Le Petit Chose*, prepared as his *thèse complémentaire* and published in Paris by Fasquelle in 1947. My own remarks borrow heavily from Bornecque's work on this subject.

2. Maupassant wrote six novels in all, five of which are, like all of Daudet's, constructed as a string of related episodes. But his most distinguished work, *Pierre et Jean* (1888), is a conscious experiment in a different mode: a depth analysis of one situation, depicting the ever widening consequences of a single episode. For a discerning analysis of Maupassant's novelistic techniques see E. D. Sullivan, *Maupassant the Novelist* (Princeton, 1954).

3. The earliest stories were composed, so far as is known, in the late summer and early fall of 1866, when Daudet was a member of the so-called *colonie de Clamart*, a group of young writers living in a suburb of Paris. The windmills at Fontvieille, one of which he adopted as the setting for his stories, were vividly in his memory, no doubt, since he had spent several months in that very region, from February to early May of 1866, writing a first draft of *Le Petit Chose*. But he neither lived nor did any writing in an abandoned windmill during those months, and the short stories themselves were probably not begun until he was back in the Paris region again. He continued work on the stories in 1868, by which time he was married and living in Paris. A visit to the windmill at Fontvieille, which now houses a charming museum of Daudet memorabilia, is a very rewarding experience, conveying as well as can be done the atmosphere of the stories in *Les Lettres de mon moulin*. But the windmill is not, alas, as usually advertised, "where the stories were written."

4. *O.C.*, III, 88.

5. The Edition Ne Varietur affords a convenient opportunity to compare the newspaper and book versions of several stories, and to see the text of newspaper stories Daudet decided never to publish in book form. In addition to the definitive text of *Les Lettres de mon moulin*, in volume III of that edition, there is given on pages 139–189 the newspaper text of the first twelve stories published in the series. These texts have repaid study, for they reveal genuine artistic preoccupations in Daudet. The extent and significance of the changes Daudet made from newspaper to book publication have for some reason escaped the notice of scholars. Yvonne Martinet,

for example, in a richly detailed study, *Alphonse Daudet (1840–1897). Sa vie et son oeuvre. Mémoires et récits* (Gap, 1940), manages to make the inaccurate remark (p. 301) that "La Chèvre de M. Seguin" was printed in the book unchanged from the newspaper version. Such a remark, missing one of the clearest instances of the application of artistic principles by Daudet in the editing of these stories, reveals how little Daudet's personal maturing as an artist has been understood, and how much the legend of his irresponsible youth has been accepted uncritically by students of his career.

6. See M. Sachs, "Manuscript Evidence Concerning *Les Lettres de mon moulin*," *PMLA*, Dec. 1959, p. 638.

7. Octave Mirbeau was the first to make the flat assertion that *Les Lettres de mon moulin* was the work of Paul Arène (*Les Grimaces*, no. 21, Dec. 8, 1883). The charge occasioned rather unsatisfactory statements from both Daudet and Arène, and a subsequent history of quite bitter but inconclusive debate among the partisans of each author. A reasonably lucid account of the known facts in the controversy can be found in G. V. Dobie, *Alphonse Daudet* (London, 1949), pp. 283–292. Some additional documentation, and the outlines of a plausible resolution of this problem of authorship can be found in: M. Sachs, "The Role of Collaborators in the Career of Alphonse Daudet," *PMLA*, March 1958; "Manuscript Evidence Concerning *Les Lettres de mon moulin*," *PMLA*, Dec. 1959; and "Alphonse Daudet and Paul Arène: Some Unpublished Letters," *Romanic Review*, Feb. 1964.

8. Both Edmond de Goncourt (*Journal*, III, 1082) and Jules Renard (*Journal*, p. 55) report hearing Daudet say—in 1889 and in 1890 respectively—that the manuscript of *Les Lettres de mon moulin* had been stolen from him. Whether this was an example of myth-making on Daudet's part, or the truth, is not known; but no manuscript answering Daudet's description has ever come to light. The only known manuscript having a connection with *Les Lettres* is a notebook in Daudet's handwriting, which has never been out of the family's possession and which is certainly too fragmentary in content to be described as *the* manuscript of *Les Lettres*.

9. See *Histoire de mes livres, Tartarin de Tarascon*, O.C., IV, vii.

10. Cited by Lucien Daudet, *Vie d'Alphonse Daudet* (Paris, 1941), p. 79.

11. See Alfred Delvau, *Du Pont des Arts au Pont de Kehl* (Paris, 1866), pp. 301–303.

12. The affinity between *Tartarin* and *L'Arlésienne* seemed so

patent to Daudet that he toyed with the idea of publishing the two
texts together in one volume. As a remark in his notebooks reveals,
Daudet felt that the two texts presented two valid facets of southern life: "Mettre en préface de *Tartarin de Tarascon,* si je le mets
dans le même volume que l'*Arlésienne:* Il y a deux midis. Le midi
bourgeois, le midi paysan. L'un est comique, l'autre est splendide. J'ai
réuni exprès ces deux études, l'*Arlésienne* et *Tartarin* comme
échantillons de ces deux midis si différents." ("Put down as a
preface to *Tartarin de Tarascon,* if I put it in the same volume
with *L'Arlésienne:* There are two Souths. The bourgeois South,
the peasant South. The one is comic, the other magnificent. I have
deliberately brought together these two studies, *L'Arlésienne* and
Tartarin, as samples of those two very different Souths.") *O.C.*,
IV, 172.

V. THE NOVELS OF REALISM: 1874-1881

1. In *Histoire de mes livres, Fromont jeune et Risler aîné, O.C.*,
V, i.
2. In the same article from *Histoire de mes livres, O.C.*, V, ii.
3. *O.C.*, V, 175.
4. *O.C.*, V, 271.
5. Daudet shared with his principal contemporaries—Flaubert,
Zola, Goncourt, and so forth—the feeling that Balzac was *the* great
novelist and the model for the kind of realistic fiction they believed
in. Tributes to Balzac abound in word and deed among them, as
can be seen throughout Goncourt's *Journal,* for example. Daudet
apparently conceived his admiration for Balzac at a very young
age, and was wont to bracket him with Shakespeare as the two
great geniuses of literature, according to Léon Daudet: "Ils m'ont
impressionné . . . tout jeune . . . Balzac, Shakespeare, Shakespeare,
Balzac, leurs noms se mêlent dans mon esprit. Je ne les sépare pas
l'un de l'autre." ("They impressed me when I was very young . . .
Balzac, Shakespeare, Shakespeare, Balzac, their names blend together in my mind. I do not separate the one from the other.")
Léon Daudet, *Alphonse Daudet,* p. 209.
6. *O.C.*, V, 11.
7. We have Daudet's own word, in his *Histoire de mes livres,* for
the specific fact that he made field trips in and around Paris to get
the background details of *Fromont jeune* exactly right. See *O.C.*,
V, vi–vii.
8. *O.C.*, V, 4.

9. *O.C.*, V, 15.

10. *O.C.*, V, 59.

11. *O.C.*, V, 169.

12. Chap. V, "Un Fait divers," and chap. VI, "Elle a promis de ne plus recommencer," pp. 171–196.

13. See especially the chapter entitled "Légende fantastique du petit homme bleu," *O.C.*, V, 199–208. For an indication of Daudet's own subsequent judgment on this invention of his, see A. Artinian, "Daudet's 'petit homme bleu,'" *Modern Language Notes*, Feb. 1954.

14. The distinguished American novelist Louis Auchincloss has offered an eloquent tribute to *Fromont jeune et Risler aîné* which is excellent evidence that the most sophisticated modern reader can still find something of value in this apparently old-fashioned work. In his *Reflections of a Jacobite* (Boston, 1961) Mr. Auchincloss states that he reread the novel, twenty years after first encountering it in college: "After twenty years I found the old charm still there, and the struggle between the good and wicked forces over the paper factory as entrancing as ever" (p. 6). Nor is he unaware of the novel's weaknesses: "Of course it is a melodramatic tale. Of course it is sentimental . . . But I still find it honest" (p. 7).

15. It seems likely that Daudet's subtitle was intended to be a direct reference to Flaubert's *Madame Bovary*, which bore the subtitle "Moeurs de province." In that way Daudet made it quite explicit to his readers in 1874 that his novel belonged in the same realistic tradition.

16. Daudet had been in the employ of the Duc de Morny, and had witnessed episodes in the short unhappy career of François Bravay, both during the period of the Second Empire. He set down an impressionistic piece about Morny's death and another about Bravay's encounter with Paris, and published them both in *Le Bien public* during 1873. These two pieces were collected in *Robert Helmont. Etudes et paysages*, published in 1874. The texts are reproduced in volume V of *O.C.*, pp. 83–86 ("La Mort du Duc de M***—Etude historique") and pp. 87–91 ("Un Nabab—Etude historique").

17. The words come from *Histoire de mes livres*, the account of *Fromont jeune et Risler aîné* composed in the 1880's (*O.C.*, V, ii).

18. For an account of the real-life basis of *Jack*, see *Histoire de mes livres*, as printed at the beginning of that novel, *O.C.*, VI, i–vi.

19. *O.C.*, V, vii–viii.

20. *O.C.*, VI, xi.

21. Oddly enough, it is Daudet himself who reports the anecdote, in the same segment of *Histoire de mes livres*, just a page after discussing his ideas on "littérature de sourd"—*O.C.*, VI, xii. This suggests what is probably true: that Daudet was not thinking of Flaubert when he described disparagingly the kind of author who overwrites and is excessively subtle. Nevertheless, most modern readers would suppose the words to be a veiled criticism of Flaubert, for the words fit no one so well as him.

22. See *O.C.*, VI, 458–459.

23. For the details of this preliminary conception, see *O.C.*, VII, 387–392.

24. *O.C.*, VII, 325–339.

25. *O.C.*, VII, 239–240.

26. That Daudet was becoming specially preoccupied with style after *Le Nabab* appears from a remark he made to Edmond de Goncourt in May 1878, while describing to him the plot of his next book, *Les Rois en exil:* "Mais tout à coup, Daudet s'interrompt en disant: 'Voyez-vous, au fond, c'est très malheureux: vous m'avez troublé. Oui, vous, Flaubert et ma femme . . . Je n'ai pas de style. Non, non, c'est positif . . . Les gens nés au delà de la Loire ne savent pas écrire la prose française . . . Moi, ce que j'étais? Un imaginateur . . . Vous ne vous doutez pas de ce que j'ai dans ma tête . . . Eh bien, sans vous, je ne serais pas préoccupé de cette chienne de langue et j'aurais pondu, pondu dans la quiétude.' " ("But suddenly Daudet interrupts himself, saying: 'You see, it's a very unhappy business for me, at bottom: you have troubled me. Yes, you, Flaubert, and my wife . . . I have no style. No, no, it's a positive fact . . . People born on the other side of the Loire River do not know how to write French prose . . . As for me, what was I? An imaginer . . . You cannot suspect what I have in my head . . . Well, without you, I would not be preoccupied with that bitchy question of language, and I would have turned out the stuff endlessly and with a tranquil mind.' ") *Journal*, II, 1239. The passage suggests not only the influence of his contemporaries on Daudet's manner of writing, but also the durability of those self-doubts in Daudet which pursued him even when he basked in the limelight of public success, as he certainly did in 1878.

27. Daudet's account of the sudden outbreak of his first serious symptoms, during the composition of *Les Rois en exil*, and his fear that he was dying, is given in *Histoire de mes livres, O.C.*, VIII, v.

28. The thought processes by which Daudet worked out incidents for his novels were often transcribed in his notebooks, and the Edition Ne Varietur has included generous samples of such material which are valuable indications of the creative process in Daudet. The incident of the piercing of the prince's eye, which occurs in chapter fifteen of the novel, is worked out by Daudet, with all its psychological potential, in a paragraph given on pp. 267-268 in *O.C.*, VIII. This passage reveals that Daudet was very much alive to the theatrical effect of the incident, but was unconcerned with its character as *accident* rather than fate. The most explicit statement that a real-life occurrence inspired the invention is made in *Histoire de mes livres*, p. iii. Daudet's reasoning seemed to be that the scene would be convincing in a novel since it had, in fact, occurred in real life—a miscalculation, it must now appear to the modern reader.

29. It was Robert de Bonnières, writing in *Le Figaro* in 1883, who charged that Daudet had first conceived the book as a defense of the Royalists and had later altered the conception out of opportunism. (See R. de Bonnières, *Mémoires d'aujourd'hui*, second series, 1885, p. 232.) Daudet gave his reply very effectively in *Histoire de mes livres*, p. viii. Among those who reviewed *Les Rois en exil* in 1879, Barbey d'Aurevilly in *Le Constitutionnel* found it to be anti-Royalist in spirit; A. de Pontmartin in *La Gazette de France* found it to be pro-Royalist. The same kind of divergence of opinion can be noted among numerous other reviewers of that year (for example, Emile Zola in *Le Voltaire* differing sharply with Jules Vallès in *La Rue*), as well as among many subsequent commentators on the book. (See the sampling of reviews given in *O.C.*, VIII, 282-294.) The original charge of opportunism made by Robert de Bonnières has often been repeated in attacks on Daudet, but the basis for it remains speculative rather than documentary. De Bonnières himself claims only that it was well known among the literary fraternity, which is hardly proof.

30. See his review of *Numa Roumestan* for *Le Parlement*, as quoted in *O.C.*, IX, 256.

31. See *Histoire de mes livres*, the piece on *Numa Roumestan* given in *O.C.*, IX, v.

32. The strongest position Daudet ever took politically was the negative one he recorded in his notebooks: "O politique, je te hais! Sous tes habits différents, la même harpie . . . Tu sépares de braves coeurs faits pour être unis, tu unis au contraire des gens qui devrai-

ent être séparés, tu rends l'honnête homme indulgent pour le coquin, pourvu qu'il soit de son parti . . . Tu es la corruption des consciences, tu donnes l'habitude du mensonge . . . tu rends l'homme indifférent aux belles choses." ("Oh, politics, I detest you! Under your varying garb, you are always the same harpy . . . You separate stout hearts meant to be united, and conversely you unite those who ought to be separated, you make the decent man indulgent toward the unscrupulous one provided he is of his own party . . . You are the corruption of consciences, you create the habit of lying . . . you make man indifferent to the finer things.") Alphonse Daudet, *La Doulou*, Paris, Fasquelle, 1931, p. 115. Otherwise there is no record of his involvement with or interest in political matters. In this, too, he is an absolute contrast to his son Léon Daudet, an outspoken and active partisan of the Royalist cause all his life, and a prime mover of the Action Catholique forces.

33. Daudet's weekly review of theater in Paris was conducted in *Le Journal officiel*, beginning in March 1874 and continuing with few interruptions until December 1880. In those days *Le Journal officiel* was not purely an official organ for government announcements, but had many news and cultural rubrics of public interest as well, like any other journal of the time. Selected articles from that series of weekly reviews have been reprinted in *Pages inédites de critique dramatique*, forming volume XVIII of the Edition Ne Varietur.

VI. THE EROSION OF OBJECTIVITY: 1881-1890

1. The idea that with his illness he was paying for the indulgences of his youth became almost a refrain in Daudet's utterances during the 1880's. For one example there is the following notation of Daudet's complaint made by Edmond de Goncourt in April 1884: "Ce soir . . . Daudet, les traits tiraillés, ses jolis cheveux maladivement défrisés, l'oeil atone, me dit, en scandant mélancoliquement ses phrases: 'Oui, oui . . . C'est que j'ai eu tout . . . tout, mon cher . . . Et je le paye aujourd'hui . . . Il y a chez moi des accidents, des accidents . . .' Et il s'arrête, regardant vaguement devant lui, comme un homme qui a peur de choses mystérieuses et troubles et douloureuses se passant au fond de son être." ("This evening . . . Daudet, his features drawn, his handsome hair uncurled in a sickly fashion, his eyes dull, says to me, sadly stressing his sentences: 'Yes, yes . . . the fact is I've had everything . . . everything, dear friend . . .

And today I am paying for it . . . There are accidents, such accidents happening to me . . .' And he stops, staring vaguely in front of himself, like a man who fears mysterious, disturbing, and painful things that are taking place deep in his being.") *Journal*, III, 335. Within a few days of that complaint Daudet brought himself—after nearly five years of symptoms and suffering—to call his illness by its name, telling Goncourt that "il s'est déclaré chez lui des accidents syphilitiques" ("syphilitic accidents have begun to occur in him"). *Journal*, III, 338. From that time forward Daudet was fully confirmed in his view that he was paying for his past. It became, indeed, a sort of mystic "life principle" with him, exploited in the play *La Lutte pour la vie* under the formula "tout se paie," and used to justify the violent end to which the wicked Paul Astier comes, after triumphing in evil. "Certains auraient voulu que le drame s'arrêtât là, plus conforme aux lois ordinaires de la vie" he wrote in his preface to that play (*O.C.*, XX, 325). "Eh bien! j'ai, moi, de l'existence une vision toute différente. J'y crois absolument à la formule du 'tout se paie'; j'ai toujours vu l'homme toucher le salaire de sa besogne, bonne ou mauvaise, et non dans l'autre vie, que je ne connais pas, mais dans celle-ci, dans la nôtre, tôt ou tard." ("Certain people would have wished that the drama had ended there, more in conformity with the ordinary laws of life. Well, for my part, I have a quite different vision of existence. I believe absolutely in the formula of 'everything must be paid for'; I have always seen man reap the wages of his toil, whether he toiled for good or evil, and not in the next life, which I do not know, but in this one, in ours, sooner or later.")

2. *Histoire de mes livres, Numa Roumestan,* in *O.C.*, IX, ii.

3. See, for example, *O.C.*, IX, *L'Evangéliste*, 197, for details of the real-life basis of this novel.

4. See *O.C.*, X, 72—and indeed all of chapter VI.

5. In an interview in 1885 with his friend Philippe Gille, a reporter for *Le Figaro*, Daudet gave his version of his brush with the Academy in 1883 and his disillusionment with it to the point of renouncing absolutely any candidacy. See Philippe Gille, *La Bataille littéraire*, 3rd series (Paris, 1890), pp. 52–54.

6. In an amusing passage Edmond de Goncourt recorded the scene when he found out what Daudet was up to: "il me confesse qu'il ne travaille pas au roman qu'il devait faire après *Sapho*. Il fait, sans l'avouer à personne, il fait pour une société internationale, une sorte de *Tartarin en Suisse,* une machine qu'on lui paye *deux cent*

soixante-quinze mille francs!" ("he confesses to me that he isn't working on the novel he was to do after *Sapho.* He is constructing, without admitting it to anyone, he is constructing for an international syndicate a sort of *Tartarin in Switzerland,* a contrivance for which they are paying him *two hundred and seventy-five thousand francs!"*) *Journal,* III, 390. The astonished italics are Goncourt's, who, seeing Daudet's sheepish air, goes on to "console" him by saying that the sum is big enough to justify a touch of commercialism, and that, in any case, Daudet does have a family to worry about.

7. Cf. A. Baillot, *Influence de la philosophie de Schopenhauer en France (1860–1900)* (Paris: J. Vrin, 1927).

8. See the poignant notation of this event, as recorded in Daudet's notebooks, printed in *La Doulou* (*O.C.,* XVII, 13).

9. The letter is in the Bibliothèque Nationale in Paris: Fonds Français, Nouvelle Acquisition 22459, no. 135–136.

10. There is now a considerable literature surrounding the "manifeste des cinq," out of which it is impossible to derive any certainties, since the memoirs and letters of those more or less directly involved agree on few points and fail to treat many key matters. Perhaps the most responsible summary of what is now known to scholarship on the subject can be found in Guy Robert, *La Terre d'Emile Zola. Etude historique et critique* (Paris, 1952), especially pages 430–431.

11. After Daudet's death, it appears, Hugues Le Roux tried to claim that he was the sole author of *La Belle-Nivernaise,* but his claim has never been substantiated, and seems highly unlikely. Cf. Dobie, *Alphonse Daudet,* pp. 248–249, note 2.

12. *O.C.,* XI, 169.

13. George Meredith's *Essay on Comedy* (1877) was followed by a considerable outpouring of critical literature in English, French, and German during the succeeding decades, on all aspects of laughter, the distinction between humor and comedy being a specially favored topic, along with national differences in comic outlook. A work like Paul Stapfer's *Molière et Shakespeare* (Paris, 1880) is a typical product of the time. For a list of studies on these subjects which appeared between 1880 and 1900, see Henri Bergson, *Oeuvres,* ed. André Robinet (Paris: Presses Universitaires de France, 1959), pp. 1554–1555. It is interesting to note, in the same source (p. 1555) that Bergson had begun to concern himself with the subject in a public lecture as early as 1884, fifteen years

before his famous study *Le Rire*. Daudet himself came under rather pedestrian analysis by a German scholar named Hermann Lindemann, in a thesis called *Alphonse Daudet als Humorist* (Meiningen, 1896), in which the distinction between English humor and French comedy is specifically exploited.

14. On July 3, 1888, Goncourt recorded as follows: "Ce soir, Daudet cause de son roman futur de *La Petite Paroisse*, dont l'embryon est en germe dans son cerveau. *L'Immortel* ne l'a pas amusé à faire, ne le satisfait pas complètement, il n'y trouve qu'une seule grande qualité, l'expérience de la vie. Il veut faire maintenant une oeuvre où il mettra de lui ce qu'il a de bon, de compatissant, sa pitié pour les misérables, les déshérités, les routiers des grands chemins. Son livre sera l'histoire d'un mari qui pardonne, et il s'étend sur la bêtise de tuer pour l'homme qui aime, qui détruit à jamais l'objet de cet amour ... 'Oui, reprend-il, ce sera une oeuvre de mansuétude.' " ("This evening Daudet is chatting about his future novel, *La Petite Paroisse*, the embryo of which is now germinating in his brain. It did not amuse him to do *L'Immortel*, it does not completely satisfy him, he finds in it only one great quality, experience of life. Now he wants to do a work into which he will put that part of himself which is kind, compassionate, his pity for those in misery, the disinherited, the wanderers of our highways. His book will be the story of a husband who forgives, and he expands on the stupidity of killing for the man who is in love, who destroys permanently the object of that love ... 'Yes, he resumes, it will be a work of gentleness.' ") *Journal*, III, 808.

15. *O.C.*, XVII, 33–34.

16. It is difficult to say just when the exact phrase crystallized in Daudet's mind, to designate his vision of himself, in his role as novelist, as akin to a shopkeeper retailing happiness. The phrase entered his conversation and his writings only toward the end of his life, finding its way, for example, into *Soutien de famille* as an author's digression of half a paragraph (*O.C.*, XVI, 62). But the general notion of using literature for healing and comfort became explicit, as has been noted, as early as 1888, when *L'Immortel* was completed and its grimness seemed evident even to Daudet. A passage in Edmond de Goncourt's *Journal* dated September 24, 1886, is especially interesting because it reveals how early the notion of himself as bringer of joy had begun to haunt Daudet. Clearly the notion was no end-of-career aberration, but something with deep roots in his personality, which evolved in him over many years.

The italics in the following are Goncourt's: "Ce matin, en se promenant sous la charmille, Daudet cause avec moi de son idée de faire un grand roman sur le peuple, où il aimerait à peindre sa personnalité telle qu'il se l'imagine, s'il avait été riche, faisant des *coups de foudre de bonheur* dans les pauvres diables d'intérieurs, et la main ouverte aux *routiers*, à ses malheureux d'affection particulière, à toutes les misères battant les grands chemins." ("This morning, strolling under the arbor, Daudet chats with me about his idea of doing a major novel about the people, in which he would like to depict his own personality as he imagines he would have been had he been rich, creating *thunderbolts of happiness* suddenly in the pitiful homes of the poor, and with his hand generously open to the *vagrants*, those unhappy wanderers who are his special affection, and to all forms of misery to be found along our highways.") *Journal*, III, 596.

VII. DISINTEGRATION: 1890–1897

1. Although there is no proof that Daudet read or saw the Ibsen play and was thereby influenced in *L'Obstacle*, we do have proof that he *wanted* to read the Ibsen play in 1890, as the following note from Daudet to Goncourt in the manuscript collection of the Bibliothèque Nationale shows: "Un service, cher ami. Avez-vous dans la *Revue Indépendante* le no. qui contient les *Revenants* d'Ibsen. J'ai un besoin urgent de lire cette sacrée pièce que Léon m'assure est belle et tout juste." ("A favor, dear friend. Have you got the issue of *La Revue Indépendante* which contains Ibsen's *Ghosts*. I have an urgent need to read that darned play which Léon [Daudet's son] assures me is fine and right on target.") Fonds Français, Nouvelle Acquisition 22458, item 288.

2. Passages from preliminary drafts of this work, which never went beyond the planning stage, are printed in *Notes sur la vie*, O.C., XVI, 88–95 and 139–145.

3. O.C., XIII, *Rose et Ninette*, 83.

4. *Ibid.*

5. The interested reader can follow—especially in the Goncourt *Journal*—the stages of concern displayed by Alphonse and Julia Daudet once Léon began to show a serious interest in Jeanne Hugo, about 1890. The wedding in 1891 was a major social event, but the misgivings of the Daudets were public knowledge, and causes for anxiety after the marriage were apparently not lacking. The marriage was, in fact, dissolved in 1895—not by divorce, but, for religi-

ous reasons, by annulment. For one indication of public rumors that a divorce was imminent, see the melancholy letter from Daudet to Goncourt in the Bibliothèque Nationale, dated 1893, and constituting item 332 in Fonds Français, Nouvelle Acquisition 22458.

6. *O.C.*, XV, 9.

7. Perhaps because it is a story for children, the Edition Ne Varietur has placed "La Fille de l'ogre," which had never previously been published in French, in volume XI, after *La Belle-Nivernaise*, where it is out of place in point of date. It was in fact solicited in person by Herzl during the winter of 1894-95, and appeared in Herzl's German translation on April 14, 1895, in Vienna's *Neue Freie Presse*.

This personal contact between Theodor Herzl and Alphonse Daudet produced more than a trivial children's tale for Easter in a Viennese newspaper. Herzl, the founder of political Zionism, was that very winter in the throes of planning a book in which he would argue for the establishment of a Jewish state and was trying to decide whether his idea made sense. He discussed his idea with Daudet, not at all deterred by Daudet's polite but frank assertion that he was an anti-Semite. Herzl reports that Daudet listened in fascination and with growing excitement, declared Herzl's vision to be a beautiful conception, and argued that the idea could be even more persuasively presented as a novel rather than a political tract. Herzl left Daudet's house much encouraged, feeling that Daudet's enthusiasm assured him he was on the right track, and moved also to think seriously about Daudet's suggestion that a novel might make more effective propaganda. A year later, Herzl published *Der Judenstaat* (*The Jewish State*) which launched the Zionist movement, and a few years after that he produced the novel *Altneuland* (*Old-New Land*) which helped inspire the movement in its work. It is an odd footnote to history that a French writer who was willing to describe himself as an anti-Semite should thus have provided vital enthusiasm, support, and inspiration for a Jewish cause at a decisive moment of its beginnings. For Herzl's account of his conversation with Daudet, see *Theodor Herzls Tagebücher* (Berlin, 1922-23), vol. I, p. 14, as well as Herzl's letter to Heinrich Teweles in May 1895, quoted in Leon Kellner, *Theodor Herzls Lehrjahre* (Vienna and Berlin, 1920), p. 155.

8. *O.C.*, XVI, 62.

9. Daudet's charm as a talker is so widely attested that a list of references here would be needlessly long. Instead I shall quote just

one sample of these testimonials to represent them all—an especially interesting one because of the particular narrative involved, and because the passage notes the effect of the performance on Daudet's illness. Under the date July 25, 1890, Edmond de Goncourt gives this account of one of Daudet's brilliant oral presentations—the more brilliant, we may suppose, because Daudet is reaching into his own past and recalling younger days, exactly as in "Premier voyage, premier mensonge:" "Ce soir Daudet parle avec une exaltation un peu fiévreuse, et comme d'un souvenir passionnant, d'un voyage de trois semaines en mer, qu'il avait fait autour de la Corse, dans une goëlette de la douane . . . [The passage continues for nearly half a page with colorful details.]Et dans l'évocation de ce voyage, il se soulève de son abattement, ses yeux brillent: c'est le Daudet d'autrefois qui a la parole." ("This evening Daudet talks, with an exaltation that is a bit feverish, and in the way one does about a thrilling memory, of a sea voyage of three weeks that he had once made around Corsica in a schooner belonging to the Customs service . . . And in the course of evoking that voyage, he rises out of his lethargy, his eyes gleam; it is the Daudet of old who has the floor.") *Journal*, III, 1210.

10. *O.C.*, XVII, 42.

VIII. CONCLUSIONS

1. *O.C.*, XVI, *Notes sur la vie*, 107. The conversation with Edmond de Goncourt is reported in Daudet's tribute to his friend, composed soon after Goncourt's death at Champrosay, in the summer of 1896. Daudet's text, which bears the title "Ultima," appeared in August 1896 as a memorial article in the *Revue de Paris*, and subsequently was made part of *Notes sur la vie* by the Daudet family.

2. Daudet first applied the phrase *littérature debout* to himself in print in his article on *Tartarin de Tarascon* for the series *Histoire de mes livres* (*O.C.*, IV, vii).

3. *O.C.*, XVI, *Notes sur la vie*, 54–55.

4. The well-known passage on this subject occurs in the article on *Fromont jeune et Risler aîné* for the series *Histoire de mes livres*, beginning: "D'après nature! Je n'eus jamais d'autre méthode de travail" ("From nature! I never had any other method of working"). *O.C.*, V, ii. But the theme was recurrent in his conversation, as much boast as confession. The following remarks, recorded by Edmond de Goncourt under the date January 27, 1878, are typical

of Daudet's way of talking about his work: "Daudet s'écrie: 'Je suis un être tout subjectif. Je suis traversé par les choses . . . Je ne puis rien inventer. Déjà, toute ma famille y a passé; je ne puis plus aller dans le Midi' " ("Daudet cries out: 'I am a totally subjective being. Things pass clean through me . . . I can't invent anything. Already all my family has been put in my books; it's not safe for me to make a trip to the Midi any more' "). *Journal*, II, 1220.

5. In the richly suggestive lectures delivered at Wellesley College, and published as *Modes of Thought* (New York, 1938), Whitehead discussed aesthetics at one point and called attention to the unhappy consequences, for the enjoyment of art, of studied harmoniousness as a standard of artistic composition: "The enjoyment of Greek art is always haunted by a longing for the details to exhibit some rugged independence apart from the oppressive harmony. In the greatest examples of any form of art, a miraculous balance is achieved . . . It is however remarkable how often the preliminary studies of the details—if preserved—are more interesting than the final details as they appear in the complete work. Even the greatest works of art fall short of perfection" ("Lecture Three: Understanding," p. 86). Whitehead's words are peculiarly useful in application to Daudet's work, for they remind us to take pleasure in the excellent details, even when these do not contribute to the harmony of the whole; and they help us understand that Daudet's works fail to be among the greatest examples of his art form, not because they are imperfect (since all art is imperfect) but because that "miraculous balance" is never quite achieved. This study has sought to show that the desired balance has been very nearly attained in the best of Daudet's works, and that wherever the balance has been upset one finds the trace of those flaws of character—uncertainty and ambivalence, particularly—that were Daudet's central weakness as an artist.

Index